T0285261

"Martin King, once again, has crafted a masterful historical work studying some of the most compelling human stories…families fighting and surviving the horrors of war. Across the ocean of time, fathers and sons, daughters and mothers, families have been severely tested in their heroic efforts to win. This collection of stories is being lived out today in Ukraine and as such, you have to add this to your library today. I met Martin in early 2019 when we both spoke at a military historical event in Las Vegas, a mere week or less before the United States began to restrict activities in response to the growing COVID-19 pandemic. Martin is a keen studier of war and an incredible storyteller, especially those stories that have had profound impacts on the lives of others, and the conflicting often devastating results. These are stories worth telling and Martin King does exactly that in this newest historical work.

–Robert G. Novotny, Brig Gen (ret), USAF

"War is a very personal endeavor. Servicemembers form inexplicable bonds as they prepare for battle and fight alongside each other. These bonds, or more appropriately stated, love, lives on, far beyond the battlefield. It is proper then, that the story of war be told through the stories of the people who experienced it. Nobody tells the story of war better than Martin King. Let Martin take you on a journey of combat through the stories of brothers, sisters, and families to experience one of life's greatest crucibles. Blood is indeed thicker than war."

–Robert Campbell Colonel, U. S. Army, 101st Airborne. (Ret)

"Martin is a master storyteller. His intensive research and unique writing style enable one to visualize the scenes and sense the emotion. Braided rope, like brother and sisterhood, is strong, but occasionally ideology snaps even the strongest bonds."

–Brigadier General (ret) Gregory J. Ihde, USAF

"Martin King, once again, has crafted a masterful historical work studying some of the most compelling human stories…families fighting and surviving the horrors of war. Across the ocean of time, fathers and sons, daughters and mothers, families tested and their heroic efforts to win. This collection of stories is being lived out today in Ukraine and as such, you have to add this to your library today."

–Brigadier General Robert G Novotny (ret) USAF

"...a story which needed to be told... definitely a volume worth reading as we look to gain all of the information possible before the primary source of the Greatest Generation is gone."

–The Journal of America's Military Past

"An absolutely essential and core addition to personal, professional, community, college, and university history collections, Blood is thicker than war is an inherently absorbing read from cover to cover."

–Midwest Book Review

"Martins ability to tie family allegiances in key historical battles over hundreds of years is unprecedented and noteworthy. Martin shows how families, regardless of their individual beliefs, rivalries, or allegiances, were critical in some of history's most pivoting and defining military engagements. Weather it was brother against brother on the bloody fields of the American Civil War, or sister working with sister fighting together under a common belief to stop the Nazis, Martin weaves the stories in such a way that it allows you to feel what they felt, whether it was the sorrow over the loss of a sibling, or the happiness and completion of reconciling with a brother who fought, just yards from you, against you and everything you were fighting for. Wars may be fought by individuals and units, but ultimately most everyone participating comes from a family that worried and grieved, or celebrated their accomplishments. This book will help you understand the emotions and critical roles that the families of those involved."

–Arthur "Art" Gordon, MAJ. US. ARMY, 1988-2015

"I've studied history for many years and I'm an author of two books myself. Martin covers the often-missed aspect of war, the personal aspect. I feel his is a much-needed reminder that wars are not fought by tanks, trucks, and artillery; they are fought by people."

–Robert R. Allen, MSGT USAF Retired

"Compelling! King mixes archival evidence with biography and history to take you into how the lives of families are affected by war... siblings fighting side by side."

–Mr. Randy Garcia President ICC The Investment Company Las Vegas

"As a Combat Veteran who thrives on remembering history, I enjoy a good read, rather than spending time reading the news, or spending hours on Facebook. I find Martin's work, honest and factual. He has the ability quite early on, to grab a person's attention and hold onto it, not just in the beginning, but also throughout the entire book. This is what I think most people are looking for when they read and purchase books. Regardless of the content of the book or the subject matter, how you portray your work and naturally flow from one chapter to the next is not something easily done, yet you seem to do this with ease. No doubt your experience in writing is obviously clear and evident in your style of writing. It takes creativity, imagination, and inspiration to perfect the writing skills to achieve this, and Martin does this time and time again. To be able to grab a person's attention, and hold onto it throughout the duration is a gift, and clearly this is what makes reading Martin's your books so enjoyable. So not only do we get a history lesson, but we crave for more as we dander through the pages. So in closing I just want to say, I tip my hat to you sir, and wish you a grand day. I will be looking forward to reading the full content of your newest edition when it arrives."

–Mark Chernek United States Marine Corps

BLOOD
IS THICKER THAN
WAR

BROTHERS AND SISTERS
ON THE FRONT LINES

MARTIN KING
with MICHAEL COLLINS

A KNOX PRESS BOOK
An Imprint of Permuted Press
ISBN: 978-1-63758-352-4
ISBN (eBook): 978-1-63758-353-1

Cover Art by Cody Corcoran
Interior Design by Yoni Limor

Permuted Press, LLC
New York • Nashville
permutedpress.com

Published in the United States of America
1 2 3 4 5 6 7 8 9 10

In Memoriam:

Dearly departed friends—Mr. Dan Goo,
whose memory will live in our hearts forever,
and Mark William Altmeyer, gone but never forgotten.

Table of Contents

PART ONE:
Destiny and dilemma.

PART TWO:
I vow to thee, my country.

FOREWORD

Martin King is a prolific writer of military history with an unrivaled breadth of knowledge and passion for his subject matter. His latest literary effort tackles the stories of siblings in conflict throughout history, at times even on different sides on the same battlefield. After reading a few excerpts, I've become even more intrigued by this subject matter, in part through personal experience. I had the privilege of commissioning my daughter into the United States Air Force and now, as a retired Air Force officer, have the good fortune of teaching at the same overseas location where my daughter is stationed. Like many of the themes in Martin's book, I've experienced firsthand the strengthening of the bonds between my daughter and I through shared experiences so unique to military life. I'm honored that a historian of Martin's caliber gave me a peek at his latest book and I eagerly await the opportunity to read the final product.

Douglas L. Haven, Lt Col, USAF (Retired)

INTRODUCTION

Through my previous books, my research, and family connections, I have a personal connection to many of the stories included in this volume. Countless popular TV series have honed in on dysfunctional families and successfully used these as their baseline: *Vikings*, *The White Queen*, and *Game of Thrones*, to name but a few. They have enthralled viewers around the world with the disagreements and machinations of family members jockeying for power, but these shows are amateurs compared to history's real brothers and sisters. So no matter how pressing, distracting, or annoying your family's problems are, there are some families here that have experienced far worse.

With this volume, I am not presuming to present the definitive scholarly work on siblings in conflict since the beginning of humankind. But through these selected stories, I hope to present thought-provoking, heartfelt, anecdotal human interest, and social history that weaves familiar themes of loyalty, love, heartbreak, and heroism among close relatives.

In most cases, families have a history—stories about sibling rivalry or sibling affection. They're usually happy to impart the tales, depending on the circumstances, but others prefer to keep the skeletons well and truly locked away in a quiet part of the house. When siblings are mentioned in the context of war, the image it inspires is one of bonding, embedded in the ideal of *esprit de corps*. The privilege of comradeship through the overarching figurative use of the word "brotherhood" has overshadowed the presence and significance of real sibling bonds. Fraternal or sororal bonds have been largely ignored as a subject of historical analysis.

Siblinghood in wartime is the primary focus of this volume, which hones in on family bonds and exposes a completely different family dynamic. Insufficient attention has been paid to fondness or love in family relationships during conflict. Despite this, as you will discover, fraternal and sororal stories are indubitably embedded throughout the history of war narratives.

During World War II, the Special Operations Executive (SOE) agents served with distinction. Back in September 2010, police were called to a small, untidy flat in Torquay. They discovered a corpse, whose only reputation with the locals was based solely on her deep affection for cats. When they looked around the "cat lady's" place, they found a small bundle of possessions that revealed a truly incredibly story of two remarkable sisters that were on the same side.

The Wars of the Roses, the English Civil War, and the American Civil War also literally pitted brother against brother.

During the Wars of the Roses, the last members of the notorious Plantagenet dynasty perpetrated a destructive chain of rebellion, revenge, usurpation, and regicide, which mostly originated within the house of York. At the core of this incomparable act of regal self-destruction was the mutually disparaging relationship between three brothers, who were all initially on the same side but harbored entirely different aspirations.

PREFACE

The names Cain and Abel, Romulus and Remus, King Richard and King John are familiar to most of us. The inspiration for this volume came from my own granddad who fought in World War I along with three of his brothers. Four went to war, but only one made it home alive. I have a brother one year younger than myself. His real name is Graham, but I think he prefers his nickname "Joe," after granddad Joe—who, although we didn't know him personally, is a legend in my family. In this volume you will find out why.

While the first chapters are based on extensive research, the latter chapters are extracted from interviews with war veterans whom I have always venerated.

As a boy I was both enthralled and inspired by the anecdotes of a select group of dear old World War I survivors who used to congregate on two park benches at the edge of the estate where I lived. One of these men claimed to have served with my granddad; he'd known and had even worked with him and his three brothers back in the day. Apparently granddad had the exemplary distinction of being a menace to both sides during World War I. I still have cassette recordings of some of those interviews, but I needed to know more.

These days it's a commonly used—in fact overused—form of address when referring to revered friends as "he's my brother" or "she's my sister." But this surrogate appropriation often leaves me cold because it detracts from the real brothers and real sisters who fought side by side, and in some cases on opposite sides during times of real conflict and real hardship.

But what of the heartbroken mothers, fathers, and other relatives they left behind? One mother who appears in this volume waved goodbye to no less than ten sons aged between eighteen and thirty-seven, all of whom were dispatched to the frontline in the World War I. She must have been overcome with pure dread at the prospect of all her boys going to war. They remain the biggest real "band of brothers" that ever served their country, but to discover how many made it back and who this dear lady was you will have to read the rest.

History is inundated with stories of love, hate, jealousy, and revenge between brothers, sisters, and families. But it isn't all misery and tragedy—far from it. It will look at the intricacies of some of these domestic relationships and explore the willingness and, in some cases, reluctance to sacrifice all for honor and glory. It will also hopefully reveal the true stories of those real brothers and real sisters who went to war or found themselves victims of it.

PART ONE:

Destiny and dilemma.

CHAPTER ONE:

GRANDAD AND THE LADS.

I f you will allow me one small indulgence, I would like to relate part of the first story in the first person. While many, such as my granddad and his brothers, were swept up by the veritable tsunami of patriotism and jingoism that triggered their lively hormones in 1914 (inducing them to join the British Army), others were conscripted.

Granddad and his brothers were all working in reserved occupations, industries considered vital to the war effort and were consequently exempt from having to join the army. But like the countless hundreds of thousands who rallied to the call to arms, they all took the king's shilling when it was offered and signed up to His Majesty's armed forces. They wanted adventure, glory, and a chance to fight for their country—but they all got much more than they had bargained for.

Four brothers went to war in 1914. Two would return, but only one would get back alive. In the summer of 1917, British and the Commonwealth forces massed behind the salient in Ypres, Belgium. Headquarters (HQ) was resolute at the prospect of forcing a breach on the inundated Flanders front. Their goal was to break through the horseshoe-shaped Ypres Salient and capture the German submarine ports of Ostend and Zeebrugge.

Before this could be achieved, it would first be necessary to take or, if need be, eradicate the Messines Ridge to the south of Ypres. Commencing in 1916, the British devised an ambitious plan to tunnel underneath the whole salient and detonate deep mines. During the preparatory artillery bombardments, more than 4,200,000 projectiles were fired at the German positions. British General Charles Harington uttered, "Gentlemen, we may not make history tomorrow, but we shall certainly change the geography."[1] Meanwhile, tunneling units beneath German lines were preparing to detonate one of the largest non-nuclear explosions of all time.

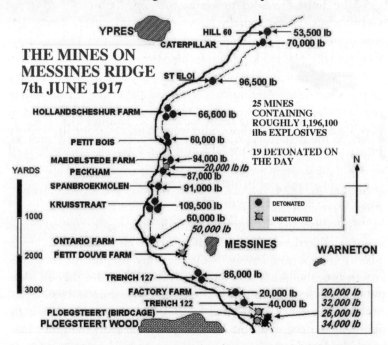

In the early morning on June 7, 1917, at 4:10 a.m. local time, nineteen of the twenty-four mines containing over 1.2 million pounds detonated almost simultaneously. It was the largest explosion ever caused by humans up to that juncture. It completely annihilated the enemy positions and created huge craters in the landscape, some of which can still be seen today.

1   "Mines in the Battle of Messines (1917)," Wikipedia (Wikimedia Foundation, December 12, 2021), https://en.wikipedia.org/wiki/Mines_in_the_Battle_of_Messines_(1917).

Belgian Chaplain Achiel Van Walleghem described zero hour in his revered war diary, "It was just 4 am and the first daylight was beginning to glimmer, when I suddenly saw the most gigantic and at the same time the most hideously magnificent firework display that had ever been detonated in Flanders, a veritable volcano, it was as if the entire south-east was belching fire. A few seconds passed before we felt the shocks. That was a veritable earthquake that lasted at least a minute. Oh, if it wasn't men being slaughtered, you would call it beautiful."[2]

The impact was so powerful that one reinforced concrete German bunker was actually blown completely upside down. The mines were even heard by British Prime Minister David Lloyd George, who was working late in his Downing Street study when the teacups rattled. The surprise was absolute and the ensuing impact was so devastating that it caused panic and chaos among the ranks of the German army. It was said that the devastation literally obliterated all those who were manning front line enemy positions immediately above the mines. In most cases, fragments of bone no bigger than a fingernail were all that remained of them. In the ensuing fight, the British, Irish, Australian, and New Zealand units succeeded in taking the Messines Ridge, but as with fruitless attacks before, it was an all too brief hiatus.[3]

Lieutenant J. Todd of the Eleventh Battalion, Prince of Wales's Own Yorkshire Regiment, wrote, "It was an appalling moment. We all had the feeling 'It's not going!' And then a most remarkable thing happened. The ground on which I was lying started to go up and down just like an earthquake. It lasted for seconds and then, suddenly in front of us, the Hill 60 mine went up."[4]

My granddad was there with one of his brothers. Early in the war, they raised so much hell that they were consequently assigned to different regiments. Apparently Grandad's brother Private John Pumford, service number 1086, was the first to be

2   Achiel Van Walleghem and Willy Spillebeen, "Oorlogsdagboeken 1914-1918," Uitgeverij Lannoo (December 6, 2021), https://www.lannoo.be/nl/oorlogsdagboeken-1914-1918.
3   Flanders State of the Art, "Anniversary of the Battle of Messines 7 - 14 June 2017 ," Visit Flanders, https://www.visitflanders.com/en/binaries/BattleofMessines_tcm13-87760.pdf.
4   Ailbhe Goodbody, "Tunnelling in the Deep," Mining Magazine (Aspermont, September 5, 2019), https://www.miningmagazine.com/mining-the-past/opinion/1263557/tunnelling-deep.

killed on May 24, 1915, when the Germans released a withering
chlorine gas attack during the second battle of Ypres. He was
nineteen years old.

The second one to lose his life was my great uncle George
Pumford, service number 49244. He was the eldest at thirty-seven
years old. The precise circumstances of his death aren't clear because
there were no major offensives occurring at the time, so his unfortunate demise was probably due to either gas or shrapnel. He was killed
on January 22, 1917. I think that he was close to granddad Joseph
Henry Pumford because Granddad would later name his first-born
son George. Brother William became a sergeant and survived the
war but after getting a "blighty one" (a wound bad enough to get
one sent back to the UK), he died tragically of an ear infection while
on the boat returning home. Bacteriology was unfortunately still in
its infancy.

Their first cousin, James Henry Pumford (Rifleman 7714),
was killed at the Battle of the Somme and is mentioned on the
Thiepval Memorial. He was just eighteen years old. His remains
were never recovered. When I decided to visit the memorial with
my wife about twenty years ago, I had a peculiar experience. I had
never visited it before, but despite this, I immediately picked out
his name from the 72,000 mentioned on the monument. I didn't
have to search for it—I just walked straight up to the panel and
there he was.

While researching Granddad's records, I noticed that he had
two serial numbers below his name: 4829 and 202084. This wasn't
unusual for those soldiers who were transferred from one regiment
to another, but this wasn't the case with Granddad Joe. I discovered
that he had been promoted to the rank of corporal and then subsequently demoted back to private for punching out a sergeant while
on duty. I've often wondered if the sergeant was his brother William,
but this has never been ascertained. Either way he sounded like one
of my lot: punch first and ask questions or make apologies later.

Mother always told me, "Your Granddad Joe had a wicked
temper and he was a stubborn old bugger." That was more or less
all I knew about the man when I began searching. Because although
I've met and interviewed innumerable veterans over the years, I

never actually knew my granddad. Like many survivors of World War I, he hardly ever spoke to anyone about his personal experiences and seldom, if ever, attended veteran reunions.

Standing at only five feet two inches, he was a diminutive Geordie miner who only opened his mouth to drink, feed, curse, and occasionally wedge a hand-rolled cigarette between his dry, thin lips. By all accounts, he could play a mouth organ, was always clean-shaven, wore a shirt and tie every Sunday, and always had a few bottles of Newcastle Brown Ale after his Sunday dinner. The only other detail mother could provide was that when she knew him, he never slept in a proper bed. He preferred the floor in front of the open hearth and once mentioned something about Passchendaele to her—with a vague inebriated reference to Hill 60—but she couldn't remember all the details.

She advised me to ask my Uncle George, who apparently knew him better than any of us. Granddad Joe had served his country with distinction in Flanders Fields and had paid a heavy price, sustaining respiratory damage that afflicted the rest of his life. The Third Battle of Ypres culminated in the deaths of 325,000 Allied soldiers and 260,000 German soldiers.

Uncle George said, "God forbid if he heard you break wind in close proximity." By all accounts, this voluntary or involuntary digestive reaction could send him into paroxysms of rage, which could reduce grown men to quivering heaps. I deduced from this that he could have used some serious behavior counseling, but there was a lot more to it than that, and I had to find out.

I have had the honor of meeting countless war veterans over the years and in my humble estimation, here was a man who was very obviously suffering from what we describe today as post-traumatic stress disorder (PTSD), but such things were rarely mentioned in those days. He had spent more than three years of his young life in the trenches on the Western front surrounded by dismembered and decomposing corpses. Of course he couldn't stand bad smells because they invoked too many painful memories. In most respects, he was no different from any other soldier who served in World War I. Confined in filth and squalor with the omnipresent prospect of imminent death, it's surprising that more of them didn't succumb to shell shock and battle fatigue. The despised British military hierarchy at the time referred to such debilitating afflictions in writing with the sinister acronym LMF (lack of moral fiber). It didn't get much more insensitive than that.

The only other thing I heard about Granddad was from an ex-miner colleague. He told that me when Britain declared war on Germany in 1939, my granddad stood at the front door of his terrace house with a personally requisitioned Lee-Enfield rifle and shouted, "Come on Hitler, I'm ready for ye yer bastard!"

Joseph Henry Pumford joined the British army in 1914, just one of the many who answered Lord Kitchener's call to arms. The year previous he and his three brothers had moved south from Durham to work in the Yorkshire coalfields. Coal mining was a "reserved occupation." They didn't have to go, but they probably considered soldiering to be less precarious than coal mining. It wasn't entirely wrong because this occupation had a particularly high mortality rate at the time.

Granddad Joe was a coal miner—a "shot firer" like my father had been. This was the job description given to those who extended the tunnels with dynamite on the coalface. In retrospect, the most natural evolution would have been for him to join one of the ubiquitous tunneling companies of the royal engineers. That would have been a logical choice, but I gather that he had enough of "being down there" and decided that the infantry would be his best option; however, joining the army's disciplined ranks was, in hindsight, not really a good option for someone who was independent-minded and quite assertive. According to one of the retired servicemen that used to gather on those park benches, "Your Granddad Joe was a good lad, but he didn't like any bugger telling him what to do," which isn't particularly conducive to soldiering.

On July 12, 1917, the Germans used mustard gas against the British for the first time. This was a bad start for the Allied bombardment that commenced four days later in preparation for a new offensive around Ypres. The battle of Messines had been relatively successful, but the ensuing delay before launching a consecutive offensive took too long. Granddad Joe was gassed on July 23 and transferred to a military hospital in Amiens. Meanwhile his brother, William, remained on active duty at the Ypres front.

First name(s)	J H
Last name	Pumford
Service number	20208
Rank	Private
Corps	King's Own Yorkshire Light Infantry
Admission year	1917
Hospital	No 39 Casualty Clearing Station
Transfer year	1917
Transfer date	24 Jul 1917
Transferred to	No 23 Amb Train
Description	British other ranks.
Archive	The National Archives
Piece	MH 106/819

Granddad Joe recovered and returned to Ypres to participate in the ongoing third Ypres offensive. It would conclude with the battle of Passchendaele, where he was present at the assault of October 4, 1917. As the King's Own Yorkshire Light Infantry (KOYLI) advanced, he got a piece of shrapnel in his shoulder that effectively ended his career in the army.

He obviously survived the war (otherwise I wouldn't be alive) and returned to his former job at the coal mine. Granddad was a heavy smoker; he died in 1953 of emphysema. This was no doubt compounded by the damage he had incurred to his lungs from the mustard gas and coal dust.

I'd like to end this chapter on a slightly brighter note. In 1998, I took my then twelve-year-old daughter Allycia to see the Queen and meet a man who was one of the last surviving veterans of Passchendaele. It was a dank, overcast, squally November morning in Ypres when I zeroed in on a 101-year-old World War I veteran comfortably ensconced in a wheelchair and protected from the driving rain beneath the Menin Gate Memorial.

His oversized jacket was sagging beneath his shoulders by the sheer weight of the medals, ribbons, and various other decorations pinned to it. I watched him for a little while, then tenuously approached and extended my hand to shake his.

"Hullo young man, what can I do for you?" he said looking up at me. Even though his marbled, old, blue eyes were glazed and reddened, they were alert, alive, and genuinely inquisitive.

"Who are you then lad?" he asked, putting his head slightly to one side as he awaited my response.

"Oh, I'm just an admirer who is deeply honored to meet a veteran such as yourself." I told him that my own granddad had fought at Ypres and had been wounded here.

"Aye lad, it was messy, very messy."

This was the kind of understatement that I'd become used to from northern British and Scottish war veterans over the years. "Messy" was the only appropriate adjective that he could produce to describe the unimaginable horrors that he had witnessed.

The arch above us contained the names of 54,896 officers and men from the British and Commonwealth forces that fell in the Ypres Salient before August 16, 1917; they had no known grave. They'd drowned in the mud or been blown to pieces. "Messy" said more than enough as far as I was concerned, but the old man added, "And do you know what young man? I still fucking hate the Germans."

I was living near Antwerp at the time, and I couldn't thank him enough for that parting statement because my daughter repeated it all the way home. By the time we arrived there it had evolved into a complete song with a sing-along karaoke chorus. She never went with me to meet veterans again. My dear wife, who imposed the lifetime ban on my daughter accompanying me to veteran memorials, asked if I could include a story of the Plantagenet's in this volume. I agreed only on the condition that I could tell my granddad's story first.

I never personally knew my granddad, or any of my great uncles for that matter, but I grew up hearing the name Passchendaele in my house. At the time, I had no idea of the significance of this name to my family or to history. Many years later, I traced granddad's footsteps from Etaples to Passchendaele and laid a wreath to my clan at the Menin Gate Memorial, where they still blow the Last Post bugle call every evening at 2000h as a mark of respect to the fallen.

CHAPTER TWO:

THE SONS OF RAGNAR WHO?

The well-known History Channel TV series *Vikings* took some serious liberties with actual history for the purposes of indulging popular fantasy; however, that doesn't detract from the fact that it introduced untold millions to the exploits of the notorious Vikings. Incidentally, the helmets worn by the so-called Saxon army in the *Vikings* series are exactly the same as those that Stannis' men wore in *Game of Thrones*. Strange, maybe they were the only helmets available from the props department when they were filming? This detail isn't very historical, though, and to those in the know, it's painfully inaccurate. Saxons simply didn't wear those kinds of helmets, which were more reminiscent of those worn by the Spanish conquistadors some five centuries later. At least none of the Vikings in the TV series had horns or wings on their helmets, which is a relief of sorts.

It's relatively safe to assume that Ragnar Lothbrok or Lodbrok existed. Two verifiable references of a particularly renowned Viking raider in 840 CE named Ragnall, also known as Reginherus, appear in the Anglo-Saxon Chronicle, which is considered to be a generally reliable source. His story was also related by the skalds of Iceland (a Scandinavian chronicle of the Viking age), 350 years after the supposed death of this most elusive of heroes.

It is, however, equally possible that the Ragnar often referred to in the testosterone-fueled Viking sagas may be a composite based on more than one actual person.

Bearing in mind that they all had anger management issues, it's entirely possible that the Ragnar often referred to in the Viking Sagas may be a composite based on more than one actual person.

For many, he is regarded as the first real Viking personage to emerge from the vague accounts of the period. In The Saga of Ragnar Lothbrok it reads, "Sigurd had a son named Ragnar, who was a large man, fair of countenance and keen in wit, great-hearted toward his men but grim to his foes."[5] This is how the erstwhile ninth-century Viking monarch and sometime dragon-slayer Ragnar Lothbrok is

5   Dom Tromans, "The Making of a Legend: The Saga of Ragnar Lothbrok and the TV Series 'Vikings," Medievalists.net, November 15, 2015, https://www.medievalists.net/2015/11/the-making-of-a-legend-the-saga-of-ragnar-lothbrok-and-the-tv-series-vikings/.

introduced to his audience. By all accounts, the real Ragnar was a fearsome Viking warlord and chieftain who was the scourge of England and France. Despite the fact that there is so much ambiguity surrounding the legend of Ragnar, it still provided sufficient fuel to the TV series makers to play around with the details as they saw fit without the need for any official disclaimer. So what about his notorious sons?

One particularly confusing aspect of the story are the multiple sources, which confirm the existence of figures that are recorded as having been either the sons of Ragnar or the sons of Lothbrok, Lagertha, and Aslaug Sigurdsdottir. But nowhere in antiquity are any of the figures referred to here as having been the actual sons of Ragnar Lothbrok. The name "Lothbrok" alone has the potential to confuse because it is written with many variations in the annals of history. The *Vikings* TV series can be definitively referred to as entertaining pseudo-history that transposes the scantest of details and proposes them as historical fact for the pure purpose of enhancing viewer stats, and hopefully getting another commission for an ensuing series. That said, according to existing records, some of the incidents and characters that appeared in the show were indeed real as far as historians are concerned.

While numerous protagonists have been called descendants of the legendary Ragnar Lothbrok, many who attempted to emulate the feats of the original Ragnar would have been referred to as a "Son of Ragnar." This was an attributed title and often regarded as a mark of honor or aspiration as opposed to a statement of hereditary genetic fact.

To fans of the TV show *Vikings*, the following names may sound familiar: Björn Ironside, Ivar the Boneless, Hvitserk, Ubba, and Sigurd Snake-in-the-Eye. It's important to note that this was the darkest of the dark ages and verifiable sources confirming their existence are at best scarce, at worst pure speculation and conjecture, except in the cases of Björn, Ivar, and Hvitserk. According to some sources, Ragnar and Aslaug had a son named Hvitserk, and in other sources he is called Halfdan. Considering that these two names never appear in the same source, it's relatively safe to assume they are probably the same person. All three are all genuine historical figures.

The Vikings were very reliable when it came to attributing nicknames to their heroes such as "boneless," "snake-in-the-eye." And "ironside." But there were some who didn't appear in the series whose nicknames were not as complimentary, such as Ulf the Squint-Eyed, (who could simultaneously look at both ends of long ship), Eirik Ale-Lover (frequently horizontal), and Eystein Foul-Fart (best avoided after a good pillage). Needless to say, the protagonists rarely had any say in the nicknames they were accorded.

The main problem in researching Ragnar is exacerbated by the fact that Vikings didn't preserve written records of their history. Therefore most of what is acknowledged is derived from the Norse/Icelandic sagas (notably *The Tale of Ragnar's Sons*), but other sources and historical accounts from conquered peoples corroborate the existence and activities of a certain Ivar the Boneless and his brethren.

In the Viking sagas, Ivar the Boneless was a man capable of exceptional cruelty and stupefying ferocity in battle. During his lifetime, he ruled over an area that extended through parts of modern Denmark and Sweden. It was said that Ivar had only limp cartilage where bone should have been, but despite this handicap, he matured into a tall, muscular, handsome man. There is much disagreement as to the meaning of Ivar's perplexing epithet "the Boneless." It may have been a hereditary skeletal condition such as *osteogenesis imperfecta* (brittle bone disease) or an inability to walk upright—which begs the question, how did they refer to him as tall? But it has been suggested that boneless was a euphemism for impotence. It was said that he had "no love lust in him."[6] It may, however, simply have referred to physical flexibility. In his defense, he was also regarded as having been the most intelligent of Ragnar's children.

Ivar's stature was such that he dwarfed all his contemporaries and in battle he led from the front in the little chariot so often depicted in the TV series. His arms were apparently so muscular that his bow was more powerful and his arrows heavier than any of those wielded by his fellow warriors. Nordic sources mention Ivar being carried on a shield by his army, which to some insinuates that he was lame; however, this is unlikely considering he was a

6   Amy Irvine, "10 Facts About Viking Warrior Ivar the Boneless," History Hit (History Hit, August 18, 2021), https://www.historyhit.com/facts-about-ivar-the-boneless/.

renowned warrior. Other sources from the period mention chieftains being ceremonially borne on the shields of enemies following a victory. The main Latin source in which Ivar is written about at length is the *Gesta Danorum* ("Deeds of the Danes"), written in the early thirteenth century by Saxo Grammaticus, which surprisingly makes absolutely no mention of Ivar being boneless at all.

The other brother of repute was Björn "Ironside" Ragnarsson, who is considered by many to be the founder and first king of the Munsö dynasty. This house ruled Sweden for many generations and is considered a protohistoric Scandinavian royal house that originated around the eighth or ninth centuries. The actual history of this dynasty isn't verifiable until the tenth and eleventh centuries when historically verifiable figures emerge.

Björn Ironside presumably reigned as king during the ninth century. His name, or rather nickname, was derived from the belief that he was rarely wounded in battle. In fact, it was thought that he was invulnerable to any wound. He grew up alongside his brothers and half-brothers and later ventured out of Sweden to conquer Zealand, Reidgotaland, Gotland, Öland, and all the minor islands. He then spent a considerable period of his life at Lejre in Zealand. One story tells how Björn and his brothers then left Zealand to avenge their half-brothers who had been killed in Sweden. Björn also conducted raids in France and the Mediterranean. According to historical accounts, after raiding the coasts of Spain, his assault force returned to pillage France and then ventured forth deep into the Mediterranean to assault the city of Pisa, Italy, which hadn't considered the prospect of a leaning tower at that time.

Progress was halted when they arrived at the city gates of Luna (Luni, as it's now called, is located in present-day northern Italy), which they wrongly assumed to be Rome. Having difficulties breaching the walls of Luna, Björn had to think of a guileful way to gain entry to the city. He sent his men to inform the bishop of the city that before Björn had died, he had converted to Christianity; it was imperative that his body was interned on consecrated ground. The city allowed the casket containing his apparently lifeless form to be brought within the city walls by a small group of guards. It was placed before the altar inside the city's church. Björn popped out of the box and fought his way to the city gates, which he then opened to allow his decidedly heathen army access. So by using his astuteness and intelligence, omitting his knowledge of geographical aspects, Björn managed to capture the city and consequently became one of the most famous Vikings in history. In the TV series, Ragnar Lothbrok used this very same deception to enter Paris.

After Luna was taken, Björn and his mighty Viking fleet raided Sicily and the coast of North Africa. On their return journey, as they passed the Straits of Gibraltar, they encountered the seaborne forces of the Al-Andalus. At this juncture, they were attacked with Greek fire. The concoction known as "Greek fire" is often referenced in antiquity. It was made from such substances as pitch, naphtha, sulfur, and charcoal. This could be thrown in pots or discharged from tubes, whereupon it apparently caught fire spontaneously and could not be extinguished with water. This particular attack allegedly disposed of forty of Björn's ships from his Viking fleet.

It is nigh on impossible to know how much of Björn Ironside's story is historic and how much is conjecture extracted from other Viking stories and attributed to him. There is sufficient proof to claim that there was someone called Björn Ironside that lived in the ninth century; however, it's highly unlikely that Björn died in battle or at the hands of Ivar the Boneless. The precise cause of his death remains a mystery, but it is widely assumed he may have died of old age or possibly illness.

A possible location could be the most prominent burial mound on the Swedish island of Munsö located in Lake Mälaren. It's also known as Björnshögen and widely considered to be the last resting place of the legendary Viking Björn Ironside. That's the assumption at least, but this has never really been definitively proven either. Christian monks recorded much of what is known of these myths and legends a few hundred years after the Viking age had elapsed. By then many of the Nordic gods had been forgotten or lost to posterity.

The third son of Ragnar and Aslaug, whose story appears in various sources, was Hvitserk, or Halfdan. Halfdan appears both in *Beowulf* and in historical records. The name literally means "half Dane," which could imply that he was of indeterminate parentage. The other name that this character is referred to is Hvitserk, which means "white shirt." Halfdan joined his brothers in their campaign to avenge the death of their father. After the success of their army in the siege of York (*Jorvik* in the Viking language) and the victory against the Northumbrian pretender kings Osberht and Ælla, Halfdan was given the command over the city. This would be a temporary position.

While his brothers Ivar, Björn, and Ubba led the great army farther southward, it was Halfdan's task to strengthen their political position in the occupied territory and subject the inhabitants to Danelaw. Danelaw was used in the part of England controlled by the Danes and dominated the laws of the indigenous Anglo-Saxons. The term was first recorded in the early eleventh century as *Dena lage*. Although Halfdan might not have been as great of a warrior as his brothers, he had remarkable political and administrative skills.

Son number four is Ubba, or Ubbe Ragnarsson, who is generally regarded as having been one of the other illegitimate sons of Ragnar. Ubba's mother is said to have been a Swedish noblewoman who died giving birth to him. He was raised in his father's court alongside his brothers. According to existing historical sources, Ubba was always in competition with his brothers Björn, Halfdan, and Sigurd but especially with their mother Aslaug, who resented Ubba because he was the son of her husband and another woman. Ubba may have been the most skilled and fierce warrior among Ragnar's sons, but he was also irascible and impetuous, which (being a Viking) didn't make him particularly unique. Most of them had anger management issues too.

During a rebellion against Ragnar's rule over Sweden, Ubba sided with his maternal grandfather Esbjörn. In a decisive battle between the armies of Ragnar and his sons on one side, and Ubba and his grandfather on the other side, Esbjörn was killed and Ubba was captured. After swearing an oath of loyalty to his father, Ubba was released from captivity, but this incident strained his relationship with his brothers, who never forgot Ubba's treason.

After the death of Ragnar, Ubba joined his brothers in their invasion of England to avenge their father. Ubba was a devout believer of the Norse gods who had no problem at all raiding monasteries and churches—which, according to the Christian population, made him the most feared of the Vikings. He advocated a total ban of Christianity within the occupied territories and had serious doubts about appointing Christian client kings to rule in the Viking-occupied territories. This inevitably led to further friction between him and his brothers. Ubba was killed in the battle of Cynwit in present day Devonshire, England, in 878 CE.

Lastly, the story of Sigurd Snake-in-the-Eye. The name refers to a defect iris that was elongated as opposed to round, which apparently resembled a "snake-in-the-eye" or "serpent eye." His name is also referred to as Sigurðr, Sigurthr, Siuardus, Siward, Siwardus, and Syuardus. The chronicles from Adam of Bremen, the *Annals of Fulda*, and the *Gesta Danorum* write about the fraternal relation between Sigurd and Halfdan. Saxo Grammaticus claims that Sigurd received his distinguishing optic trait in battle, as the result of a war wound.

So to get a bit of background, it's imperative to look at the accepted historical details of the era. One of the first recorded rape, loot, and pillage ventures by the Vikings occurred in the year 793 CE when Viking ships attacked and ravaged the monastery at Lindisfarne on the east coast of England. By 800 CE the Anglo-Saxons ruled kingdoms and territories in the British Midlands, the largest of which was Mercia (527–879 CE). For the purpose of clarification, Mercia was one of the Anglo-Saxons' heptarchic kingdoms centered on the valley of the River Trent and its tributaries, in what is now the Midlands of England. Mercia was bordered to the south by the kingdom of Wessex, to the west by Wales, north by Northumbria, and to the east by East Anglia. Even though a powerful warlord ruled the kingdom, he didn't provide sufficient protection against Viking raids. The warlord would "talk the talk" but would not necessarily "walk the walk," unless it was in the opposite direction of the hairy marauders.

Accompanied by his brothers Halfdan and Ubba, Ivar crossed the North Sea to England and led the invasion of East Anglia in 865 CE. There, he unfurled the Viking raven banner and terrified East Anglians to such an extent that they made peace with the invaders and even provided them with horses, albeit under duress.

After the conquest of East Anglia in 866 CE, they used these horses to head for York, the capital of the Anglo-Saxon kingdom of

Northumbria. The Vikings probably chose York as their prime target because at that time there was civil war in Northumbria, and they thought that this would make an invasion of the territory easier. It is difficult to get a clear understanding of the actual size of the attacking force, which is simply referred to by Anglo-Saxon chroniclers as the "Great Heathen Army." Some say it was comprised of two—or perhaps three—thousand men, but others have suggested it may have numbered as few as three hundred. The army was sizeable enough to establish temporary settlements in the areas where they disembarked. On the whole, they got on extremely well with the indigenous Yorkshire folk and intermarried. This northern British/Viking heritage is still omnipresent in Yorkshire, particularly at weekends, and more specifically after flagons of ale have been consumed.

Halfdan and Ivar the Boneless led the Viking army that attacked the York on November 1, 866 CE. It was All Saints Day, an important festival in the city's calendar when many of the town's leaders, along with Northumbrian kings Ælla and Osberht, would have been in the cathedral. The carefully planned surprise attack was successful, but the two kings were not taken prisoner.

During Northumbria's civil war, King Ælla of Northumbria had usurped the throne from King Osberht, who had ruled for the previous eighteen years; however, they agreed to put their differences aside and unite against their common enemy. It took a full four months for them to organize and join forces. The following year, sometime around March 21, 867 CE, the Anglo-Saxon army stormed York's city walls and managed to break through the first line of defense. The Viking army, who had been spending the winter farther north on the banks of the River Tyne, then had the task of supporting the garrison in place and defending York against Ælla and Osberht's joint forces. The Northumbrian *Anglo-Saxon Chronicle* recorded that there was "an excessive slaughter made of the Northumbrians."

Both Ælla and Osberht were taken prisoner and killed in revenge for the cruel execution of Ivar's father, Ragnar Lothbrok, who was allegedly thrown into a snake pit on Ælla's orders. York was now firmly held by the Vikings and would remain in their hands for the majority of the next eighty years.

In apparent retribution for the death of Ragnar, Ælla was subjected to the unimaginably agonizing death often referred to in the Nordic sagas as "the blood eagle," a horrific, ritualistic Viking method of torture and execution. The torture would begin by making an incision from the nape of the neck to the pelvis, detaching the ribs of the victim from the spine, breaking the ribs, and then extracting the lungs through the wound in the victim's back so they resembled blood-stained wings. The victim would be kept alive throughout the ordeal whenever possible to add to the spectator's enjoyment. Salt was then liberally sprinkled in the exposed flesh.

This depiction of murder may have stemmed from a potential misinterpretation of a skaldic verse present in *The Saga of Ragnar Lothbrok* that mentions death by the mark of an eagle; however, this is a possible mistranslation that has prolonged one of the most widely accepted modern stereotypes concerning Vikings, who are frequently portrayed as bloodthirsty, murderous brutes. But this also distracts modern audiences from the importance of Vikings in their other role as peaceful settlers who built towns and villages and established lucrative trading routes across the known world.

After the conquest of Northumbria in 866 CE and East Anglia in 869 CE, it is believed that the Great Heathen Army added to their numbers when the Viking "Summer Army," under the command of King Bagsecg (also known as Bægsecg or Bagsec), arrived with reinforcements.

In 870 CE, Halfdan led an invasion into Wessex and took the field on six occasions against the new king of Wessex, Alfred, who successfully resisted and repelled the attempted Viking incursion into his kingdom. Halfdan had no other option at the time than to accept a truce from King Alfred. Halfdan's army then retreated to the Danish-occupied city of Lunden (London) and remained there during the winter of 871/872 CE.

In 873 CE, they were compelled to return to York yet again because their puppet King Egbert and Wulfhere, the archbishop of York, had been driven out by a rebellion. Wulfhere had clearly reached some agreement with the Vikings and was regarded as their ally. The rebellion was mercilessly crushed and Wulfhere was restored to his cathedral, but Egbert had died and had to be replaced by another puppet ruler. The Vikings now felt that York was secure, which enabled them to safely spend the winter of 873/874 CE in Lincolnshire. In 874 CE, the Vikings conquered Mercia and divided it in two halves. According to the skaldic saga, Sigurd and Björn returned home after the capture of York. Sigurd didn't return alone. He took King Ælla's daughter, Blaeja, as his wife, and she gave him four children. After the death of his brother, Halfdan, Sigurd became the king of Denmark sometime around 877 CE. It's generally assumed that he died in battle in 891 CE. After a series of campaigns against other kingdoms, part of the Great Heathen Army returned to Northumbria in 876 CE. According to the *Anglo-Saxon Chronicle*, Halfdan then became the first Viking king of Northumbria. He "shared out the lands of the Northumbrians and they proceeded to plow and to support themselves."[7]

The legendary Danish king Harthacanute (1018–1042 CE) may have been a grandson or a great-grandson of Sigurd, though neither claim is verifiable.

Precisely where and how Ivar died isn't entirely clear. Professor Martin Biddle of the University of Oxford and his wife Birthe claim that the skeletal remains of a nine-foot-tall Viking warrior, discovered during excavations at the churchyard of St. Wystan's in Repton in southern Derbyshire, may be that of Ivar the Boneless. But this is pure speculation.

Another prominent character from the TV series was the shield maiden Lagertha. Historically, there is no hard evidence that proves the existence of formally trained female warriors in ancient Scandinavian culture, but that didn't deter Hollywood. Viking sagas make some references to powerful female warriors, but later assessments determined that shield maidens were nothing more than a symbolic incarnation of idealized womanhood, similar to the handmaidens of the god Odin, who were known as the Valkyries. Death in combat and access to Valhalla, the Viking version of heaven, feature prominently in these stories, but it's safe to assume that these women warriors were nothing more than an aspect of Viking legends.

The story of Lagertha is also referred to in the *Gesta Danorum*, which details how she met Ragnar and how he killed a bear and hound that guarded her home. She was so impressed with this feat that she married Ragnar, but there is no mention of any of the sons

7   David A.E. Pelteret, ed., *Anglo-Saxon History: Basic Readings* (Routledge, 2021).

depicted in the TV series. According to the same reference, the happy couple had one son called Fridleif and two daughters, whose names are not recorded. There is, however, mention of their divorce and Ragnar's request for help during a domestic civil war, where-upon Lagertha sent 120 ships to assist her ex—but maybe that was in the prenup.

One of the primary sources for the stories of our beloved protagonists was, as previously mentioned, the *Gesta Danorum* by Saxo Grammaticus, but it should be pointed out that Saxo's accounts do not faithfully reflect all the information contained in the Old Norse material that he draws from extensively. Saxo heavily modified and edited his source material, making it nigh on impossible to reconcile his narratives with the broader Old Norse framework. Once scholars accurately identified the sources and compared them to the material he recorded, it became glaringly obvious that Saxo had altered them dramatically to fit his personal narrative and indulge his own misogynistic, ideological requirements.

Inspired by a profound affection for Old Norse legendary sagas, Saxo includes characters ad hoc from Germanic folklore into his narratives intermixed with a basic medieval Christian understanding of Classical culture. Therefore, these accounts cannot be considered reliable. Saxo was capable of being diplomatic with the truth. He rationalized his narratives from myth, and then added, subtracted, and amended as he saw fit. But does it matter?

Incidentally, the place referred to as Kattegat in the series is a fictional Viking settlement. The Kattegat is actually the name of a sea region located between Sweden, Denmark, and Norway. There are several large cities and major ports in the shallow sea known as the Kattegat, including Gothenburg, Aarhus, Aalborg, Halmstad, and Frederikshavn.[8]

Vikings is a highly entertaining TV series that deserves every accolade as long as it isn't seen, or regarded as, an accurate historical account. But that shouldn't prevent anyone from thoroughly enjoying the entertaining (and somewhat bloodthirsty) antics of Ragnar, his wives, and their sons.

---

8   "Kattegat," Wikipedia (Wikimedia Foundation, February 3, 2022), https://en.wikipedia. org/wiki/Kattegat.

My father was a born and bred Yorkshire man. They used to say, "Yorkshire born, Yorkshire bred, strong in the arm and thick in the head," which isn't entirely inaccurate, but there are exceptions. My Dad always said, "I'm descended from Vikings, which make you half a Viking." Consequently, I was only allowed to wear one horn on my Woolworths play helmet. The first time I heard the name Ragnar was at the York Castle Museum, the first museum I ever visited when I was a mere ten years old. As I've mentioned earlier, the Viking name for York was Jorvik, and the Viking legacy is everywhere in the north. They had a magnificent display at the museum all about the northern Viking heritage. I was hooked and have been ever since. Ragnar lives!

CHAPTER THREE:

THE LIONHEART AND THE LACKLAND.

During their reign, the Plantagenet dynasty was the most affluent royal family in Europe, bar none. They ruled England for over 300 years, from 1154–1485, and held a significant portion of France. Their name derives from *planta genista*, which is Latin for "yellow broom flower." This was also the emblem that the counts of Anjou wore on their helmets and shields. They were among one of the most murderous and treacherous collectives ever to hold sway. Stories of their evil, manipulative ways have long since been ingrained in history and captured the imaginations of both historians and readers alike. Two of the best-known kings from this motley crew were King Richard I, *Coeur de Lion* (lionheart), the brave one, and King John (nicknamed Lackland, because he didn't own much territory outside England), who wasn't all that brave.

Richard made a name for himself as a renowned crusader, who always led from the front, but his affections for England were questionable to say the least.

The Magna Carta granted by King John at Runnymede only remained in effect for a few short weeks. John grudgingly agreed to the document under duress from his barons. He even managed to get excommunicated by the Pope.

In many Robin Hood movies and TV series, King Richard the Lionheart is often portrayed as the courageous warrior who returns from his crusade to the green and pleasant land to release his merry souls of England from the clutches of his wayward brother, the apparently evil King John. What's even more astounding is how many people actually believe this; such is the all-persuasive power of contemporary media. So was it really just a case of good King Richard and bad King John?

The truth of the matter is considerably more complex and deeper than TV and cinema's errant portrayals of these two disaffected brothers from this highly dysfunctional family. It's nothing short of remarkable that there is a proud statue of King Richard mounted on his steed and holding up his sword of justice outside the British bastion of democracy, the Houses of Parliament. The fact is that Richard probably didn't speak a word of English and didn't particularly care for his subjects, except for tax reasons. He much preferred being in France, where he would eventually meet his demise.

Richard I was born on September 8, 1157, and became, among other things, king of England (from 1189–1199), duke of Aquitaine, count of Poitiers, duke of Normandy, lord of Cyprus, and count of Anjou. He was also the great grandson of Godfrey de Bouillon, the man whose successful first crusade led to him being crowned the first Christian king of Jerusalem. Godfrey staunchly objected to being called "King of Jerusalem" because in his fervently pious mind there was only ever one king, namely Jesus Christ.

Richard and his brothers were not renowned for harboring profound respect for their father. When Richard was only seventeen years old, he conspired with his other brothers to organize what became an unsuccessful rebellion against Henry II. When Richard's eldest brother, Henry the Young King, died in 1183, Henry II basically offered Richard Normandy and Anjou in exchange for the province of Aquitaine, which the king intended to give to his younger brother John. This suggestion didn't go down all that well with Richard, who regarded the offer as a base insult, which in turn led to further dispute with Henry II.

Henry II was the person who inadvertently gave the order to assassinate Thomas Becket of Canterbury, when he allegedly uttered the words, "Will no one rid me of this turbulent priest?" A couple of bored knights in proximity overheard and replied something to the effect of, "Leave it with us boss, we're on it."

As the relationship between Richard and his father deteriorated, Richard defected to the Capetians (a dynasty of Frankish origin often referred to as the House of France), and with the support of Philip Augustus, he drove Henry II out of Le Mans and to an early death. Richard became King Richard I and received the entirety of his father's lands owned in the Angevin, or Plantagenet, empire. The unusually close relationship between Richard and Philip Augustus raises some questions regarding Richard's sexuality. Was Richard the Lionheart gay and would Sean Connery have portrayed him if he had known?

Roger of Hoveden, a renowned court chronicler of the day, was in a position to gather the facts as he interpreted them during those tumultuous years from 1192–1201. Roger had previously reported in 1187 that Richard and King Philip of shared a bed,[9] but it was common for people of the same sex to do this at that time. It was generally seen as an expression of trust and not intended for the purpose of sexual gratification. In medieval times, it was common practice for men to kiss or hold hands, which was usually construed as political gestures of friendship or peace.

So it's probably wrong to assume that an act that had symbolic significance 800 years ago has the same implications by contemporary standards. It should be pointed out, though, that no such aspersions were cast against Philip Augustus. Roger further states that, "Richard and Philip ate from the same dish, at night slept in one bed and had a strong love between them."[10] Truth be known, Roger wasn't a great fan of Richard the Lionheart, and his writing can be interpreted in a number of ways depending on one's perspective.

Richard's future wife, Berengaria of Navarre, was brought to his court in March 1191, which was, at that time, located at Messina, Sicily. It wasn't Richard's first venture into the realm of intended nuptials. Richard's father arranged for his nine-year-old son to be

---

9   Helen Castor, "Why Richard I Shared His Bed with the King of France," *The Guardian* (Guardian News and Media, March 19, 2008), https://www.theguardian.com/uk/2008/mar/19/monarchy.france.

10   *England in the Middle Ages: the Angevins 1154-1216* By Peter Simpson

betrothed to French King Louis VII's daughter Princess Alais, who was also nine years old. But the wedding never happened, probably because piñatas and goody bags hadn't been invented.

Berengaria accompanied Richard on his journey east when he embarked on his legendary crusade, possibly in an attempt to emulate his illustrious great-grandfather Godfrey de Bouillon. It is, however, a fact that he didn't provide his wife Berengaria with any children, but that could have been due to his frequent absence. On the other hand, Richard's failure to provide offspring from his union could be interpreted by some as further proof of his inclinations. But these assumptions are precisely what occur when one applies twenty-first century perceptions to medieval ideologies. During his reign, Richard physically spent less than two years in the British Isles. But over his lifetime, while on his notorious wanderings, he did manage to father two illegitimate children. There is no conclusive proof that this steel-jawed warrior was anything but precisely that.

His brother John is historically regarded as having been a weak, duplicitous, and vicious person—a traitor, usurper, and even murderer—who was eventually excommunicated by the pope and compelled by his oppressed barons, along with the archbishop of Canterbury at their head, to sign the famous Magna Carta.

Stories about his life describe him as the evil conspirator who plotted against his glorious and magnanimous brother Richard and attempted to seduce Matilda Fitzwalter, otherwise known as Maid Marian. Robin wouldn't have been happy about that, if he had actually existed, and there is still no definitive proof that he ever did (try telling that to Hollywood). Contemporary chroniclers and historians are still inclined to rely on myth and bias to enhance their interpretations.

Historically, Richard's name is more likely to be associated with the name of his famous adversary Saladin rather than that of John, although John did give the Lionheart some cause for serious concern.

Saladin, or Al-Nasir Salah al-Din Yusuf ibn Ayyub, was a Sunni Muslim Kurd born in the city of Tikrit, Iraq—the same place as Saddam Hussein. In his lifetime, Saladin rose to power, became the first sultan of Egypt and Syria, and founded the Ayyubid dynasty. News of his exploits had reached many in Europe including Richard. It was the mercy he displayed to the Christian citizens of Jerusalem after its capture, among many other things, that earned him a place in history.

In the autumn of 1187, when news of Saladin's recapture of Jerusalem reached Europe, people were undeniably animated and moved. Passions were further inflamed when it was even alleged that the elderly and infirm Pope Urban III died of grief when he heard that the Holy City had fallen to the Muslims, but this was more than likely medieval conjecture intended to enrage the consciences of European Christians.

In late October 1187, Urban's successor, Pope Gregory VIII, issued the papal bull *Audita tremendi*, calling on the people of Europe to launch a new crusade to retake the Holy Land. It blamed the calamity primarily on the sins of the Franks who had occupied Jerusalem for eighty-eight years since the time of Godfrey de Bouillon. The pope further insisted that Christians living in Europe were equally culpable of even allowing a Muslim force to dominate the Holy Land.

However, religion being an omnipresent force at the time, signing up to the crusades would absolve the potential participant of all past sins, no matter how great. That appeared to do the trick.

In late November 1187, a few weeks after the papal bull was issued, Richard was among the first western princes to take the cross, which meant he was signing up to participate in the crusade. It was a rather extraordinary decision at that time, considering his attention was preoccupied with his need to defend the duchy of Aquitaine and ensure his succession to the Angevin empire now that Henry II had shed his mortal coil.

It is, however, also entirely possible that Richard regarded the planned Third Crusade as an opportunity to cement his legend a great warrior. When Henry II died in July 1189, Richard inherited his throne and his vast empire. Once he had these opulent resources at his disposal, he began earnestly making preparations, and "merry olde England" was seen as a good place to impose huge taxes on his subjects that became known as the "Saladin tithe." Under this administrative umbrella, Richard sold vast amounts of land and property in order to raise money for his crusade. It was even jested that Richard would have sold London itself if he could have found a buyer. So England was good for something then?

Stringent and ruthless economic planning became tantamount to the new king's considerations because he had decided to travel to the Holy Land by sea. Building and hiring ships would entail vast financial expenditure, but a sea journey would be markedly swifter than a laborious, time-consuming expedition over land. In time, Richard's crusading army would become a disciplined and effective fighting force assembled by faith and maintained by punitive penalties for all transgressions.

It's perfectly feasible to propose that a further impetus for Richard was maybe an irrepressible urge to emulate his illustrious great-grandfather Godfrey de Bouillon. King Richard embarked on the Third Crusade with the intention of retaking Jerusalem from the renowned Saracen-commander Saladin and the Muslim occupiers to reestablish it as a Christian city.

After Richard had taken Cyprus in 1191, he joined King Philip of France who was dealing with the siege at the port of Acre, gateway to the Holy Land. Once Richard's army disembarked and threw themselves into it, Acre fell in just five weeks—but a dispute arose between the lionhearted one and his former dear friend Philip of France. The two monarchs divided the property of Acre equally, but tensions soon resurfaced because each king supported a different claimant to the throne of Jerusalem. Only weeks after Acre fell, Philip decided to abandon his participation with the crusade and leave the Holy Land along with his army.

The Lionheart then went on to meet Saladin's forces at what became known as the battle of Arsuf. Up until that juncture, Saladin's army was undefeated. By September 7, the crusaders were just twenty-five miles away from Jerusalem's port of Jaffa, and Saladin was determined to prevent their further advance. If Richard's forces could take Jaffa so soon after the fall of Acre, Saladin's reputation and his position as the fearless, noble defender of Islam would become seriously compromised.

The battle of Arsuf commenced when Saladin's army numbering around 30,000 emerged from the wooded hills onto the plain north of Jaffa. It was an unwelcome surprise for the first crusaders that arrived at the battlefield who hadn't really expected any concerted opposition to their march. It was then that the rigorous discipline of Richard's crusaders became significant to any chance of achieving victory against this vastly numerically superior force of seasoned Muslim warriors. Moreover, most of the crusaders were wearing chainmail and armor in searing heat as opposed to the light linen clothing worn by the Saracen army.

Consecutive waves of Muslim cavalry attacked the marching crusader army but were effectively repulsed every time. Throughout this terrible initial onslaught, King Richard's priority was focused on maintaining formation as they moved forward. He was well aware that a break in the line could prove potentially fatal. He watched dismayed as two impetuous knights broke ranks and began pursuing Saladin's cavalry, followed by hundreds of their fellow crusaders. Richard had little option at that moment than to order his whole army into the fray. During the ensuing chaotic melee, Richard's men adeptly repelled two fierce Muslim counterattacks and launched renewed charges, which eventually forced Saladin's army to flee from the field in apparent disarray.

Although victorious, Richard the Lionheart's leadership at the battle of Arsuf has raised questions among some historians. His role as a resolute and effective commander may have been exaggerated over the many centuries that have passed since the event. Although he didn't plan this encounter, under the circumstances he merely reacted as he saw fit. There is, however, no doubt that the success of the crusaders in reaching Jaffa marked a pivotal moment in the Third Crusade. Saladin's army had been seriously mauled, but they were still more or less intact. The battle of Arsuf had definitely damaged their morale, but this was probably because it was Saladin's first major defeat at the hands of the crusaders. His apparent invincibility had been compromised and that was a bitter blow.

It's at this juncture, with the port of Jaffa comfortably in the hands of the crusaders, that disagreements began to arise between Richard and his leading nobles. Disconcerting news had reached them concerning Ascalon, a castle some thirty miles to the south, which safeguarded Saladin's communication and supply route to Egypt. Saladin had preempted Richard's assault on the stronghold and had taken the painful decision to sacrifice the castle. He instructed his men to break down the city walls and render the place indefensible.

Richard insisted that it was integral to capture this port as a means to weaken Saladin and protect crusader supply lines in preparation for an eventual siege of Jerusalem. Well that's what he told his nobles, but it would later transpire that Richard's primary intention was to conduct raids into Egyptian territory, as opposed to venturing inland to secure the Holy City some forty miles east of Jaffa.

His nobles, being an obstreperous lot, vehemently disagreed. They wanted to move on Jerusalem as soon as they could. The multitudinous members of the clergy and pilgrims that had accompanied the crusade inevitably supported this move and rallied to the cry of "Deus vult" (God wills it). Collectively they remained resolute that getting to Jerusalem had to be the main objective and imperative of the campaign. What these religious zealots didn't know was that behind the scenes, Richard had been conducting negotiations with Saladin concerning the division of Palestine between the crusaders and the Muslims. With the purpose of achieving this goal, Richard even discussed the possibilities of making a truce with Saladin's brother Al-Adil. In an attempt to sway his hand, Richard even offered his own sister Joan to become one of Al-Adil's wives. It's not particularly surprising that Joan didn't react favorably to this suggestion. "You've done what? I'm not marrying him." In fact, it's surprising that Al-Adil agreed to the union because, although European personal hygiene was at best questionable, Muslims were particularly stringent when it came to maintaining a clean body.

Meanwhile the Knights Templars and Hospitallers, supported by some local warlords, defended Richard's plan wholeheartedly, and also agreed that a foray to the east would leave their supply lines dangerously exposed. Despite their fervent objections, Richard, being a pious man, inevitably bowed to pressure from the clergy and began marching his troops toward Jerusalem. As they progressed inland, torrential winter rains heaved down and powerful gusts of wind yanked tent pegs out of the ground. The inclement weather rusted armor, bogged down the horses, and turned the barely discernable roads into virtually impassable quagmires, which impeded further advances. It didn't bode well.

Then in the spring of 1192, Richard was faced with increasing pressure both internally and externally. To make matters worse, messengers arrived from Europe bringing news that his younger brother Prince John was attempting a coup d'état. By May 29, the king was also informed that his former close friend, the formerly beloved King Philip, was conspiring to support John, which prompted the Lionheart to fear for the safety of his Angevin lands. Richard didn't take the news well at all. He descended into an all-consuming depression and refused to speak to anyone for days on end. Something had to be done.

Meanwhile, Saladin wasn't fairing much better. His devout commitment to jihad had intensified, but his capacity to effectively resist the crusaders had been diminished, and he was facing potential divisions within his army. He had been fighting for six long years and, for much of that time, had been debilitated by a recurrent mystery illness.

During Richard's second attempt to reach Jerusalem in June 1191, he halted his army's advance at Beit Nuba, a mere twelve miles from the Holy City. Then to many of his crusaders' chagrin, he once again retreated. It was claimed that on that second occasion, Richard actually saw the formidable high walls of the Holy City for himself. It was all to no avail because on both occasions the crusaders reacted to the tactical retreat with voluminous wailing and gnashing of teeth.

Richard decided that he'd had enough, and there were more important pressing matters to attend to closer to home. After signing a truce with Saladin, he chose to abandon the crusade.

The Treaty of Jaffa, agreed to on September 2, stated that in return for a three-year truce, Palestine would be partitioned. Saladin would retain control of Jerusalem. Ascalon's fortifications would be destroyed again. The crusaders would be allowed to retain Acre, Jaffa, and the narrow coastal strip between the two port towns. Most importantly, Christian pilgrims would be permitted access to the

Church of the Holy Sepulchre in Jerusalem. Barely one month after the Treaty of Jaffa was signed, three groups of crusaders were allowed to travel to Jerusalem and visit the Holy Sepulchre unmolested. Richard wasn't among them. Despite later depictions, he never physically met Saladin face-to-face. Six months later, the noble leader of the Saracen army who had displayed mercy, humility, and great intelligence died a broken man. The cause of his death has never been definitely ascertained, but there is one theory that it was possibly typhus.

Now it was time to deal with that wayward, conniving, curmudgeon brother John. Richard's journey home from the Holy Land was beset by bad luck. He was delayed by a shipwreck near Venice. It was then that he was taken prisoner by Duke Leopold IV of Austria, and subsequently handed over to Holy Roman Emperor Henry VI to be incarcerated while ransom demands were agreed upon. Those Habsburgs were terribly duplicitous. Such abductions were common practice in the Middle Ages and a great way to top up royal coffers when required.

During King Richard's absence, John was at his treacherous best. Richard had made a name for himself as a renowned crusader who always led from the front. But despite this, there were still those who were only too willing to conspire against him. The main perpetrator of the unrest was younger brother John, whose most prominent and powerful ally was now King Philip II of France—who had, as previously mentioned, fallen out with Richard and returned home early from the crusade. Any insinuation that it was a lover's tiff will be completely discounted here.

Matters reached a pinnacle in 1193 when John decided to orchestrate a rebellion against his captive brother. Despite John's barefaced temerity, the majority of the barons in England were reluctant to betray their monarch, King Richard the Lionheart. It should be noted that John didn't plan his villainy independently. After paying homage to Philip, he attempted to persuade the English that Richard was dead, but failed. Naughty John's aspirations were further exacerbated by news from the Continent warning him of Richard's impending release from prison. When this information was delivered to Philip, he wrote "the devil is free" ("quia diabolus jam solutus erat").[11] Fearing the return of the king, John left England posthaste for Normandy—but within a few months, he returned and was compelled to kneel in front of his brother and beg his forgiveness.

Ransomed and returned to England in 1194, Richard spent the remaining years of his life waging war in France against Philip Augustus, the one who had been actively conspiring with John to seize Richard's lands on the continent. Richard regained most of his lands from the French before being mortally wounded by a crossbow bolt at Châlus-Chabrol castle. After contracting gangrene, he died on April 6, 1199. His posthumous reputation as warrior king and pious defender of Christendom has remained largely intact to this day.

Throughout the onset and ensuing early years of King Richard's reign, chronicler Roger's sympathy had remained decidedly biased toward John as a focus of English sentiment; however, he does remark that he distrusted John's volatile temperament. When the news of Richard's incarceration by the Austrians became known, Roger lashed out at John, accusing him of being guilty of basest ingratitude. "Breaking the bond of brotherhood, he entered into a bond with death and a pact with Hell!"[12] In this, and ensuing events (as previously mentioned), John hadn't autonomously planned his villainy. But as his status weakened, he appeared constantly at the beck and call of King Philip of France.

Those who attempt to uncover the real story of King John usually go out on the supposition that he was unfairly maligned, and that in reality he wasn't nearly as bad as legend implies. In the twentieth century, some historians put forward a case in King John's defense, arguing that his traitorous behavior was largely based on Shakespeare's play and nineteenth century contrivance and that his misfortunes as a ruler were mostly down to simple bad luck. This assessment has resounded in some quarters of the popular imagination to such an extent that John is now often seen as being the victim of a posthumous smear campaign, a Plantagenet king no worse than most others, often misreported, and grossly misunderstood. But this isn't the case either—the truth is considerably more damning.

11   *Rerum Britannicarum Medii Ævi Scriptores, Or, Chronicles and Memorials of Great Britain and Ireland During the Middle Ages*, vol. 36, 1864.
12   Ruth Coons 1893- [From Old Wallerstein. Creative Media Partners, LLC, 29 Oct 2018

The Middle Ages in England were an exceptional time when remarkable cruelties were metered out against a subjugated population who struggled under the punitive feudal laws of the day. Feudalism was, for all intents and purposes, just another name for slavery. It was a time when one could be blinded, castrated, or even killed by the king's officials for just about anything from stealing a loaf of bread to poaching game from the royal forest. That's where we derive the saying "fair game."

On May 27, 1199, John was crowned king of England. Several months later, in 1200, John stirred the pot by ending his marriage to Isabella, countess of Gloucester, and marrying Isabella, daughter of the duke of Angoulême (in western France) who was already engaged to Hugh X de Lusignan. Isabella was a remarkably popular name with the aristocracy back then. Upsetting a family as powerful as the Lusignans was not considered a wise move. To make matters worse, John sought to rule his English barons by fear and intimidation. This was received like a digestive malady in a dungeon.

He cast damning aspersions regarding their vows of homage and fealty and demanded degrading gestures of submission. Among these were demands that nobles' sons be sent to his court as hostages in return for their fathers' loyalty. The barons were naturally hesitant to turn their sons over to him after rumors spread of his perpetration of political assassinations—most notably the death of his nephew, Arthur, duke of Brittany, possibly even by his own hand. King John became ignominiously known as the "Lackland," largely because he was not expected to inherit significant overseas territories when he ascended the throne.

Another pivotal moment in John's troubled life was the signing of the famous Magna Carta on June 15, 1215. This document implied that the king of England would be compelled to observe and respect the laws of the land. Although not originally proposed as a bill of rights for the common man, two of its provisions evolved to become such and were reflected in the Fifth and Sixth Amendments to the American Constitution. John never had any intention of respecting the Magna Carta, which he probably assumed would take out all the fun of being king and doing precisely whatever he wanted with impunity.

The truth is that the charter granted by King John at Runnymede only remained in effect for a few short weeks. The king had only grudgingly agreed to the document under some duress from his barons, but at no given time did he have the intention of respecting it or abandoning the omnipresent powers which the Plantagenets enjoyed. The problem was John enjoyed his power a little too much.

By 1211, trouble was also brewing between John and the pope. John was wholly dissatisfied with the pope's decision to appoint consecrated archbishop Stephen Langton as the archbishop of Canterbury. Fanning the flames of discontent, King John then openly refused to bow to Rome. He objected vociferously to Langton's appointment, refused him entry to England, and confiscated the estate of Canterbury. This led to the whole of England being placed under an interdict in 1208, closely followed by the king's excommunication the following year. As a result, church services were prohibited in England except in the case of baptisms and the administration of the last rites.

In contemporary portrayals of King John, much is made of the collusion between the king and the sheriff of Nottingham. But at the time Robin Hood was supposed to have been kicking around Sherwood Forest, Nottingham didn't even have a sheriff. The title of "sheriff of Nottingham" was created in 1449, roughly seventy years after the first literary reference to Robin Hood appeared in "The Vision of Piers Plowman" written by William Langland. It's the first known reference in English verse to the mythical outlaw Robin Hood and was written shortly before Geoffrey Chaucer penned *The Canterbury Tales.*

While agrarian discontent had begun to eradicate the hated feudal system in England, Robin Hood is depicted as an antiestablishment rebel who steps up to the plate to protect peasants and murder government agents and punitive wealthy landowners. He is the product of wishful thinking, someone whom the peasants would have loved and honored. The only problem with that is that Robin Hood remains a powerful legend, a figment of writers' imaginations—nothing more and nothing less. The actual legend came to prominence due to the chaos inflicted on the general populace during the reign of King John in the early thirteenth century.

There are numerous versions pertaining to precisely how King John died, but the truth is whatever caused his death has never been conclusively established. Some say it was poison, but it was more than likely dysentery that brought this unpopular king's reign to a welcome end. This could also be the inspiration for the idiomatic phrase "in deep shit" because John was definitely an exemplary candidate.

So, bad King John isn't all that far removed from the truth but good King Richard is a little overstated? Richard was courageous, chivalrous, and magnanimous in victory, but he wasn't really a great king of England. The Plantagenets would endure, but by the time a fresh domestic feud erupted between future royal aspirants, the end was already in sight.

Outside the noble Houses of Parliament stands the mounted statue of Richard the Lionheart. I saw it for the first time when I was fifteen, but living at that time in proximity to Sherwood Forest, I grew up hearing about this brave king of England and how he saved Nottingham and Robin Hood. The other side of the coin was King John and the evil sheriff of Nottingham, which I later discovered was pure conjecture. Richard I's association with his kingdom and his subjects was fraught with disaffection and disdain. He doesn't really deserve to have a statue at all.

CHAPTER FOUR:

SIBLING RIVALRY IN EXTREMIS.

The tale of the House of York during the Wars of the Roses is indeed a study of sibling rivalry in extremis. It reveals a withering sequence of events, which culminated in rebellion, revenge, fratricide, and regicide. At the core of this matchless act of dynastic hari-kari was the mutually destructive relationship between three notable royal siblings, who were all, surprisingly enough, on the same side (well, for most of the time at least).

This chapter is quintessentially about three ambitious brothers who concealed rather different aspirations: Edward IV, who became king; Richard III, who also made it to the throne; and the rather less significant brother-in-the-middle George, duke of Clarence, who badly wanted to be king but, despite his treacherous machinations, never actually got that far. This chapter will refer to the names George and Clarence; but for clarity's sake, they were one and the same person. All the events occurred during a particularly violent time in British history that paved the way for the ensuing Tudor dynasty. It would mark the end of the violent, double-dealing, murderous reign of the notorious Plantagenets.

The most significant person to become embroiled in this vitriolic domestic dispute was Edward IV, eldest son of Richard, duke of York. Edward IV was born on April 28, 1442, at Rouen in Normandy.

In his late teens he already stood an impressive six foot, four inches. Moreover, Edward was irrefutably the most powerful and effective general to grace either side during the Wars of the Roses, but he is rarely referred to as the "Warrior King," which he indisputably was. Among other achievements, he was the first monarch to marry one of his subjects, namely Elizabeth Woodville a.k.a. "The White Queen." French-born Edward would become Edward IV, the first king of England who actually spoke English.

Edward's marriage to Elizabeth Woodville only served to exacerbate his brother George's deep sense of insecurity. Brotherly love solved some of the problems, but not all of them.

The year 1460 was cataclysmic when his father had attempted to seize the crown from his ill-fated Lancastrian adversary Henry VI. But this was a brief sojourn for the Lancastrians because one year later, they were effectively dislodged and sent scurrying for the hills by Edward (who then claimed the throne of England).

The initial impact of Edward IV's reign was a panacea for the maligned people of England who had suffered greatly during the chaotic reign of his predecessor. There's little doubt that at the onset of his reign Edward walked the walk and talked the talk with great authority. He was a handsome, immoral, fighting machine who rarely did anything by half measures. His motto, *comfort et liesse* (comfort and joy), was incredibly appropriate because he reveled in luxury, debauchery, and ostentation. He dressed in the finest robes and exuded self-confidence to the point of distraction.

But this seemingly impenetrable exterior disguised a darker side to Edward's character. He was quite possibly one of the most self-indulgent, manipulative monarchs who ever held court. He had a voracious sexual appetite fueled by manic narcissism and a level of insensitivity that didn't always endear him to his advisors or his relatives. Together with his propensity to be remarkably impulsive and unscrupulous on occasion, it was inevitable that he would make enemies.

Many of the errant characteristic traits that Edward displayed during his lifetime would be reflected in his notorious grandson Henry VIII, which validates the old adage about the apple not falling far from the tree. The other comparison with Henry VIII was of a more physical nature. In his later years, Edward IV devolved from being a physically astute, handsome man to a corpulent, volatile, avaricious monarch.

It wasn't Henry VIII but his elder brother, Arthur, prince of Wales, who was expected to lead the Tudor dynasty. But Arthur died young in 1502, and two decades later, Henry's marriage to Catherine of Aragon was declared invalid, on the grounds that she had been his brother Arthur's widow. Later on, Henry VIII developed a unique way of curing migraines using an axe or sword and a wooden block. It is often speculated that Henry's position as a second son—raised and mollycoddled by his mother and sisters while Arthur was sent away to Ludlow—greatly affected his later attitudes and inevitably damaged any prospect he had of qualifying as a marriage guidance counselor.

Edward IV's activities in the 1460s fueled the gradual implosion of sibling relations within the House of York, in particular with his brother Clarence and with his prominent cousin, the hugely influential, so-called Kingmaker Richard Neville, earl of Warwick. Edward would eventually refute and disregard him.

Warwick was doubtless a vain and arrogant man who had the propensity to dangerously overestimate his own importance on a number of occasions. Consequently, his feverish ambition often clouded his judgment. He was a man whose coming of age coincided with the outburst of national rage induced by exorbitant taxes at the end of the disastrous Hundred Years' War. His birth strategically placed him at the head of one of the great cliques in the nobility at that time, a position that he would eventually exploit. How he dealt with the problems, which inevitable necessity placed before him, has long since graced the annals of military history.

Edward's father Richard, third duke of York and aspirant king, was killed at the battle of Wakefield on December 30, 1460, by a Lancastrian army commanded by the vindictive Queen Margaret of Anjou, wife of King Henry VI. Simply killing and disposing of an opponent wasn't enough for the victors in those wicked old days. After the battle, King Richard's head was reputedly impaled on a spike at the Mickelgate entrance to the city of York, along with that of his young son, the seventeen-year-old Edmund, earl of Rutland, who had been the future King Edward IV's closest brother. He was abducted after attempting to escape the battlefield and summarily executed near the Chantry Bridge in the Yorkshire town of Wakefield.[13]

So it was up to surviving son Edward to continue hammering home the Yorkist cause. After defeating Lancastrian armies at the battles of Mortimer's Cross and Towton in early 1461, and at the tender age of just nineteen, he effectively deposed King Henry VI and took the throne for himself. Those battles precipitated the Wars of the Roses (1455–85) between the houses of Lancaster and York, respectively. Edward IV became arguably the most successful king to reign during the Wars of the Roses.

In the early years of his reign, he focused his affections on his two remaining brothers; his overprotective fraternal inclinations accentuated the substantial age gap between them. Richard was eight, George was eleven, and Edward was nineteen when he ascended the throne. Thanks to the bloodthirsty bitterness between the houses of York and Lancaster, the lives of the two younger boys

---

13   My great uncle Clifford threw a local policeman from that very same bridge into a freezing River Calder in 1959, and then immigrated to New Zealand and was only heard from in dispatches. All his sons are on my Facebook page.

had been particularly turbulent during their formative years, and this would resonate with both of them in one shape or another for the rest of their natural lives.

Early in 1461, in the aftermath of their father's death, they were promptly whisked out of the country for their own safety to Flanders under the protection of the all-powerful Burgundians. Upon returning to England in June of that same year, they discovered how radically things had changed during their absence. Big brother Edward was comfortably ensconced on the throne, rendering the brothers second and third in line. George and Richard were consequently granted royal titles in accordance with their new status. While George was appointed duke of Clarence (a formerly Lancastrian title that had initially belonged to the second son of Edward III), Richard was proclaimed duke of Gloucester. There was an immediate disparity between these two titles, which didn't bode well. One title delivered a substantial amount of land and wealth, the other didn't really compare on either level.

Due to exceptional circumstances, Edward, George, and Richard all found themselves exceptionally wealthy and powerful. But power ultimately corrupts and these positions were at best tenuous, at worst downright precarious; however, this kind of nepotism wasn't unusual among royal families during the Plantagenet dynasty, and Edward had every intention of bestowing land and titles to his brothers along with honoring the powerful warlords who had supported his original claim to the throne. The price for being granted titles was unquestioning loyalty and fealty to the crown—anything less could have dire consequences.

Middle brother George, the duke of Clarence, had just reached his teens when he began to display all the attributes of a restless, testosterone-fueled young man. He may have possessed a rapier-sharp wit, along with being highly intelligent and astute, but he already displayed the propensity to be incredibly disobedient and snotty whenever the mood took him. Clarence knew full well that once Edward took a bride and had children, he would automatically move down the pecking order, and this prospect appeared to have troubled him greatly. His title and the lands he owned had been appropriated from their previous Lancastrian incumbents, who would inevitably attempt to reclaim these when the time was right.

George, no shrinking violet, would grow to fervently resent his older brother King Edward IV and his collusions to prevent George's marriage to Isabel Neville, the older daughter of his Yorkist cousin (the previously mentioned Richard Neville, earl of Warwick).

Edward's marriage to Elizabeth Woodville only served to exacerbate George's deep sense of insecurity—but he discovered an ally. By this time, the Woodville family was progressively dominating the king's inner circle (an expression that has multitudinous connotations, depending on one's perspective of course). Meanwhile, the earl of Warwick was becoming equally estranged from the man whom he claimed he had made king of England. In July 1469, in defiance of Edward's express wishes, George married Isabel Neville in the Église Notre-Dame de Calais.

When George was just nineteen, he became Warwick's son-in-law, and then "the Kingmaker" explicably transferred his allegiance to the Lancastrian cause. Like a rabid realty salesperson, he convinced George that he could dramatically improve his circumstances if he so desired. Warwick seriously overestimated his own authority, which culminated with the all-too-malleable George initiating open rebellion against his own brother. In 1470, alongside Warwick and a French-supported Lancastrian army, Edward was removed from the throne and forced into exile while Henry VI was restored to the throne, albeit temporarily. The newly appointed and anointed king of England rewarded George, duke of Clarence, by making him the sole heir to the throne; however, it was a hollow, unsustainable promise that wouldn't reach fruition.

By the spring of 1471, George had slowly started to realize that his erroneous allegiance to Henry VI was not going to serve his best interests. He grovelingly repented his impetuosity and made amends with his estranged brother, the deposed King Edward IV. They then joined forces and prepared to meet the Lancastrian army shoulder to shoulder.

On April 14, 1471, Warwick was killed at the battle of Barnet, a decisive engagement in the Wars of the Roses. He had been nicknamed "the Kingmaker" for his fervent desire and effort to control and assist aspirant kings of England. In hindsight, the title was a misappropriation because he didn't really do all that well. After unsuccessfully attempting to flee the battlefield, Warwick was struck off of his horse and killed against the strict wishes of Edward IV who had wanted him taken alive. Warwick's mortal remains, along with those of his brother, were publicly displayed at St. Paul's Cathedral to dispel any potentially disparaging rumors pertaining to his survival—and to confirm to the doubters that "the Kingmaker" was very dead indeed.

The resounding Lancastrian defeat at the battle of Barnet, along with the subsequent battle of Tewkesbury the same year, secured the throne of England for Edward IV once more. This time it would be a more permanent arrangement.

On the outside, the brothers appeared to be happily reunited, but this was a feint, an extremely thin veneer. In truth, it was a very uneasy alliance. One of the reasons for the underlying animosity that remained between them was that during the Lancastrian rebellion, both the father and the brother of Edward's (White) queen had been executed on the orders of brother George. This naturally did not win the duke any friends at court, and slowly but surely his ties with Edward began to unravel. It's at this juncture that the fiercely loyal, dependable, and obedient youngest brother Richard began to make his presence known.

Although Richard had followed Edward into exile in 1470, he was his physical and intellectual antithesis. He had a diminutive stature, and at age eighteen, he was already displaying signs of the disease that would blight his life. Although quite rare, scoliosis usually occurs during the growth spurt just before puberty. Though most cases can be totally mild, some sufferers develop spinal deformities that increase in severity as they mature. Severe scoliosis can be agonizingly painful and disabling; however, this didn't prevent Richard from displaying extreme courage on the battlefield in support of his brother, King Edward IV.

What transpired after Clarence and Edward were reunited was a classic downward spiral plagued by suspicion, paranoia, and deep resentment. It was never going to end well for these brothers.

On the outside, Richard seemed to be everything that George wasn't. Fiercely loyal, he had fought with remarkable ferocity and tenacity in the battles of 1471. Growing up in the shadow of the avaricious, volatile brother George, Richard learned to hold his peace and bide his time. It's possible that he was driven by a desire to maintain some semblance of cohesion amid these fragile allegiances.

When George married Warwick's widowed daughter Isabel Neville, he knew full well that in the event of her father's death he would inherit all his estates; however, Edward IV had other ideas on the subject. He rewarded his youngest brother's fidelity by establishing him as Warwick's de facto heir in the northeast of England. Much to George's profound chagrin, the expansive estate would be divided between the two younger brothers. Edward openly consented to Richard's ambition to marry Warwick's younger daughter Anne, which only served to exacerbate the existing problem.

George's discontent deteriorated, and Edward IV's suspicions regarding the middle brother and his potential usurpation came to a head when, in early 1478, George was found guilty of treason and condemned to death by his brother, the king. George, duke of Clarence, was executed in the privacy of the Tower of London, allegedly in a vat of Malmsey wine of dubious vintage.

Despite all the domestic turmoil, Richard remained silent and submissive. Throughout the previous years, he had gradually maneuvered himself into a position that made him practically indispensable to Edward. When Edward died in 1483, his son was proclaimed Edward V. Richard nominated himself as the natural candidate to run the country as protector until the twelve-year-old boy-king reached maturity.

Richard's dualistic maneuverings had served him well on the battlefield and cemented his position as his brother's right-hand man, but driven by a peculiarly corrosive mix of self-serving unscrupulousness and susceptibility, he wasn't widely regarded as someone who was aptly qualified to ascend the throne of England.

Although the last surviving brother Richard had promised to serve as the boy-king's protector until he came of age, he had begun to display distinctly paranoid behavior, like his older brother George. Richard firmly believed that the Woodville family was conspiring against him. Moreover, he became hypercritical of his late brother's reign claiming that Edward IV had descended into a chasm of depravity and lasciviousness that had inflicted terrible suffering on the good people of England. Then he fanned the flames further and dropped a social bomb when he claimed that Edward

IV's marriage to Elizabeth Woodville was invalid, and that all his sons from this marriage were illegitimate. This was little more than a convenient excuse that allowed Richard to present himself as the only legitimate heir. He even went as far as persuading Parliament to declare Edward IV's sons illegitimate by law.

Edward IV's two sons were incarcerated in the Tower of London. There are many who believe Richard III was responsible for their murders, but till this day it has never been conclusively proven. At the time it was of little consequence because the rumors had been circulated, and as far as the public was concerned Richard did it. It was this that compelled former Yorkists loyal to Edward IV and the princes to seek an alternative leader in the shape of Henry Tudor, an exiled Lancastrian who didn't really have much royal blood at all. More importantly, it was a damning indictment of Richard III's brief reign as monarch.

On August 22, 1485, at the battle of Bosworth, Richard III led a mounted cavalry charge in a concerted attempt to personally kill Henry Tudor. It didn't go exactly according to plan. During the ensuing fighting, Richard became surrounded by Tudor's supporters, who effectively dispatched him with multiple blows. His body wouldn't be discovered for 700 years.

In August 2012, a team of archaeologists from the University of Leicester unearthed his mortal remains in the grounds of a former monastery that had become a public car park. Ensuing examination of the exhumed remains confirmed that eleven wounds were inflicted at or around the time of his death. Nine blows to his skull and two to other parts of his body suggested that he was indeed ferociously attacked from all sides, probably by more than one assailant. This is consistent with the contemporary accounts of his death.

History is indeed written by the victors, and according to the Tudors and William Shakespeare, Richard was hunchbacked, with a withered hand and limping gait; however, further investigation revealed that although there was a slight curvature of his spine, it was not sufficient to have rendered him cripple. He didn't have a withered hand either. Forensic facial reconstruction proved that he bore no resemblance to Quasimodo whatsoever. It was further revealed that he probably had blond- or light-colored hair, in contrast to existing portraits.

Edward IV became arguably the most successful king to reign during the Wars of the Roses. His aptitude for strategic and tactical matters was highly developed, but he proved to be somewhat less talented when it came to diplomacy.

Edward, George, and Richard would be consigned to history as the brothers who took infighting to the next level. The Wars of the Roses was a civil war, begun in harmony but inevitably ended in acrimony—though it wasn't the first and it wouldn't be the last.

One dynasty later, the dysfunctional Tudors would hardly present a face as the ideal family. The person who became the legendary Queen Elizabeth I was Henry VIII's second surviving legitimate child; her ever-so-slightly wayward sister, "Bloody Mary," was Henry's eldest daughter. But neither sister had any qualms about accepting the succession going to their younger brother, Edward VI. He didn't stick around too long, and in 1553, after Edward's premature death, marked differences between the sisters led to Elizabeth being imprisoned in the Tower, for her own protection, then scary Mary, who would meet her untimely and cruel demise there. This wasn't a typical case of sibling rivalry. The core of the dispute was intrinsically down to having different religious persuasions and whether the Catholic Mary or the Protestant Elizabeth had the best claim to the throne. Elizabeth won that particular domestic battle, and many ensuing conflicts. But that's another story. Next up are those Scottish rapscallions the Stuarts.

> Near my father's home was a large hill with ruins on it. We knew it as Sandal Castle. I later discovered that it was the focal point of the battle of Wakefield that occurred during the Wars of the Roses and toppled a king from his throne. This was my introduction to the Plantagenet dynasty. The other place of great significance was the Chantry Bridge in Wakefield where a crown prince was murdered. The location had another significance to my family. It was the place where Uncle Clifford threw a policeman into the Calder River, the night before he immigrated to New Zealand. Cliff was a legend in my house.

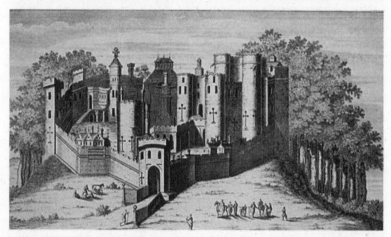

Richard, 3rd duke of York (born Sept. 21, 1411–died Dec. 30, 1460), aspirant King, was killed at the Battle of Wakefield 30 December 1460 along with his young son, the seventeen-year-old Edmund. Their heads were impaled on spikes at the entrance of the city of York.

CHAPTER FIVE:

UNCIVIL WAR.

I n the turbulent wake of the Plantagenet and the Tudor dynasties came the Stuarts. James VI of Scotland became James I of England, and the stage was set. His reign was greeted with high expectations, but these soon dissolved when the true nature of the man prevailed. He was lazy, narcissistic, and arrogant for a start, and had a displeasing tendency to lecture Parliament, which didn't go down too well. Adding oil to the fire, he further damaged his popularity by arranging a marriage for his son Charles with the Catholic Bourbon princess Henrietta Maria. Because of her Catholicism, she was never officially crowned queen. The whole premise of monarchs, such as James acting with impunity, further exacerbated a very tenuous situation. With the ascension to the throne of Charles I, things didn't improve. In fact, they gradually deteriorated as opposing factions and parties became further alienated from one another.

The first two years of the English Civil War proved relatively successful for King Charles I and his forces, but his reign didn't end well.

It all cumulated with the English Civil War that began in 1642 and ended in 1651. This really did pit brother against brother and family against family in a series of violently pitched battles and skirmishes that began with a monarchy and a king and ended with a republic and a dictator.

There are a few periods in history that fire imaginations like the exploits of the Cavaliers and Roundheads. In a nutshell, the Roundheads were fervent supporters of Parliament who (in most cases) had distinct religious persuasions of the puritanical nature. They fought against Charles I of England and his supporters, commonly known as Cavaliers or Royalists, who supported absolute monarchy and the divine right of kings to rule with relative latitude, but not impunity as it transpired.

The nickname "Roundhead" comes from the men's habit of cropping their hair close to their heads rather than wearing it in the long, flamboyant style of the Cavaliers. The Parliamentarians and their low maintenance haircuts wouldn't have won any awards for style. Their attire was distinctly lacking in both color and design, which was the veritable antithesis of the Cavalier dress sense. Cavaliers loved color and ostentatiousness. Their assembled armies would have presented a veritable feast of pageantry and glamour.

The civil war began, in earnest, in the county of Nottingham on August 22, 1642, when Charles I proudly raised his royal standard as a signal for his supporters to rally by his side and prepare to fight. The English town of Nottingham proved to be a precursor of the starkly divided loyalties, which would transpire on both sides as the war gathered momentum.

The actions at Nottingham prompted King Charles I to move on to Shrewsbury to gather more support for his cause. This left the Parliamentarians (Roundheads) free to garrison the castle with their own soldiers.

Nottingham was, in many respects, archetypal of many English towns and families that were compelled to cope with divided loyalties. Two brothers living in Holme Pierrepont Hall in Nottingham had distinctly contrasting views on the subject of loyalty and royalty. Henry, marquess of Dorchester, openly and actively supported the king while William, his brother, was a close friend and supporter of future dictator Oliver Cromwell. Being on opposing sides—and with their mother still living at home—would have no doubt prompted some interesting conversations at the dinner table.

The two brothers may have harbored distinctly opposing views regarding their allegiances, but after the civil war, William adopted the "blood is thicker than water" stance and managed to favorably negotiate the return of his former estates on behalf of his Royalist brother. This didn't necessarily imply that they would live out their lives in relative harmony, but at least past constancies could be, to some extent, assuaged.

There were two other brothers from the same mother who also harbored distinctly opposing ambitions: Simonds and younger brother Richard D'Ewes. When they lost the steadying influence of their mother at a young age, and by the time of their father's death in 1631, the two brothers had developed noticeably dissimilar characters, as brothers have a tendency to do. Richard was destined to follow a decidedly different path to that of his elder brother. Simonds had become a lauded and respected lawyer. But despite being given baronetcy by the king, he subscribed zealously to Parliamentarian ideologies that openly condoned his commitment to severe Presbyterianism. Richard, on the other hand, wasn't in the slightest perturbed by his brother's politics and preferred the more flamboyant approach of the Cavaliers.

One of the reasons that so much is known about these two brothers is due to Simonds D'Ewes being a prolific diarist and writer, who made frequent scathing remarks about the Royalist cause. On one occasion, as he observed the dealings at the royal court, he wrote, "Atheism, profaneness and ignorance now reign,"[14] which could be alternatively described as, "God won't mind, who gives a damn, Oliver who?"

His younger brother Richard D'Ewes would eventually serve King Charles I as a Royalist lieutenant colonel and die early in the war in 1643. Meanwhile Simonds was becoming increasingly disillusioned with the Parliamentarian cause. His loyalties were further tested when he witnessed the execution of two women who were merely protesting for peace. It was an unfortunate time when the social status of women was only marginally higher than that of a domestic pet. Simonds' disillusionment with appointed Lord Protector Oliver Cromwell's governance culminated with his expulsion from Parliament in 1648. He died shortly thereafter, but his legacy remains somewhat notable thanks to his prolific and revealing scribbling.

The first two years of the war had proved relatively successful for King Charles I and his forces—and in all fairness, those flamboyant Cavaliers did present a more resplendent presence on the battlefield.

---

14   J. Sears McGee, *An Industrious Mind: The Worlds of Sir Simonds D'Ewes* (Stanford, CA: Stanford University Press, 2020).

The original "Great Dictator" who abolished Christmas (among other things), which didn't go down particularly well with anyone at the time. After the restoration of the monarchy Cromwell's body was exhumed and hanged in chains at Tyburn, London. Then, after his head was severed and displayed on a pike outside Westminster, the rest of his mortal remains were thrown into a pit. The head remained on display until 1685.

In 1645, the Roundheads appointed the dour, pious individual Oliver Cromwell, a confirmed and committed Puritan, as their commander. Often maligned by historians, Cromwell rigidly transformed the dissident Parliamentarian forces into what became known as the "New Model Army," which (in a relatively short time) became a highly disciplined and efficient military organization and would serve as a template for future British armies.

There is no doubt that he understood the semantics of seventeenth century warfare and employed his profound knowledge on numerous occasions.

The armies were usually arrayed in a standard formation with Royalist and Parliamentary armies lined up directly facing each other. Infantry brigades of musketeers and pike men would usually occupy the center ground flanked by cavalry. Heavy artillery was positioned to the rear where they could release their projectiles in a parabolic arc at the enemy over the heads of their own infantry.

Smaller caliber cannons, loaded shotgun-like with nails and scrap iron in canvas bags, were positioned in front of the infantry, not unlike the canisters that would be used much later in pitched battles to disperse oncoming infantry and cavalry. Many soldiers wore armored breastplates. These offered a modicum of protection, though infantry were more inclined to wear heavy leather tunics, which were completely insufficient against gunfire but were often thick enough to deflect sword blows and swipes.

The standard issue pikes could vary in length between twelve- and eighteen-feet long and were usually quite cumbersome. Using these pikes to repel a cavalry charge would allow the musketeers armed with matchlock muskets to fall back behind the lines of pike men. Matchlock muskets were rather inaccurate, only really effective at short range and, on some occasions, downright precarious. Difficult to reload if it rained, these weapons were often rendered completely surplus to requirements.

One of Cromwell's renowned tactics was to employ swift moving, mounted dragoon infantry armed with primed short-barreled muskets to soften up the ranks of Royalists before committing to his main assault. This often procured the desired effect of inflicting casualties among the Royalist men and officers, which could, in turn, disrupt their command and control.

Not intransigent to the opinions of his fellow officers, Cromwell could also be regarded as a consultative leader, someone who established strong relationships with his fellow soldiers; whom he referred to in writing as his "faithfullest and most experienced Captains."[15] His competence didn't end there either because he frequently displayed remarkable skill and leadership in the thick of the fight. He appeared to have possessed an intrinsic knowledge of strategic requirements and had a notable acumen for tactical maneuvers.

Before the hacking, shooting, gouging, and stabbing commenced, a respected member of the clergy would bless the respective combatants. The Parliamentarians fervently believed that God was indisputably on their side, and that when the occasion arose, they would take the field with divine assistance. The problem was that the other side believed this too, which would have confused God terribly.

15   Martyn Bennett, "Why Oliver Cromwell May Have Been Britain's Greatest Ever General – New Analysis of Battle Reports," The Conversation, June 20, 2017, https://theconversation.com/why-oliver-cromwell-may-have-been-britains-greatest-ever-general-new-analysis-of-battle-reports-79301.

As early as 1634, future republican Oliver Cromwell had already become disillusioned with the monarchy and believed that much of England was still living in sin, having way too much fun for their own good. It was this fact—and his unshakeable conviction that Catholic beliefs and practices needed to be completely eradicated from the church—that galled him to distraction. He even considered immigrating to a freshly established colony in the Americas but was prevented from leaving by the government that he would someday control. There is no record of the pilgrim fathers breathing an audible sigh of relief that Cromwell didn't cross the Atlantic, but it's possible that they did.

Parliamentarians besieged the town of Newark, England, from 1643 to 1646. After a devastating outbreak of plague conditions in the town became so intolerable in May 1646, Charles I ordered the town to surrender. Disguised as a clergyman, he made his way to Southwell. There, at the poplar tavern the King's Arms, he surrendered to the Scottish Covenanter Army, who escorted the king back to their camp at Kelham, near Newark. But although Charles I had surrendered, the civil war was far from over.

Cromwell's supporters seized control of Parliament by ousting the majority of members who wanted a restricted monarchy with constitutional guarantees for the rights of the people and Parliament. Cromwell decided to establish the "Rump Parliament," a compilation of one hundred core members who promoted the idea of completely removing all traces of monarchy in favor of a total republic. This, in turn, provoked another round of fighting and even though Cromwell's supporters were in the minority, they now controlled a highly disciplined army that effectively vanquished the cause of royalist Cavaliers within a few months.

It's often overlooked that the Scottish Covenanters made a significant contribution to Parliament's victory in the first English Civil War, but their tepid support proved to be incredibly volatile because during the second (1648) and third English Civil Wars (1650–51), they switched sides and supported the king.

At the time of Charles' arrest they were perfectly prepared to have him remain as king, on the premise that he left the Scottish church alone and established a new Church of England that would be administered along the lines of the Scottish Presbyterian Church. Officers and soldiers treated the king with profound respect, but in the evening (under the pretext of rendering him due honor) a strong guard was placed at his door. Either way, the civil war was effectively over for the monarch. The war may have been over, but many families still had to contend with divided loyalties within their domestic confines.

Here follows the tale of two brothers divided by both political loyalties and religion. Early on in the English Civil War, author of the renowned "Paradise Lost," John Milton, decided that the pen was mightier than the sword. Milton's father was a moneylender; needless to say, they were not the most popular people in the community. He and his wife, Sara Jeffrey, had three children: Anne, the oldest, followed by John, and then Christopher. Thomas Young, a Scottish Presbyterian, privately tutored John and may have influenced his eventual ideologies on religion and politics because they maintained contact with each other for many years thereafter.

When poet John took the side of the Parliamentary forces, he could have easily become embroiled in a fight with Christopher Milton, his brother younger by seven years, a fervent Royalist, and eventual papist. Their father, John Sr., attempted to remain neutral during the conflicts because, at various times, this perpetual free-loader lived with Royalist son Christopher, and at other times with the Parliamentary subscriber son John.

The junior John Milton married his first wife Mary, the daughter of a Royalist and Roman Catholic country squire, Richard Powell of Oxfordshire, which effectively set him up for political and religious household turmoil. It's safe to say that it wasn't a happy marriage because a few short weeks later she said a "Hail Mary" and left him. But as the war raged on and the Royalist forces appeared to be losing ground, they were later reunited, which was probably a matter of convenience rather than anything else. Whatever the reason for Mary Powell's initial desertion of John, he was inspired enough to publish a pamphlet titled *The Doctrine and Discipline of Divorce* in 1643. The ideas that John expressed in this pamphlet are widely accepted these days, but in the 1640s, they were considered so frighteningly radical that John acquired the ignominious nickname "Milton the divorcer."

In 1645, Mary Powell returned to John. Charles I had lost the battle of Naseby along with any reasonable hopes of military victory. Mary's family had remained staunch Royalists throughout the war but as Oliver Cromwell's army looked like impending victors, these avowed Royalists now found their position in society becoming increasingly volatile. As King Charles's power faded, they were unceremoniously ejected from their home in Oxford, and John got much more than he bargained for. Within a year of Mary's return to John, her entire family had moved in with them, which must have cheered him up to no end. He complained bitterly at this juncture that he was surrounded by "uncongenial people,"[16] but this domestic difficulty was resolved a few months later when John almost dislocated both wrists waving at all the Powell relatives as they packed their belongings and moved back to Oxford.

In 1649, there's every possibility that John attended the execution of Charles I, although this has never been definitely ascertained. He definitely put himself forward in favor of the regicide. A committee from the Council of State asked him to accept the position of secretary for foreign tongues. He accepted this position, but his eyesight was already failing (possibly due to glaucoma). Although he could no longer read by candlelight, he didn't hesitate at this great opportunity for public service.

With the death of Oliver Cromwell in 1658, John's political fortunes took a serious downturn. As the Royalists gained power, John took the wise decision to go into hiding at the home of a friend, where he remained until Parliament passed the Acts of Oblivion, pardoning most of those who had opposed Charles I. Oliver Cromwell's body was exhumed and put on public display by some grudge monkeys who weren't as forgiving, but they would get theirs eventually.

Moreover, the Royalists didn't forget that John had vigorously defended Cromwell's government in 1649 when he wrote a scathing personal attack on Charles I comparing him to Shakespeare's Richard III (mentioned earlier in this volume) and claiming that Charles was a consummate hypocrite. Up until the Restoration period, and despite going blind by 1652, John continued to write in defense of

---

16   John Milton, Paradise Lost (Penguin Classics, 2003).

Oliver Cromwell's eventually despised Protectorate period. Dictator Cromwell's popularity waned quickly when he imposed extremely stringent religious laws on his subjects. He even had the barefaced audacity to cancel Christmas.

After Charles II was crowned, John was inevitably dismissed from governmental service and eventually imprisoned. Payment of outstanding fines and the intervention of notable friends, maybe even his younger brother and prominent Royalist lawyer Christopher Milton, contributed to John's subsequent release.

After the restoration of the monarchy, Christopher, along with many other eminent statesmen of the day, converted to Catholicism. There is every possibility that Christopher may have converted for political motives because shortly after his conversion, he was knighted by King Charles II's brother, King James II (James VII of Scotland) and raised to the Exchequer Bench by his fellow Catholics. The reason James became king was because, although his philandering brother Charles fathered no less than eighteen illegitimate siblings, he died without leaving an official heir to the throne. This begs the question, "Who in England is related to King Charles II?" The answer, "Just about everybody." James II wouldn't be king for long, though, because England feared another Catholic monarchy. He was deposed just three years into his reign.

In his personal writings, eminent brother John mentioned Christopher's religious leanings toward Catholicism years before the latter's conversion, and indicated that it inspired many heated exchanges. Clearly, if the two brothers had argued passionately about the subject for years, as John's writings appear to suggest, it would be more probable that Christopher's conversion was genuine. But being a remarkably intelligent man and a qualified lawyer, Christopher would have doubtless been aware of the potential benefits of embracing Catholicism during the brief reign of the Catholic James II.

During the tumultuous period that followed the Restoration, John Milton was forced to abandon his home in Westminster, which he had occupied for eight years. He took up residence in the house of a friend on Bartholomew Close, among other places. Eventually, he settled near Bunhill Fields. On or around November 8, 1674, at the age of sixty-six years old and after being married three times,

John died of complications from gout, which was known back then as the "rich man's malady." Sir Christopher died in 1693 and was buried on March 22 in the church of St. Nicholas in Ipswich.

On the British throne today are the descendants of Elizabeth of Bohemia, not of her brother, Charles I. When Charles I's eldest surviving son, Charles II, was succeeded by his own younger brother James, the latter's unpopularity and fervent Catholicism led to his eventual deposition in 1688. The "Glorious Revolution" of that year introduced James' Protestant daughter Mary and her husband, the Dutch King William of Orange. The Act of Settlement of 1701 effectively secured the throne for the Protestant Hanoverian dynasty ensuring that no Catholic monarch would ever occupy the English throne again. That remains law until this day.

During the Queen's Silver Jubilee celebrations in 1977, some people in the north of England and in Scotland put posters of Oliver Cromwell in their windows. These party poopers were ubiquitous. "Whose side were we on in the civil war, Dad?" I recall asking at the time. "That depended on who was winning lad. We were on our own side, but never on our backsides," he replied. Some significant civil war battles occurred in the north and I had the occasion to visit many of these battlefields in my youth. It engaged my interest then and still does today.

CHAPTER SIX:

SHAH JAHAN AND HIS FOUR SONS.

There are some who claim that the war of succession that occurred in the Indian subcontinent in the 1700s was the inspiration for George R. R. Martin's book *A Song of Ice and Fire*, the series of novels that the TV show *Game of Thrones* is based on. The name of Shah Jahan is inextricably linked to the magnificent Taj Mahal, the beautiful white marble mausoleum built in Agra between 1631 and 1648 and dedicated to his profound love for his favorite wife Mumtaz Mahal. According to the official court chronicler Qazwini, the relationship with his other wives "had nothing more than the status of marriage. The intimacy, deep affection, attention and favor which His Mughal Majesty had for the Cradle of Excellence [Mumtaz] exceeded by a thousand times what he felt for any other."[17] Needless to say, Shah Jahan was utterly devoted to Mumtaz, who was his constant companion and trusted confidante. Her passing broke his heart, hence the amazing monument.

Life under Shah Jahan was generally peaceful all in all, but toward the end of his reign the empire was experiencing some formidable challenges. Shah Jahan wasn't a person to evade potential

---

17   "Emperor Shah Jahan: About Shah Jahan," Taj Mahal (Department of Tourism, Government of Uttar Pradesh), http://www.tajmahal.gov.in/about-shah-Jahan.aspx.

danger, so he initially reversed this trend by suppressing an Islamic rebellion in Ahmednagar, repulsing the Portuguese in Bengal, and capturing the Rajput kingdoms to the west and the northwest beyond the Khyber Pass. There was more to follow; however, these challenges would emanate from those closer to home, a little too close for comfort in one example. Nevertheless during his lifetime, Shah Jahan established a highly effective military machine sufficient in repelling all potential assailants, which culminated in a reign that experienced relative stability and subjects thriving under his rule.

Another facet to his reign was the promotion of historiography and the arts, which became instruments of propaganda. Exquisite artworks supported by wonderful poetry expressed and extolled specific state ideologies. These elements combined maintained the status quo while the hierarchical order actively promoted balance and harmony. All was well. The sheer magnificence, opulence, and resplendence of Shah Jahan's court was widely admired and respected by many European travelers. Some time in the late seventeenth century, the jeweler Tavernier valued the Shah's Peacock Throne—and all those rubies, sapphires, and emeralds—at around $892,580,000.00 in today's money.

The Shah was a Mughal—and just to clarify, the name "Mughal" (or "Moghul") is derived from the Persian word for "Mongol," as in the all-conquering, rampant horde that originated in Central Asia. They terrified the living daylights out of all their adversaries and were descended from the famous Mongol ruler Temüjin, also known as Genghis Khan. Like the famous Mughal leader Shah Jahan, Genghis also had four sons, who didn't really get on terribly well with each other.

Shah Jahan's eldest and apparently favorite son was Dara Shikoh. The name means "Equal of Darius," who was arguably the greatest early Persian emperor that ever lived. But Dara didn't have any of the emperor's aspirations to rule and conquer. He was regarded as a gentle soul, a deep thinker, and a modest lover of literature who was very philosophical in his approach to life, the world, and just about everything.

Dara reveled in the debates of fellow intellectuals and possessed little or no knowledge of warfare, but that was probably his father's fault. Shah Jahan had noticed Dara had neither the temperament nor the inclination to learn the ways of war, so he actively encouraged him to pursue his desires unabated. Some even claim that Dara laid the foundation stone of the famous Golden Temple at Amritsar, but this assertion is embroiled with polemic opinions.

Being first in the line of succession, he was naturally expected to follow Shah Jahan; however, Shah Jahan's devotion was such that Dara hadn't been schooled in the art of warfare, which would ultimately prove to be to his detriment. On the Indian subcontinent, Dara is still widely renowned as an enlightened paragon of the harmonious coexistence and could even be described as someone who was a genuine mystic, which isn't a bad accolade at all. Could be just another way of saying that he was a very sensitive person who loved reading.

He was a dedicated follower of the Persian perennialist mystic Sarmad Kashani and subsequently developed a close friendship with Sikh Guru Har Rai. To some extent, Dara Shikoh could even be described as a philanthropist because he devoted considerable time and much effort toward finding a common mystical language between Islam and Hinduism. Bearing this noble aspiration in mind, in 1657, he completed the translation of fifty Upanishads (late-Vedic Sanskrit texts of religious teachings, which form the contextual foundations of Hinduism) from their original Sanskrit into Persian, so that notable Muslim scholars of present and future generations could study and learn from these writings.

Dara's translation is known as the *Sirr-i-Akbar* (*The Greatest Mystery*). His most famous work, *Majma-ul-Bahrain* (*The Confluence of the Two Seas*), was also devoted to a revelation of the mystical and pluralistic similarities between Sufic and Vedantic theories.[18] He sought to unite and find common ground between two significant religions rather than divide them, a worthy aspiration that continues today in some parts of the world. Dara was a bit of a happy hippy who really had no other agenda, and this would ultimately prove to his detriment.

Dara had the eye for beauty and is also credited with the commissioning of several exquisite examples of Mughal architec-

---

18   "Majma-ul-Bahrain," *https://en.wikipedia.org/wiki/Majma-ul-Bahrain*, February 4 2022.

ture, some of which can still be seen today. Among them is the tomb of his wife, Nadira Begum, in Lahore; the shrine of Mian Mir also in Lahore; and the Dara Shikoh Library in Delhi.

On September 10, 1642, Shah Jahan formally confirmed Dara Shikoh as his heir and bestowed the title of *Shahzada-e-Buland Iqbal* (Prince of High Fortune). He also gave Dara the authority to command an army of 20,000 infantry and 20,000 cavalry, which wasn't necessarily a wise decision as previously observed. Dara had absolutely no interest in military matters. Being the recipient of so much affection and so many titles naturally inflamed jealousy among his brothers. On September 6, 1657, the illness of emperor Shah Jahan triggered a desperate struggle for power among the four Mughal princes: Aurangzeb, Dara Shikoh, Shah Shuja, and Murad Bakhsh. Realistically though, only two of his sons had any feasible chance of emerging victorious.

Meanwhile, Shah Jahan's affection and devotion for Dara, and his increasing taciturnity toward Dara's younger brother Aurangzeb, grew by the day. The situation was further inflamed when, in 1645, Dara was appointed governor of Allahabad, and his father refused Aurangzeb the right of a crown prince to reside in the venerable "Red Tent." Aurangzeb's patience reached a breaking point when he was banished from entering the royal court for a whole seven months. It didn't bode well. During this time, Aurangzeb's hatred and bitterness toward his father and elder brother simmered and festered as he meticulously planned his revenge.

Meanwhile, the two other brothers were also feeling somewhat overlooked. Shah Shuja, the second son of emperor Shah Jahan and his wife Mumtaz Mahal, was born June 23, 1616. During his life, he participated in various empirical military campaigns and gained valuable experience both as a general and as an administrator. His nose may have been put ever so slightly out of joint when at only ten years old, he was offered as a hostage on behalf of his father. It was one way to extinguish the flames of a pre-pubescent mind if nothing else, but it probably didn't go down well with the lad.

Power in the Mughal empire was indeed a fickle and volatile thing. People could go from hero to zero in an instant. This was the case with the incumbent governor of Bengal. In 1639, Shah Jahan dismissed him and appointed his son Shah Shuja as a replacement. Then in 1642, Shuja was also handed the province of Orissa, which he ruled (along with Bengal) until 1647 when he was requested to accompany Shah Jahan in his campaign against the rebels in Afghanistan. The campaign was short, and upon his return from Afghanistan in 1648, he was reappointed as governor of Bengal. He was again recalled a second time in 1652, when he was stationed at Kabul from April to July.

In 1657, Shah Jahan's health deteriorated and his four sons geared up to contest their apparently dying father's throne. At that time Dara was forty-two; Shuja, a year younger; Aurangzeb, almost thirty-nine; and Murad Bakhsh, the youngest, was thirty-four. One year later, in September 1658, Shah Jahan continued to be on his deathbed, but court physicians remained insistent, probably out of fear for their own lives, that the emperor would recover. While he was incapacitated and the other brothers, except Dara, asked, "Is he dead yet?" Dara Shikoh assumed the role of the ruler. This inevitably infuriated his brothers, and almost immediately, Shuja and Murad Baksh sought independent provinces in an attempt to claim what they regarded as their rightful slice of the imperial pie. Aurangzeb had assembled an army of his own.

Muhammad Murad Bakhsh was born October 9, 1624, the youngest son of Shah Jahan and Mumtaz Mahal. Murad is often described as a gallant swashbuckler, brave as a lion, and extremely forthright in his opinions. Although not politically gifted, he fervently believed in ruling by the sword. He had proven his worth on the field of honor on a few occasions, and his after-battle parties were legendary. His fellow soldiers remarked that Murad was the man who could be relied upon during a violent melee. He was fatuous in council, and according to official historians, reckless in a debauch. Murad's recklessness would follow an inevitable road to perdition.

Murad epitomized the life and times of the seasoned warrior, but he did have the propensity to disobey his illustrious father on a number of occasions, which inevitably led to arguments and frustrations between the two. There was one time in 1646 when Shah Jahan dispatched a huge army to Afghanistan, led by Murad, to capture the Uzbek-ruled city of Balkh. It was supposed to be an attempt by the Mughals to reclaim their ancestral lands in Central Asia, which the Uzbeks had taken from them during the time of Genghis and his fun-loving horde. Wishing to avoid any confrontation, Balkh's Uzbek ruler fled the city as Murad's army approached. When Murad took possession of the city, he wrote to his father requesting a transfer to another city because he had absolutely no desire remain in Balkh any longer than he had to. Precisely what prompted the written request isn't overtly apparent, but it could have been motivated by the dread of the impending harsh Central Asian winter. Murad was well aware that winter's snow could completely eradicate the narrow roads for several months and cause almost insurmountable logistical difficulties for the Mughal armies.

Unfavorable environmental conditions had already exacerbated Murad's forces when they arrived in Balkh and occupied the city. They were all rightfully concerned about what lay ahead. According to contemporary chroniclers, the prince's aversion to spending the winter in Balkh was shared by the rank and file of his army. Murad's nose was definitely put out of joint when Shah Jahan flatly refused his request to move back to Hindustan. The rejection could have been motivated by the fact that although the city had been effectively taken, the surrounding region was still under enemy control.

The ability of the Mughals to wage war depended largely on their ability to utilize available resources such as local livestock, crops, firewood, and water. During expansive military campaigns, their armies even attempted to subjugate the landscape by felling trees, leveling the earth, and bridging rivers. Simultaneously, environmental factors such as climate, ecology, and landscape influenced how campaigns, such as the one in Afghanistan, were conducted, so maybe Murad was right to object to his father's refusal to allow him to return to base. He reluctantly acquiesced to his father's wishes and remained in Balkh until his elder brother Aurangzeb replaced him in 1647.

Much to the surprise and delight of the court physicians and to the dismay of at least three of his sons, Shah Jahan recovered from his illness. Now the stage was set for a humongous confrontation between the siblings. To this day, Aurangzeb remains one of the most hated men in Indian history. Among other things he was a cruel despot who brutally murdered enemies, including his own brothers. This game of thrones culminated at the battle of Samugarh when three of the brothers squared off against each other. Aurangzeb's significantly smaller, but better disciplined, army arrived on the field carrying orange and yellow banners while Dara decided to erect red tents. Apart from traditional armor, Dara employed large cannons, swivel guns, and muskets.

Both Aurangzeb and Dara were armed with matchlock muskets and seated on war elephants. Brother Murad Baksh commanded Aurangzeb's left flank. Dara began by making the eternal military blunder of dividing his massive force as he awaited the arrival of his son Sulaiman Shikoh, who was commanding an army of 40,000 strong.

The battle began with salvos of cannon fire from both sides. Murad, as impetuous as always, didn't wait for Aurangzeb's order to attack and moved against two of Dara's most prominent commanders, whom he effectively dispatched. So before the battle had even gathered pace, Dara had lost two of his best men. He vainly attempted to remedy the situation, but heavy artillery fire forced him to dismount his elephant, which promptly turned about and charged through his own ranks as it deserted the field. This gave the erroneous impression to his men that Dara had been either killed or had fled.

Consequently, thousands of Dara's army surrendered on the spot. It was game over when Aurangzeb granted immediate amnesty to these troops and encouraged them to join his army. Now more powerful, determined, and formidable than ever, Aurangzeb was ready to march on the royal palace at Agra and exact his revenge.

In the wake of the battle of Samugarh, Aurangzeb would imprison both his brother Murad and Shah Jahan. He chased Dara around the subcontinent for a while. After seeking refuge with a duplicitous ally in Punjab, Dara was double-crossed and handed over to Aurangzeb. Magnanimous and vengeful in victory, Aurangzeb paraded his captor in Delhi and then callously ordered him to be beheaded. Dara's decapitated head was sent to Shah Jahan. Aurangzeb's attention now focused on subjugating his most dangerous rival, his own aging father. How different things could have been if Dara would have beaten Aurangzeb in battle. The basic truth of the matter is that despite commanding a considerably larger army than Aurangzeb, Dara simply didn't possess the military prowess and tactical acumen required to obtain a victory; fighting simply wasn't his thing.

Sometime after the battle, Aurangzeb sent his son Muhammad inside the fort of Agra where he overcame the guards and transformed the palace into a jail. Shah Jahan became Aurangzeb's reluctant prisoner, remained a captive for a further seven years, and was subsequently never released. Although he was provided with all the facilities his old age demanded, father and son would never see each other face-to-face again.

After Aurangzeb had occupied the throne by force, Shah Shuja, the second son and governor of Bengal, also waged a war against him. But he was defeated and is believed to have fled to eastern India where he eventually died.

Murad, the able warrior who had actively supported his brother Aurangzeb, discovered to his chagrin that this loyalty would eventually count for nothing. Murad was accused of expropriating funds from the royal treasury and consequently assassinated.

Aurangzeb became widely reviled as a malicious, religious fanatic who sought, among other things, to violently oppress the indigenous Hindu populations. He is even blamed by some for setting conflicts in motion that would result in the creation of a separate Muslim state in the subcontinent, a problem that resonates to this day. He did, however, become one of the most powerful and wealthiest rulers of his day. His nearly fifty-year reign (1658–1707) had a profound influence on the political landscape of early modern India, and his legacy continues to influence India and Pakistan. It is often claimed that his exploits ultimately led to the fall of the Mughal empire.

Aurangzeb proved that in the real world the bad guys also win sometimes. Some consider him the most ruthless and intolerant ruler India has ever experienced. His punitive actions against Hindus, such as banning all the religious celebrations and imposing heavy taxes, resulted in dividing his subjects piecemeal.

His own son would eventually orchestrate a rebellion against him, which would inevitably fail, forcing the lad to flee to Afghanistan where he died in exile.

Apart from his four diametrically opposed sons, Shah Jahan also had three beautiful daughters: Jahanara, Roshanara, and Gauhar. Of these three, Jahanara, the eldest, was regarded as a compassionate and sensible person. Risking her own life, she even attempted to persuade Aurangzeb to abandon his evil ways but didn't succeed. She remained with her father Shah Jahan until his death. He died in 1666 at the age of seventy-six. His body was laid in a tomb near the magnificent Taj Mahal mausoleum, dedicated to his beloved late queen.

> Growing up, I had the luxury of living between two substantial migrant communities. One of these was Indian/Pakistani and the other was West Indian, mainly Jamaican. A friend of mine back then, Hakam Dosanj, was part of the Sikh community. He told me about Amritsar, the Taj Mahal, and the story of Shah Jahan's sons. I loved the food and still do, but more importantly, Hakam's whole family was incredibly knowledgeable concerning the history of India. This time was filled with great company, wonderful stories, and terrific food. Later, there was some Jamaican influence, which I prefer not to divulge here. Being in close proximity to these communities opened my mind, and I made some marvelous friends. This was the meaning of life to me.

CHAPTER SEVEN:

THE QUEEN'S FAVORITE.

Not a great deal is known about the military career of General Charles Churchill, younger brother of the illustrious John Churchill, the duke of Marlborough—though they did take the field together on a number of occasions. Not incidentally, during the English Civil War, their father was a renowned Cavalier called Winston Churchill. Does that name ring any bells?

Insert Caption: The 1st Duke of Marlborough was the hero of Blenheim and a major English celebrity, except for writer Jonathan Swift and a few other detractors who disliked Marlborough intensely.

Charles Churchill joined the English army as an ensign in the Third Regiment of Foot in 1674, during the reign of King Charles II, and would later be promoted to colonel. In 1690, he was promoted again, this time to brigadier general, and then to major general in 1694. His astute political machinations led him to be elected as a member of Parliament for Weymouth and Melcombe Regis in the first general election of 1701, but he would eventually be blacklisted for opposing preparations for war with France, which his brother John would lead.

John enjoyed a quite remarkable career as a courtier, soldier, and diplomat, first during the English Restoration of Charles II, then James II, and afterward under William III. When King William and Queen Mary died without any surviving offspring, the crown passed to another younger sibling. Mary's sister, Anne, came to the throne under the Act of Settlement of 1701, which effectively secured the throne for the staunchly Protestant Hanoverian dynasty. At the onset of her short reign, it was the morbidly obese Queen Anne who made John her trusted advisor and captain general of all forces, which serendipitously coincided with the outbreak of the War of the Spanish Succession. Churchill's wife, Sarah, had been the Queen's "favorite" for many years, but Abigail Hill would eventually usurp her position. Queen Anne would endure eighteen pregnancies but fail to produce an heir (that's another story).

In 1702, Charles became a lieutenant general and was simultaneously appointed colonel of the Coldstream Regiment of Foot Guards, one of Britain's oldest and most respected regiments. At Blenheim in 1704, he served with distinction under the auspices of his elder brother John Churchill, who had been appointed first duke of Marlborough in 1703 by Queen Anne in gratitude for his services.

There's no denying that the duke was an excellent soldier and a talented strategist whose career spanned the reigns of five monarchs. He had an intrinsic grasp of logistics that evaded most other army commanders of the day, to the detriment of his many adversaries.

At the battle of Blenheim, arguably the duke's most famous victory, General Charles Churchill commanded the center of the allied line. His army initially consisted of sixty-six squadrons of cavalry, thirty-one battalions of infantry, and thirty-eight guns and mortars, collectively twenty-one thousand men of whom sixteen thousand were English.

The first duke of Marlborough wasn't particularly optimistic about his prospects when he embarked on the campaign that would incorporate the battle of Blenheim. On February 20, 1704, he wrote to his wife Sarah, "I am extremely out of heart."[19] His apparent pessimism wasn't entirely unjustified regarding what had become known as the Grand Alliance, or the United Provinces and Austria (which, at that moment, seemed to be on the verge of implosion).

The two great powers, France and Spain, prepared to converge on the imperial capital of Vienna, which was already under threat by a concerted Hungarian uprising in the east of the empire, and only a scant force held the western approaches. While the French Marshal Villeroi contained the Anglo-Dutch army in the Netherlands—and his colleague Vendôme threatened to invade the north of Italy—Marshal Tallard was moving to join forces with the elector of Bavaria in preparation for final march down the River Danube.

The crises that were unfolding in southern Europe seemed reassuringly remote to many English and Dutch statesmen, and only Marlborough and a couple of those in the know truly grasped the gravity of situation. The duke, who was fifty-four years old at the time of the events, was at the pinnacle of his power and influence. His unsullied reputation as a consummate statesman and a gifted military man was at an all-time high. He had a lot to lose.

It would be the first time in over fifty years that the fortunes of the ostentatious "Sun King" Louis XIV would be reversed by one titanic encounter, which would place Marlborough in a seemingly unassailable position of wealth and power. The British Lord Treasurer Godolphin was among the first to be informed of Marlborough's intentions. "I think it absolutely necessary for the saving of the Empire to march with the troops under my command in order to take measures with Prince Lewis of Maiden for the speedy

19   William Coxe et al., *Memoirs of John Duke of Marlborough: With His Original Correspondence: Collected from the Family Records at Blenheim and Other Authenic Sources: Illustrated with Portraits, Maps, and Military Plans* (London: Longman, Hurst, Rees, Orme, and Brown, 1818).

reduction of the Elector of Bavaria."[20] Bold words from a confidant man, but at that time he was masking his trepidation concerning the Dutch troops who were going to support his offensive. Marlborough's fears would be allayed when they turned up at the battlefield with 21,000 soldiers and not a wooden clog in sight. It was a bit touch and go there though.

During the ensuing battle, brother Charles led the British troops that secured the passage of the River Nebel and physically captured the village of Blenheim, a feat that saw him rewarded with the title "Lieutenant of the Tower of London."

Meanwhile, the Duke became quite possibly one of the world's first media sensations when his exploits at Blenheim triggered a massive reaction in the London newspapers. News of his victory was disseminated extensively throughout a magnanimous nation. According to firsthand reports, on the morning of the famous battle, the duke received the Holy Sacrament from his chaplain, Doctor Hare, and upon mounting his horse, he said, "This day I conquer or die," or equally stirring words to that effect. This could also have been consummately engineered propaganda. He became the willing subject of some rather astute merchandising from those wishing to cash in on his popularity, including the man himself.

One widely distributed head and shoulders portrait of the duke depicts him in full armor wearing a huge lace cravat, a long, full-bottomed periwig, and the Great George of the Order of the Garter. This combination of aristocratic dignity and military prowess was widely reproduced as an engraving by the printer John Smith just after Marlborough's victory at Blenheim. It was sold so extensively that it became the default portrait of the hero and demand was so enthusiastic that the printing plates quickly wore out and had to be redone.

It was indeed a tremendous victory and there was more to follow. In April 1706, the duke of Marlborough returned to the Low Countries (Belgium, the Netherlands, and Luxembourg) to commence the campaigning season. He discovered that the French army under Marshal Villeroi had established a defensive line behind the Dyle River (in present day Belgium) and there didn't appear to

---

20   Jeroen Deploige and Gita Deneckere, *Mystifying the Monarch Studies on Discourse, Power, and History* (Amsterdam University Press, 2006).

be any indication of any prospective intent to move from this relatively safe position.

Marlborough surreptitiously disclosed stories to the French high command that he was planning to assault the important fortress town of Namur. To his surprise, his ruse appeared to work when Villeroi's army began to move forward. It is, however, more likely that the particularly abrasive and scathing letters from his hissy monarch King Louis XIV, who demanded a victory in Flanders, prompted Villeroi's displacement. It was his vanity in extremis and a futile attempt to restore French prestige that had been severely impaired by the battle of Blenheim.

So at the battle of Ramillies, Charles served under his brother again. On the morning of the battle, Marlborough was unable to clearly study all the enemy dispositions to any great extent due to restricted visibility caused by an early morning mist. Consequently, he decided to deploy in a seemingly conventional manner, with infantry holding the center, flanked by regiments of cavalry on both wings. Charles was, once again, tasked with controlling the center position.

The focal point of Marlborough's attack was the small hamlet of Ramillies, a settlement of around two hundred people situated on the slopes above a river. Charles ordered four brigades of footmen to attack the village, which broke the enemy's main battle line and eventually delivered another resounding victory to the duke of Marlborough. His rapid exploitation of the victory enabled him to capture both the city of Leuven and the Dyle River from the French. The towns of Mechelen, Lier, and Aalst also surrendered to the allies, followed by Ghent, Bruges, Damme, and finally Antwerp and Brussels. These places were not regarded as Belgian at that time because Belgium simply hadn't been established as a country yet. For that attribution, it would have to wait until 1831.

Within a fortnight of the battle of Ramillies, Marshall Villeroi had fallen back to the French border leaving almost all of Flanders and Brabant to Marlborough's forces.

In the same year as the Battle of Ramillies, brother Charles decided to resign his lieutenancy of the Tower of London to serve as the governor of Guernsey, which he held from 1706 to 1711. By this time, his health was beginning to suffer and he had taken to drinking heavily. He also abandoned any future political aspirations and consequently never stood for Parliament again. He died December 29, 1714, aged fifty-eight, which wasn't a bad tally considering that life expectancy for males in the eighteenth century was between thirty and forty years old.

Marlborough's next battle would be fought without the assistance of his brother Charles. The bloody battle of Malplaquet in 1709 would introduce the duke to the electoral prince of Hanover, who would later become King George II of England; however, Marlborough's personal fortunes took a downturn when he failed to bring the war on mainland Europe to a conclusive and successful end. He may have achieved a tactical victory at Malplaquet, but it was a fraught and messy affair that consumed the lives of thousands. It's been claimed that every European nationality was represented during this battle, where over two hundred thousand troops were present.

Marlborough was justifiably criticized for the terrible casualties incurred by the allies. This resulted in his enemies, both domestic and foreign, claiming that he was more concerned with his own advancement and aggrandizement than with the lives and well-being of his loyal soldiers, which was, in retrospect, rather unfair.

Marlborough's capacity for providing excellent logistic support and ensuring that his troops were well tended to was always a priority of his. Malplaquet was his final field battle. Now he would have the unenviable task of confronting the increasing numbers of his detractors on the home front.

Supported by his closest allies, he attempted to retain what influence he could muster during the reign of Queen Anne, but the emergence of duplicitous party politics eventually rendered his position untenable. He continued to insist on a strong commitment to the continental war, but his position as chief advisor and leading minister of Queen Anne depended largely on the volatile monarch's favor. By 1708, the deterioration of the relationship between the Queen's favorite and Churchill's wife, Sarah, had already begun to undermine Marlborough's position and status.

Marlborough's situation with Parliament and Queen Anne eventually became indefensible. One of the duke's main critics was the author of *Gulliver's Travels*, Jonathan Swift. In one of his most influential pieces, *The Conduct of the Allies*, he condemned the war as a waste of money, of no use to England, and only helping the despised Dutch. He was especially vitriolic in verbally attacking the duke of Marlborough. Swift also claimed that the war was started and continued only for the personal amelioration and enrichment of the Churchills, and even had the temerity to claim that Marlborough wanted to be king.

The unnerving prospect of an army general seizing power and establishing a stringent system of arbitrary rule, as had occurred under the dictatorship of Lord Protector Oliver Cromwell, was the clincher that exacerbated the existing fears among contemporaries. According to Swift, the majority of the British public were opposed to prolongation of the war on the continent. Thankfully, there were also many among the public and the hierarchy who stoically supported and defended Marlborough to the hilt.

In late 1711, Marlborough was charged with misappropriation and receiving unlawful perquisites from army suppliers. As Marlborough pointed out, these perquisites had been customary for a commander-in-chief on the continent, and whether the charges were justified or not, they gave sufficient ammunition to his enemies to enable the government to push for his dismissal. On December 31, 1711, Anne dropped her trusted counselor and military champion, which was a decision of political necessity rather than a sign of personal mistrust. The reaction to the duke's dismissal was lauded by his enemies and lamented by his supporters. It disseminated disappointment and frustration among his soldiers, whom he had led to many victories and for whom he had shown unusual care, to such an extent that they had even named him "the Old Corporal."

Marlborough became erroneously regarded as the only impediment to Queen Anne's wish to bring the war to a conclusion. Although it appears to have been common knowledge that the duke had no objection to accumulating wealth, this fact only fueled further scathing assaults by his critics.

John Churchill, first duke of Marlborough, prince of the Holy Roman Empire, and victor of Blenheim may have inspired ignominy when he was dismissed, but when he died on June 16, 1722, his passing was widely mourned by the British public. A state funeral was held for him in London. The volatile and duplicitous world of politics may have been his nemesis, but the public never forgot their hero. His legacy of greatness is intractable, irrefutable, and his reputation as a great commander remains completely intact to this day, otherwise he wouldn't still be written about (but don't forget his brother Charles).

British WW2 leader Winston Churchill and the late Lady Diana Spencer are both descendants of the female line of John Churchill, duke of Marlborough, and his wife, Sarah, the first duchess of Blenheim Palace, which remains one of the largest and most ostentatious stately homes in the whole United Kingdom. When the only son of John and Sarah's marriage died, their second surviving daughter, Henrietta, was allowed to inherit the title of second duchess of Marlborough after her father's death. When Henrietta died, the title was passed down to the family of her sister, Anne Churchill, who married Charles Spencer (1706–1758). He became the third duke of Marlborough, hence the name being altered to Spencer-Churchill. It is from this matrilineal line that the present-day Spencer-Churchills are descended.

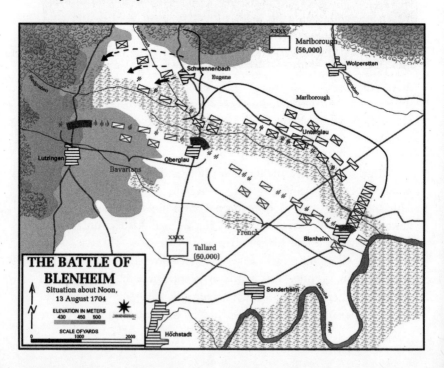

My history teacher in middle school (sixth to eighth grade) was a duke of Marlborough fanatic and a serious nut job. He was a World War I veteran who had some serious anger management issues and was probably suffering from PTSD. When he wasn't beating kids within an inch of their lives, he would extoll the virtues of the duke of Marlborough. The only thing that could assuage his violent temper was retelling tales of derring-do attributed to the duke. I would discover later that most of what he told us was historically inaccurate. Therefore, I made it a point to unearth everything I could about Marlborough back then and spent untold hours in the local mobile library. The actual library had been incinerated, along with most of the school I attended. To claim that it was a rough neighborhood is a gross understatement. Local stray dogs hunted in packs, and the police only visited my area under duress. My hand would always shoot up first whenever the teacher had any questions on the subject of Marlborough, so he liked me, which did absolutely nothing for my popularity. I was never the Queen's favorite, but I became the history teacher's favorite. It was then that I discovered that no one loves a schmoozer, and I've never been one since.

CHAPTER EIGHT:

FOR THE REVOLUTION.

Men in the dark look different from women in the light. That was one opinion at least. Two American sisters (they were actually sisters-in-law, but that's close enough), who never physically joined the Continental army, decided to do some ad hoc cross-dressing to suit their own mischievous intentions. During the sieges of Augusta and Cambridge that began on May 22, patriotic fervor was ignited among the locals. While the Martin family's seven sons were away fighting the British, Mrs. Elizabeth Martin remained at home with her two daughters-in-law and her youngest son. Her husband, Captain Abram Martin, had served with George Washington in the Virginia militia during the French and Indian War. Native Americans had killed him on September 3, 1771 (aged fifty-five), while he was surveying land in North Georgia at the personal behest of George Washington.

While comfortably ensconced with their mother-in-law and pining for their absent husbands, the wives of the two eldest Martin sons were determined to do something to help the cause. This could have been inspired by those log cabins rarely having more than one room, and, in all fairness, close proximity to a mother-in-law over a sustained period of time could have induced innumerable responses.

Insert Caption: These two cross-dressing women cleverly disguised themselves by donning their husband's clothes and intercepting some important British dispatches.

In the case of Rachel and Grace Martin, it was all down to some intel they had inadvertently received regarding a courier conveying important dispatches to one of the British HQs. The sisters heard that to avoid detection, the courier traveled the road at night guarded by two British officers. They decided to risk their lives to intercept him and apprehend the papers, whatever they were. For this purpose, the two intrepid, mother-in-law-challenged women cleverly disguised themselves by dressing up in their husbands' clothes. They managed to get a hold of a couple of pistols to complete the deception, and then set about to put their task in hand.

It was a pitch-dark, moonless night when the women hid in bushes beside a dirt track that ran through a dense forest and waited. It wasn't long before the sound of approaching hooves caught their attention. As soon as the courier appeared, flanked by two guards, they leapt to their feet and pointed the pistols at the small party. They demanded the immediate surrender of the courier and the dispatches. Whether they lowered their voices or applied facial hair to complete the effect is not known.

In any case, they were probably a little taken aback when the courier obediently handed over the papers. Once they had obtained what they wanted, they rushed home through a secret path in the forest and got changed, which in the 1800s would have taken a while. Then they wasted no time in sending the documents by a trusty messenger to General Nathanael Greene.

The blighted courier and his guards returned by the road they had taken and stopped at the house of Mrs. Martin to request accommodation for the night, as weary travelers tend to do. The hostess asked why they returned so soon after they had passed. They replied by displaying the empty satchel and explaining that two rebel lads had callously robbed them. This inspired the curiosity of Rachel and Grace Martin. One of them asked, "Had you no arms?"[21] The officers answered that they had arms but were waylaid so suddenly that they didn't even have time to draw their weapons.

The following morning the three men left the premises completely unaware that the ladies who had shown them such warm hospitality were the same ones that had robbed them the previous night. The matriarchal Mrs. Martin considered it a job well done. She was a native of Caroline County, Virginia. When war broke out, she had nine children, seven of whom were sons old enough to bear arms. When the first call for volunteers was made, Mrs. Martin eagerly encouraged her sons to join the Continental army to fight the British.

There was another incident at her house when Colonel John Cruger, who was commanding the British at Cambridge, along with several British officers, stopped at her house for some refreshments. One of the British asked how many sons Mrs Martin had? She answered that she had eight, pointing out that seven of them were away fighting for their country. The officer raised his eyebrows and

---

21   "Grace and Rachel Martin," Women of America (American History & Genealogy Project), https://www.ahgp.org/women/grace_and_rachel_martin.html.

asked if she had enough of them? To which Mrs. Martin replied, "No sir," replied the matron proudly, "I wish I had fifty."[22] Hopefully Cruger avoided the soup.

There was another occasion when Loyalists had ransacked her house while the sons were absent. They slashed open the feather beds and scattered the contents. When her sons returned shortly afterward, she told them to get after the marauders who had trashed the sleeping arrangements and deal with them. Precisely what transpired after this event isn't known, but one time a badly wounded Continental soldier had been left in Mrs. Martin's care. During the war, Loyalists constituted about one-third of the population of the American colonies. She kindly nursed and attended the man whose name isn't known until he had recovered. A party of Loyalists, who had heard that he was there, arrived with the sole intention of taking the wounded man's life. Mrs. Martin managed to successfully hide the man until the Loyalists had left the premises.

Of the seven brothers, six survived. The eldest, William M. Martin, was a captain of artillery who served with distinction in the sieges of Savannah and Charleston but was killed at the siege of Augusta as he positioned the cannon.

It was said that not long after his death a British officer took it upon himself to relay the tragic news to the mother of this brave young man. He arrived at the house and asked Mrs. Martin if she had a son in the army at Augusta. She nodded. Then the vindictive officer sneered, "I saw his brains blown out on the field of battle." He had expected Mrs. Martin to breakdown in tears but she reacted quite differently. She stood face-to-face with the officer and said defiantly, "He could not have died in a nobler cause!"[23]

It is generally accepted that the Irish rarely back down from a fight. One patriotic family, which had five sons and sent four of them to war as officers in the revolution, attested to this fact. They all fought with great distinction at some of America's most crucial Revolutionary War battles, eventually earning special honors from General George Washington himself at the battle of Yorktown.

---

22   Elizabeth Ellet, *Revolutionary Women in the War for American Independence: A One-Volume Revised Edition of Elizabeth Ellet's 1848 Landmark Series,* ed. Lincoln Diamant (Westport, CT: Praeger, 1998).

23   Ibid.

Their father, Thomas Butler, was an immigrant from Kilkenny, Ireland, a skilled gunsmith, and a patron of the church. He had moved with his wife, Eleanor, and their two sons, Thomas Jr. and Richard, from County Wicklow, Ireland, and settled in Pennsylvania in 1748. Their last three sons, William, Percival, and Edward, were all born in the colonies. The sons would fight together and apart with great distinction during the Revolutionary War.

In 1776, Richard received a commission as a major, was quickly promoted to lieutenant colonel, and then sent to join Morgan's Riflemen, who were attached to the Eleventh Virginia Regiment. He received well-deserved credit for the constant state of readiness in that unit. Richard participated in the American victory at Saratoga and then led troops in the assault on the British positions at Yorktown. After British General Charles Cornwallis was forced to surrender, George Washington personally chose Richard to place the flag on the former British fortifications. Unfortunately, Baron von Steuben got there before him and claimed the honor for himself. When the war ended, Richard became a farmer but enlisted again as a major in 1791.

Richard's younger brother William earned a commission as a captain in 1776 and was promoted to major during October of that year. William was wounded as he stood beside General Benedict Arnold at the battle of Saratoga. He then fought in Canada. After being promoted the rank of lieutenant colonel, he fought defensive actions against Native American tribes and participated in the successful Sullivan-Clinton Expedition to break the Iroquois Confederacy and its British allies in 1779. William later became a senator but never gave up his position in the army. He died in 1789.

The third brother, Thomas Jr., was commissioned as a first lieutenant in early 1776 and promoted to captain later that year. At the battle of Brandywine he displayed great courage in rallying retreating colonials and thwarting a British attack. This action earned him accolades from Washington. Later, he fought at Monmouth and was cited for defending a redoubt against a powerful assault, which allowed his older brother Richard to escape while the British forces were engaged. On one occasion in 1803, Thomas was court-martialed on multiple counts but managed to have all the charges quashed except one regarding his wig. Despite vociferous objections, he flatly refused to remove his Unionist wig, even for the army.

Then there was Percival, whose resumé was equally impressive. He was commissioned first lieutenant in the Third Pennsylvania Regiment, on September 1, 1777, when he was only eighteen years old. He wintered at Valley Forge, served in the battle of Monmouth, and was present at the capture of British General Cornwallis. After that he headed south and remained there until the close of the war. He moved to Kentucky in 1784, and married Miss Hawkins of Lexington. He was the only survivor of the old stock, the original American army that went south when the war of 1812 began. In time he became the adjutant general of the state of Kentucky, and in that capacity joined one of the detachments of troops sent out from the state.

The youngest son to grab his flintlock and participate in the revolution was Edward. He was too young to fight in the initial stages of the revolution, but in 1778, at the tender age of sixteen, he was made an ensign in his brother Richard's regiment. He was later promoted to the rank of lieutenant on January 28, 1779, and transferred to the Fifth Pennsylvania Regiment on January 17, 1781. He was again transferred to the Third Pennsylvania Regiment on January 1, 1783, and discharged on November 3, 1783, when the Continental army was officially disbanded. He had remained in the army until the end of the war, by which time he had attained the rank of captain.

Three of the four remaining brothers served together at St. Clair's Defeat, also known as the battle of the Wabash, the battle of Wabash River, or the battle of a thousand slain, which took place on November 4, 1791, in the Northwest Territory. Remarkable that a battle lost had so many different names. Richard, who commanded the wing of the army in which Thomas served as a major and Edward as a captain, was mortally wounded and evacuated to the center of St. Clair's encampment, where he was soon joined by the gravely wounded Thomas. Before the retreat began in earnest, Edward arrived to remove his brothers, but could only take one. Richard insisted that the other brother be saved, and Edward succeeded in carrying Thomas to safety.

When Native Americans began kicking up a storm on the fron-
tiers and while the five sons were absent from home in the service
of the country, the old father decided to offer his services to the
army. The neighbors remonstrated, but his wife said, "Let him go, I
can get along without him, and have something to feed the army in
the bargain, and the country wants every man who can shoulder a
musket."[24] Or, in other words, he might have been a miserable swine
and she wanted to see the back of him—but that's pure speculation.

Surrounded by a large party of senior officers during a dinner,
General Washington raised his glass to propose a toast to the Butlers
and their five sons. General Marquis de Lafayette wrote of the
brothers: "When I wished a thing done well, I ordered a Butler to
do it."[25] Many landed gentry back in the United Kingdom would
have concurred wholeheartedly but wouldn't have insisted on the
fraternal aspect.

There were few who played more of a role in American history
than Great Britain's brothers George, Richard, and William Howe.

These fortunate brothers were born with a proverbial silver
spoon big enough to paddle a canoe with. They all hailed from
the privileged classes, as did most of the British military's high
command at the time. Moreover, their family was exceptionally well
connected. Their father, Emanuel Scrope, second viscount Howe
(the name alone sounds like a Dickensian villain), was a renowned
member of parliament and served several years as the royal governor
of Barbados before succumbing to disease in 1735. The British army
always considered Barbados a precarious posting owing to the high
number of military fatalities incurred by tropical diseases.

George Augustus, the eldest son, was born in 1725 and
earmarked for a prominent position in the British army from a very
early age. By the time he was twenty, George was made an ensign in
the First Foot Guards. During the Jacobite rebellion, he served as an
aide-de-camp to the infamous duke of Cumberland, the third and
youngest son of King George II. It's safe to assume that he witnessed
the merciless butchery the duke inflicted against the highland

24   "Lt. Edward Butler," The State Society of the Cincinnati of Pennsylvania, https://paso-
cietyofthecincinnati.org/gallery_post/lt-edward-Butler/.
25   Shane Oliver, "The Fighting Butlers," The Historical Marker Database, November 13,
2021, https://www.hmdb.org/m.asp?m=185765.

clans at the battle of Culloden in 1746. George also fought with the British army during the War of the Austrian Succession (1740–1748), which was followed by the Seven Years' War (1754–1763), also known as the French and Indian War. This conflict can be seen in many respects as a world war because it drew in every European superpower of the time and affected five continents: Europe, North America, South America, West Africa, and Asia. The conflict divided Europe into two coalitions, one led by Great Britain and the other by France.

When the French and Indian War was officially declared in 1756, George first served as a colonel of the Sixtieth Regiment of Foot (Royal Americans) and was then posted to the British colonies to command Fifty-Fifth Regiment. The Seven Years' War cemented Britain's position as the most dominant European country in the world, but their overbearing dominance in the colonies would eventually incite justifiable rebellion.

George was a particular favorite of William Pitt (the elder) and a few other notable members of Parliament. This favorable status enhanced George's promotion to brigadier general. At the battle of Ticonderoga in 1758 he was second in command to Major General James Abercromby.

George led by example and earned a favorable reputation with colonial provincials as a soldier's soldier. They greatly admired his ability to abandon the "silver spoon" treatment and pitch in—live as they lived, including sleeping on the ground. There's no doubt that George learned a lot from them too, particularly their irregular style of waging war, which contradicted all previous notions he had. The British Army had been stringently trained in fighting on open plains and had little concept of this guerilla style of warfare. Brigadier General George Howe was courageous, innovative, and most importantly, deeply respected by the men serving under him. On July 6, 1758, while personally leading an advance force against French forces, Howe was struck square in the chest by a musket ball that catapulted him off his garters and killed him instantly.

The baton now passed to Richard (1726–1799) and William (1729–1814), his younger brothers. But despite having fought in the War of Austrian Succession and the French and Indian War, their war against the continental army would be a different matter entirely. In 1758, William proved his bravery by leading the light infantry under Brigadier General James Wolfe at Quebec. William's ensuing career in the colonies, which was intended to suppress the rebellion and reclaim the place as a British possession, turned into a catalogue of chaos and a serious learning curve for the imperial authorities. Richard and William, who was a member of Parliament, urged the government to display restraint in the hope of averting an armed confrontation with the colonies. Unfortunately their pleas fell on deaf ears.

When tensions were reaching a boiling point in 1774, William voted against the Coercive Acts and, later that year, informed his constituents that, "If a war with America should come and I should be offered a command in the British Army, I will decline."[26] Up until his arrival in May 1775, the British government was continuously at odds in regarding how to deal with the rebellion.

While most members of Parliament thought that the rebellion could be mercilessly crushed by the military, many questioned the appropriateness of doing so. These polemic perspectives resulted in an indeterminate policy that wavered between coercion and concil- iation, between a punitive war to impose peace and an attempt to negotiate a settlement through appeasement. By the winter of 1775, Britain considered the situation in the colonies as a strictly mili- tary problem and held on staunchly to the belief that the sword alone could subjugate these upstart revolutionaries. So when the war finally arrived, William displayed his acumen as a politician and promptly accepted a posting to the colonies.

In its arrogance, Great Britain incorrectly assumed that in him it had the commander that it wanted to deal with the developing insurrection. William doubtlessly represented the cream of the British army. As a battle-hardened officer, he was widely consid- ered as being the best and most experienced commander that the British army had to offer at that time; however, the only thing he really proved was his consistency to not be very good. During the two years that he commanded the British forces, he bungled almost

---

26   Brian Joseph McHugh, *Sir William Howe: A Study in Failed Strategic Leadership* (Pick- le Partners Publishing, 2014).

every operation. It ultimately culminated in his resignation from his command and ensuing return to Great Britain with his reputation in tatters and the revolutionary cause in a considerably better condition than it had been before his arrival.

It all kicked off in Boston for Major General William Howe in May of 1775, barely one month after the battles of Lexington and Concord. He got his baptism of fire at the Battle of Bunker Hill. Despite this being a British victory, William completely failed to capitalize on his position controlling the heights where he still had troops in reserve who were relatively fresh. As the rebels retreated, he ignored General Henry Clinton's sound advice and missed a perfect opportunity to decisively defeat them. Consequently, the Battle of Bunker Hill became a rallying cry to the Americans. William would be equally consistent in failing to follow-up any tactical successes with decisive action.

It soon became an irrefutable fact that General William Howe had neither the strategic ability nor the skill to maintain the position he had accepted. Up until that point he had only commanded a brigade and had little or no interest in the studying tactical machinations of his colonial adversaries, which would inevitably lead to his demise.

Richard's path would follow the nautical branch of the British military. In June 1755, he led a pursuit of some ships that were transporting French regulars to Canada near Nova Scotia. On that occasion, he succeeded in capturing eight companies. Over the following decade, Captain "Black Dick" (as Richard was known for because of his dark complexion) experienced an almost meteoric rise in rank, eventually being appointed commander of Britain's North American naval forces in February 1776. Working with his brother William, he would attempt—and ultimately fail—to bring the colonial rebellion to an amenable conclusion.

Even though the Howe brothers failed to end the war on the battlefield and at sea, they always clung to the faint hope that they could establish peace through dialogue as opposed to bloodshed. In this capacity, they both displayed a certain reticence to fight those whom they considered to be fellow countrymen.

After William's resignation, Richard retained his command and successfully helped evacuate Philadelphia in June 1778. He also managed to score a victory against a combined Franco-American force in Rhode Island later that year, but afterward he packed his sizeable coffers and returned home as well. The saga of the Howe brothers in America is triumphant, tragic, and tinged with irony. During the French and Indian War, they had fought bravely to secure the colonies for the king; during the revolution, they lost them for him. They did, however, secure their place in history.

I often heard calls for revolution and independence in my youth, which still resonate today. The '60s and '70s were a turbulent time in the north of England and in Scotland. Industrial disputes were rife and riots were happening in the main towns all the time. Whereas some of my fellow students were wearing Che Guevara and Chairman Mao T-shirts, the unrest instilled in me a kind of empathy for the American Revolutionary War and the main protagonists. There was a popular TV series at the time called *The Last of the Mohicans*. I found it inspiring. The subject was rarely approached in class, so I had to find out for myself. That was the spark that ignited my fervent passion for all things connected to the Revolutionary War. Nobody ever told us that King George was crazier than a dog in a hubcap factory.

CHAPTER NINE:

THE ROAD TO WATERLOO.

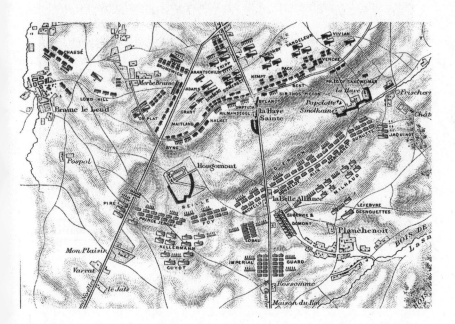

At an auction in the UK in 2020, a unique collection of war medals awarded to four brothers who served in the Napoleonic wars (initially valued at $76,000) fetched nearly double their predicted price. Up until that time, the set had remained in the Maclaine family's possession for two hundred years along with the stories of how these medals were achieved. These proud Scottish soldiers were John, Archibald, Murdoch, and Hector, who all served as officers in the British army in different capacities.

Archibald and his twin brother Murdoch were born January 13, 1777, at Scallasdale on Mull, the second largest island of the Inner Hebrides, which lies off the west coast of Scotland. His fellow officers in the British Twentieth Regiment of Foot described him as a most promising officer and brave to a fault. Murdoch was a captain. Precisely how he obtained the commission isn't entirely clear. Because he came from a prestigious and wealthy clan, it is unlikely that he rose through the ranks since at that time the British army could hardly have been described as a meritocracy.

In fact, buying a commission was common practice for those with dashing aspirations to be an officer of a prestigious cavalry or infantry regiment of the British army. It was also a very effective way of relieving one's family of hormonally-challenged, pouty teenagers. The countess of Mornington, in a fit of despair, once remarked, "I vow to God I don't know what I shall do with my awkward son Arthur," who was appointed as an ensign in March 1787, in the Seventy-Third (Highland) Regiment of Foot, and later became the duke of Wellington.

Paying for your rank was the usual method of obtaining a commission in the army from the seventeenth to the late-nineteenth century, completely bypassing the need to receive a promotion for outstanding conduct or by way of seniority. Formally, the purchase price of a commission was used as a cash bond for good behavior, liable to be forfeited to the army's accountants in the event of cowardice, desertion, or gross misconduct. Precisely how gross the misconduct was assessed depending largely on the situation.

For the lesser privileged among us, the other way of joining up was referred to as "taking the king's shilling." Once this shilling had been accepted, it was nigh on impossible to get out of the British army, which at the time wasn't widely regarded as a particularly viable career prospect. Scurrilous recruiting sergeants often had to use less-than-honest methods to secure their "prey," such as getting the prospective recruit blind drunk, placing the shilling into his pocket, and then hauling the victim before the magistrate the following morning while still badly hungover to get him to legally accept the fact that he was now in the army.

On some occasions, the king's shilling was hidden in the bottom of a pewter tankard. The earnest drinker could later discover, to his profound chagrin, that he had unwittingly accepted the king's offer. As a result of this dishonest practice, some tankards were made with glass bottoms. One man was hanged in 1787 for enlisting, taking the bounty, escaping, and reenlisting on no less than forty-seven separate instances.

Thankfully, Murdoch wasn't conned into joining up, but his first commission was definitely bought. He participated in one of the only battles fought by the British against Napoleon Bonaparte's French forces in Italy. It all happened in 1806 at the battle of Maida in Calabria. The battle demonstrated the superiority of the classic British double line against the French column, a method that would be used to repel attacking French on numerous consecutive occasions during the Napoleonic Wars, up to and including the epic Battle of Waterloo.

The battle of Maida was the result of Britain being asked by Russia to dispatch an expeditionary force into the Mediterranean and to support a possible joint expedition against French troops stationed in the Kingdom of Naples's eastern ports. Italy didn't exist as an official country at that time.

The town of Maida lies just sixty miles north of the Strait of Messina. The pitched battle that occurred there was a result of the War of the Third Coalition that pitted France and its allies against a coalition that was eventually comprised of the Napoleonic superpowers (Great Britain, Austria, and Russia) and augmented by the lesser Kingdoms of Naples, Sicily, and Sweden. At the time, France's aggression in Italy had induced Austria and Russia to join Britain in its continuing conflict with France. It was to be Britain's first European land battle in the Napoleonic Wars. Along with the preceding French Revolutionary wars, the Napoleonic Wars constitute a twenty-three-year period of recurrent conflict that concluded with the epic Battle of Waterloo and Napoleon's second abdication on June 22, 1815.

The commander of the British army's expeditionary force on the momentous day was Major General Sir John Stuart. His army numbered around fifty-two hundred infantry equipped with eleven guns. The opposing French force commanded by General Jean Louis Ebénézer Reynier checked in with six thousand men, which included some fifteen hundred cavalry and six guns.

The battle began when soldiers of the French First Light Infantry rushed forward toward the double line of a British light battalion. As the French advanced across the level plain in Calabria, British cannon balls smashed into their ranks. When they were at around 250 yards away from the British line, the artillery gunners switched to case shot, which consisted of shells filled with hundreds of musket balls and pieces of metal that scythed through the forward French ranks and eliminated them in whole rows. The French would have then tasted the devastating force of precision British musketry.

A well-trained British infantryman in the early 1900s could fire and reload his standard-issue Brown Bess musket three times a minute, which considering that this took nineteen separate actions was no easy feat. Facing off against disciplined British infantrymen at that time was not a particularly endearing prospect. On the day at 150 yards, the British light infantry came into the fray and opened its first volley. Owing to their exemplary musketry skills, at least half of their shots hit their target. The second volley was released at eighty yards. A badly wounded French general of the First Light Infantry continued to bravely wave his men forward into this veritable storm of iron and lead. The British fired their third volley at twenty yards, which inflicted further horrific carnage and decimated the oncoming French ranks. Colonel Sir James Kempt sent Corsican Rangers, supported by the light company of the Twentieth Regiment, across the shallow River Lamato to clear French skirmishers from the scrub on the far bank. Kempt would later be appointed to lead the Eighth British Brigade at the battle of Waterloo. Young and eager Captain Murdoch Maclaine, a captain in the Twentieth Regiment, was mortally wounded. He was the only officer to be killed at the Battle of Maida in 1806.

Although the name of Maida isn't really well known, news of the battle caused a sensation in Britain. Consequently, a pub was built in Middlesex, situated to the northwest of London and named the "The Hero of Maida." The pub sign displayed a portrait of General

Stuart. In due course, as London's city boundaries extended, the area around the pub became known as Maida Vale.

Another brother fought with the British expeditionary force through the Peninsular War in Spain and Portugal, which lasted from May 2, 1808, up until April 17, 1814. Captain Hector Maclaine first served with distinction in the Sixty-Fourth Regiment in the West Indies and Surinam. Getting a posting to the West Indies was incredibly precarious for British soldiers at the turn of the nineteenth century. Many of them died of malaria, typhoid, dysentery, and other jungle-related diseases during their tour of service. At least Hector didn't catch one in the forehead from a native sniper while he was there. By all accounts, he was considerably less impetuous than his brother John.

In 1811, he joined the Fifty-Seventh Regiment in Portugal with the rank of captain during the height of the Peninsular War. He was attached to General Rowland Hill's Second Division, a division that endured some of the bitterest fighting of the campaign that would ultimately eject Napoleon's army from Spain and Portugal.

The Peninsular War was one of those rare Napoleonic British army expeditions to the European continent. They were often faced with perilous objectives, taking on French forces in Portugal and Spain, in an attempt to fracture or maybe even break Napoleon's hegemony in mainland Europe. The duke of Wellington's diminutive army was occasionally at risk of being totally annihilated. It was certainly in Britain's self-interest to assist in liberating indigenous populations in Europe from Napoleon's tyranny, and it was this fact that helped motivate popular and political support for the war on the British home front.

Hector fought valiantly at the battle of Vitoria, where he was commanded by General Arthur Wellesley (who became the duke of Wellington in 1814) against Joseph Bonaparte, brother of the French Emperor Napoleon Bonaparte. Napoleon had imposed his brother on the Spanish people as their king. Then Hector went on to fight with the British army at Roncesvalles, the Pyrenees, Nivelle, Tarbes, Orthez, and Toulouse.

Commanding the light companies of General John Byng's brigade, Hector experienced the full-on horrors of Napoleonic warfare from the front and was frequently involved in hand-to-hand skirmishing. At the battle of Nivelle, Hector was severely wounded and received a medal for distinguished conduct. After the Napoleonic Wars had concluded, he remained in the army and served in North America and France. He departed this life on January 15, 1847, aged sixty-two.

The most illustrious name of the four Maclaine brothers was definitely that of Archibald. During his rise to become a colonel of the Fifty-Second, he served in the campaign of 1799 against Tippoo Sultan in the Polygar War in 1801 and in the Maratha wars of 1802, 1803, and 1804. During the 1799 campaign, he was so severely wounded at the Siege of Seringapatam that he had to remain in hospital for a whole year. Eventually, in 1804, due to his severity of his wounds, he was compelled to return home. After he had sufficiently recovered, he went on to serve in the Peninsular War in 1810, 1811, and 1812.

It's safe to say that General Sir Archibald Maclaine had a distinguished military career. He is best known to historians and admirers for his intrepid defense of the fort of Matagorda (near Cadiz, Spain) in 1810 while serving as a captain in the Ninety-Fourth Regiment. At the time, the attacking French forces, commanded by Marshal Nicolas Jean-de-Dieu Soult, heavily outnumbered the then-Captain Maclaine and his small force.

In his report to General Thomas Graham, Captain Maclaine wrote, "The whole of the night of the 21st and morning of the 22nd, I employed in endeavoring to repair the parapet of the southeast face, composed of sandbags, which, from the very heavy fire of twenty-one pieces of cannon (most of them 32-pounders) the enemy had totally demolished, so that the men at the guns were completely exposed. We continued to replace the sandbags and fill up the breach so as to put ourselves in a tolerable state of defense: and at daybreak in the morning (April 22nd) the enemy opened with a salvo from all his batteries. We returned the fire with the same spirit and success as yesterday, but the fort soon became a complete ruin and nowhere afforded any shelter for the reliefs."[27] Four of the

27　　Wellington's Men Remembered Volume 2: A Register of Memorials to Soldiers Who Fought in the Peninsular War and at Waterloo: M to Z
by Janet Bromley and David Bromley | Jan 31, 2020

seven guns were now disabled and put out of action, and the bomb-proof casemate in which the magazine was lodged was blown in, entirely exposing the powder barrels.

General Stuart came over from General Graham during the early morning to report on the state of the garrison. On his return, the evacuation of the fort was ordered and a naval officer, Captain Stacpole, was sent with boats from the British squadron to relieve the garrison of their duty. The defenders' casualties at the end numbered 83 out of the 147 who had originally formed Captain Maclaine's command.

Maclaine had courageously held the fort from February 22 until April 22, 1810, when he was ordered to evacuate. His actions resulted in his promotion to major of the Eighty-Seventh Regiment. For several years, he commanded the Seventh West India Regiment and subsequently became a full colonel in the Fifty-Second Regiment.

When Maclaine's battalion left Cadiz, Richard Wellesley, first marquess Wellesley (a British diplomatic agent at Cadiz), personally wrote to his brother General Arthur Wellesley, duke of Wellington. He proudly mentioned Archibald Maclaine. "You know that Maclaine who behaved so gallantly at Matagorda is in the Ninety-Fourth."[28] Maclaine was afterward known among his acquaintances and among old Army officers as "the Hero of Matagorda."

The duke of Wellington, who commanded the allied troops during the Peninsular Wars and at Waterloo, had also served with distinction in India. It's safe to assume that Archibald would probably have known the man who would become the "Iron Duke."

In a dispatch to Lord Liverpool, General Graham wrote this of Captain Maclaine in connection with the defense of Matagorda: "It would be an injustice to the Service not to recommend him in the warmest manner to your Lordship's notice." The result was the promotion "without purchase" of Captain Maclaine to the Eighty-Seventh Royal Irish Fusiliers on October 4, 1810. By all accounts, Maclaine was much admired by the officers in the Second Battalion, Eighty-Seventh Infantry Regiment, so it's safe to assume that there would have been a great deal of resentment if his promo-

---

28   Arthur Wellesley Wellington, *Supplementary Despatches, Correspondence, and Memoranda of Field Marshal Arthur Duke of Wellington: Expedition to Denmark* (London: John Murray, 1860).

tion had not been from within. With his new regiment, he took part in the Battle of Barrosa in 1811, where he was severely wounded for the sixth time in his career and had his horse shot from under him.

In the *London Gazette* October 12, 1816, it was announced that "His Royal Highness the Prince Regent had been pleased, in the name and on behalf of His Majesty, to grant unto Archibald Maclaine, Esq., Lieutenant-Colonel in the Army, and Companion of the Most Honorable Military Order of the Bath, His Majesty's royal license and permission that he may accept and wear the supernumerary cross of the royal and distinguished Spanish Order of Charles the Third, which his Catholic Majesty Ferdinand the Seventh, King of Spain, has been pleased to confer upon that Officer, in testimony of the high sense which that Sovereign entertains of the highly distinguished intrepidity displayed by him in the arduous defense of Fort Matagorda, in 1810, in the memorable Battle of Barrosa, in 1811, and the capture of Seville, in 1812."

Archibald's contribution to and subsequent career in the British army cannot be underestimated. He was appointed colonel of the Fifty-Second Regiment of Foot in 1847, promoted to lieutenant general in 1851, and then general in 1855. (These commissions were earned, not purchased.) His death occurred in London on March 9, 1861. By that time, he had reached the grand age of eighty-nine years old.

The eldest of the four brothers, Major John Archibald Maclaine of the intrepid Second Battalion, Seventy-Third Regiment, fought at the famous battle of Waterloo, the last definitive engagement for the British and allied troops in the Napoleonic Wars. In 1809, recruiting difficulties meant that the Seventy-Third lost its status and dress, which simply meant that they would be outfitted in normal British infantry uniforms as opposed to wearing the kilt. (This would inevitably increase the British Army's laundry bills because kilts didn't require undergarments of any description.) It did, however, manage to raise a Second Battalion from local militia companies at Nottingham that same year. This was in effect the start of their road to Waterloo.

On June 18, 1815, the duke of Wellington had never personally taken the field against an army commanded by Napoleon Bonaparte himself. At the time of the epic battle both commanders were forty-six years old. Wellington had the unique distinction of never having lost a major battle against his adversaries throughout his career, which was encouraging for the British and allied troops whom he commanded at the battle of Waterloo.

The duke was a great believer in steadfast musketry, and it's generally accepted that had it not been for the unflinching steadiness of the British infantry at Mont-Saint-Jean (Waterloo), it is more than probable that the duke of Wellington would have had to retreat from the field. He wasn't at all convinced that he could defeat Napoleon, and he had placed fourteen thousand troops in the town of Halle, roughly twelve miles to the northwest of the battlefield, just in case he had to make a quick getaway.

One eyewitness who was in close proximity to the action on the day said, "It was very ridiculous…to see the number of vacant spots that were left nearly along nearly the whole of the line, where a great part of the dark-dressed foreign [allied] corps had stood intermixed with the British, when the action began….The same field continued to be a wild one the whole of the afternoon. It was a sort of dueling-post between the two armies, every half-hour showing a meeting of some kind upon it….The smoke hung so thick about, that, although not more than eighty yards asunder, we could only distinguish each other by the flashes of the pieces."[29]

Lord William Beresford, who earned his fearsome reputation as a great commander in the Peninsular War and would have known John's brother Hector, remarked that at the Battle of Waterloo, "Never did I see such a pounding match. Napoleon did not maneuver at all, he just moved forward in the old style in columns, and was driven off in the old style. I had the infantry for some time in squares, and we had the French cavalry walking about us as if they had been our own. I never saw the British infantry behave so well."[30]

Because so many wonderful accounts of this momentous battle have been written over the years, this chapter will avoid getting too deep into the actual semantics of this encounter on that field of gentle rolling hills.

---

29   William Henry Fitchett, ed., *Wellington's Men: Some Soldier Autobiographies,* https://www.gutenberg.org/files/62571/62571-h/62571-h.htm.

30   Philip Haythornthwaite, *British Napoleonic Infantry Tactics 1792-1815* (London: Osprey Publishing, 2012).

The Second Battalion, Seventy-Third Regiment fought at the Battle of Quatre Bras on June 16, 1815, where fifty-three men were killed and wounded. At the subsequent Battle of Waterloo on June 18, the French cavalry charged the regiment on no less than eleven consecutive occasions. The day hadn't started all that badly for them because the opening bombardment didn't seriously affect the regiment, who had been ordered to lie down behind the ridge. In fact, some of them even fell asleep.

Later on that fateful day when they had formed a square with the men of the Thirtieth Regiment, there were many horrific incidences of soldiers literally being blown to pieces or decapitated by canon shot. The effect of an exploding shell against men standing and kneeling in close proximity was devastating. One shell could easily kill or wound seventeen men. The inside of the battalion squares soon filled up with dead and dying men writhing in agony. One man was quoted as saying, "We were nearly suffocated by the smoke and the loud cries of the wounded was most appalling."

It is unimaginable how these men coped with the deafening sounds, sickening sights, and the asphyxiating stench of this battle. The nauseous odors of burning buildings and gunpowder mixed with the smell of blood, sweat, vomit, and the human detritus of thousands of men and horses must have been beyond terrifying. After the initial artillery bombardment, the British and allied units were given the ominous order "to prepare to receive cavalry." This was the standard instruction to form battalion squares. For roughly two hours, between 4:00 p.m. and 6:00 p.m., Marshal Michel Ney led ten thousand French cavalry in wave after wave of relatively futile charges against these densely packed allied squares. Among them was a square formed by the Thirtieth Regiment and the Second Battalion, Seventy-Third Regiment who remained steadfastly in square without breaking throughout the whole terrifying ordeal.

Each time the cavalry came within musket range, roughly twelve paces from the square, the three or four deep ranks of infantrymen poured volleys of musket fire at them, causing their horses to rear up and veer away. Many eyewitnesses claimed that when the projectiles hit the steel harnesses of the cuirassiers and carabineers, the sound resembled that of a violent hailstorm. The French cavalry didn't manage to break a single British square that day and the stead-fastness of the British infantry at Waterloo became a byword for future generations.

Every single soldier present that day had a one in four chance of being killed or seriously wounded. During a terrible pounding by French artillery, Major John Maclaine's body was literally blown in half by a cannon ball. The battalion lost six officers and 225 men were killed and wounded, the second heaviest casualties suffered by a line infantry regiment at Waterloo. John is one of the twelve senior officers buried in the crypt of the official British Waterloo memorial in the cemetery of Evere, near Brussels.

So the incredible stories of four brave brothers, whose lives were full of adventure and action, were worth considerably more than an obscure collection of medals that were auctioned off in 2020. Each one of them was a genuine hero.

These days I live about forty-five minutes north of the famous battlefield. I know the story and the place intimately. Twenty years ago, I used to organize battlefield tours of Waterloo and the surrounding areas. I also have a great love of antiques but not necessarily those of a military nature. Some time ago, I received an email from an antiques mailing list that I subscribe to. It mentioned the auction of medals from one family that had sent sons to the Napoleonic Wars. I wanted to know more about them, so I began some research and discovered that although only one of the men had fought at Waterloo, they were a remarkably interesting set of brothers indeed.

CHAPTER TEN:

WE SAW HISTORY.

The following story is about two young sisters, who are often referred to in local history to as the "Army of Two," so they deserve a mention in this volume. In the state of Massachusetts, the antics of Rebecca and Abigail Bates are widely remembered in folksongs, poetry, and local lore. The story of a lighthouse keeper's two daughters, who saved their town from British marauders during the War of 1812, has no doubt been exaggerated and embellished throughout the centuries—but it's still worthy of note. With some legends, if examined with close scrutiny, it's occasionally possible to discover some elements of truth and determine the facts from the conjecture.

Their antics are widely remembered in folksongs, poetry, and local lore—but did they really turn back the British Navy? This is the stuff of legend...but how much of their story was true?

It's an established fact that by 1814, Britain's navy was committing a naval war of harassment along the East Coast of America. Part of their modus operandi was to harass small towns or harbors and occasionally dispatch marines to ransack these places to procure supplies. There were even recorded instances of the British war ships setting fire to American vessels while they were anchored in the harbors. In June and July of 1814, British ships had invaded Scituate harbor on no less than three previous occasions, and at each incursion they destroyed fishing vessels and stole others. The local militia gallantly stood guard against any troops intending to land, but the situation for them and the inhabitants was becoming untenable.

Simeon Bates was the keeper of the local lighthouse where they all lived, situated at Cedar Point in Scituate on the shores of Massachusetts Bay. Rebecca, according to her obituary, would have been twenty years old and Abigail was about thirteen. Early in September 1814, a British man-of-war was sighted offshore preparing to launch barges in the direction of the lighthouse. For reasons best known to himself, Simeon Bates was absent without leave (AWOL) and not manning the lighthouse at the time, so only his wife and the two girls were on hand to do anything, if they could.

They suspected that the militia would not be able to make it to the harbor in time, so they decided to hide from view and play a fife and drum to make the enemy think the soldiers were on their way. According to the story, the impromptu duet played a meager rendition of "Yankee Doodle" as loudly as they could. On hearing this, the British stopped rowing their barge and promptly returned to the warship, which then departed the town of Scituate, much to the relief of the young musicians.

Considering the adage about things sounding too good to be true, the most pertinent question here is did this all really happen. According to historical records, the British blockaded Scituate harbor on no less than three occasions between June 11 and July 9 in 1814. A written history of Scituate published in 1931 claimed that "ten vessels, fishing and coastal craft, were lost." It also claims that the barges belonged to the British frigate seventy-four-gun *Bulwark*.[31]

The British did not disembark when they were burning the ships in the harbor on June 11. Six days later, according to committee reports from the Thirtieth United States Congress, "a British ship-of-war, two brigs, and several small craft came to anchor near Scituate harbor." Colonel John Barstow's militia was called out July 9 when a British warship, tenuously identified as the *Bulwark*, demanded provisions from the townsfolk, who were in no mood to provide any sustenance to the British navy. The militia remained on guard that summer, but the British did not reappear. Was this because two young ladies had played "Yankee Doodle?"

Over the years, some have questioned the veracity of this story in its entirety, but it should be pointed out that the Bates sisters never once defaulted from their original version of events. Later in

31   Samuel Deane, *History of Scituate, Massachusetts, from Its First Settlement to 1831* (Boston, MA: J. Loring, 1831).

life, they took to retelling it, and even went as far as providing affi-
davits attesting to its accuracy. So, if they said it happened, well,
maybe it did. What right do irascible historians have to debunk
the story of these two heroines? Just for the record, the first version
of "Yankee Doodle" appears to have been written by British army
physician Dr. Richard Shuckburgh during the French and Indian
War. It was a satirical observation of New England's "Yankees," an
appropriation apparently coined by British General James Wolfe,
the victor of Quebec.

Two other sisters, Juana Gertrudis Navarro Alsbury and Maria
Gertrudis Navarro, witnessed history at the Alamo firsthand. They
didn't wear uniforms or brandish any arms, but by all accounts, they
personally experienced the main events that transpired at the Alamo.
In 1836, this famous standoff was between a group of Texan and
Tejano (Texas-born Mexicans) men against Mexican forces led by
deluded dictator President General Antonio López de Santa Anna.
The domestic fortunes of these two sisters alone were worthy of a
reality TV show; they moved around more than chess pieces.

Juana and Maria Gertrudis Navarro were the daughters of
José Ángel Navarro and Concepción Cervantes, and nieces of José
Antonio Navarro (one of the men who signed the Texas Declaration of Independence). Following the death of their mother, the
two sisters moved in with their aunt Josefa Navarro Veramendi,
her husband Juan Martín de Veramendi, and their daughter Ursula
Veramendi (who became the wife of a certain notable American
called James Bowie).

In February of 1836, Juana, her second husband Dr. Horatio
Alsbury, and her son Alejo Pérez (from her first marriage to Alejo
Pérez Ramigio) were living in San Antonio de Bexar in the newly
declared Republic of Texas when the town was captured by the
Mexican army on February 23. Under the auspices of her adopted
sister's husband James Bowie, Dr. Alsbury left San Antonio with
Juana, her son, and younger sister Maria and took up residence in a
local mission station there known as the Alamo.

They remained on site during throughout the siege that began
on February 23, 1836. The mission station, which was garrisoned
by two hundred men under the command of lieutenant colonel

William Barret Travis, fell to the attacking Mexican army that was estimated to have numbered around six thousand men. The final assault began on the morning of March 6, 1836, at 5:30 a.m. Around that time, Juana was helping to nurse James Bowie, who had fallen ill. Despite inconsistent accounts regarding his death, the most popular, and probably the most accurate one, claimed that he died in his bed while defending himself against Mexican soldiers.

William Barret Travis was shot through the head on March 6 as he directed fire on the north wall, according to his slave, Joe (who was among the very few who survived the battle). Renowned frontiersman and congressman, David "Davy" Crockett also died on the morning of March 6 fighting alongside remaining Alamo defenders. Their dead bodies were unceremoniously cremated.

Many years after the siege, journalist and Texas Ranger John S. Ford interviewed Juana regarding her experiences during the battle. According to his summarized account, the Navarro sisters "were in a building not far from where the residence of Col. Sam Maverick was afterwards erected," which would have put them in one of the houses on the west wall during the final battle. Ford wrote that, "They could hear the noise of the conflict, the roar of the artillery, the rattle of small arms, the shouts of the combatants, the groans of the dying, and the moans of the wounded."[32]

Juana claimed that during the battle, Mexican soldiers entered the room where she and Maria were holing up. They broke open a trunk and took valuables belonging to Juana and her family and slaughtered two of the Alamo defenders right before their eyes. After the Alamo had fallen, the sisters were brought to their father's home.

There are some who seriously doubt the veracity of Juana's story. Susanna Wilkerson Dickinson also survived the Alamo, and long before suing people for defamation became a popular American pastime—a few short months after the battle—she accused Juana of being the legendary Mexican woman who carried Travis' parley message from the Alamo to Santa Anna on March 4. Susanna also claimed Juana left the Alamo with her father before the siege on March 6. It should be added that most references refute this claim in its entirety.

---

32   Bill Groneman, *Eyewitness to the Alamo* (Guilford, CT: Lone Star Books, 2017).

Historians often have the propensity to cite the Battle of the Alamo as having provided sufficient time for Samuel Houston to organize the newly formed Republic of Texas. Their intention was to ultimately repel the Mexican army, which they did most effectively at the battle of San Jacinto on April 21, 1836.

After the fall of the Alamo, Santa Anna headed east toward what would become the city of Houston. There, he was defeated and captured by General Sam Houston on April 21, 1836. After his release six months later, Santa Anna traveled to the United States before returning to Mexico. In 1838, he rose against the French, losing a leg in battle (which would have severely afflicted his capacity to rise anywhere, but he did regain some popularity). He led the armies against the United States in the Mexican-American War, which lasted from 1846–1848.

After his defeat, Santa Anna would see Mexico lose half of its territory to the United States. He went into exile until 1853 when he returned to power. Two years later, Santa Anna would sell a small portion of land to the United States, known as the Gadsden Purchase, a move that effectively ended his political career. He died aged eighty-two in Mexico City on June 21, 1876.

In 1841, Maria married José Miguel Felipe Cantú, with whom she had eight children. She died in 1895 at age seventy-eight, so being a waddling baby machine didn't badly affect her longevity. Juana's second husband, Dr. Alsbury, was killed in 1847 during the Mexican-American War. She then married Juan Perez, a cousin of her first husband. She must have believed in keeping it in the family.

Juana became a prominent citizen of Texas and died July 23, 1888, at her son's home at Rancho de la Laguna on Salado Creek, in east Bexar County, where she is buried. That's the assumption at least. Other information gives her burial place as a Catholic cemetery in San Antonio. She would have been seventy-six or thereabouts. Her exact age at the time of her death isn't known, so this is purely an estimate. During her life, her signature appeared on numerous Bexar County land documents and in the state archives on legal petitions to the Texas legislature. She petitioned the legislature in 1857 and received a pension for the personal belongings she lost at the Alamo and for her services.

Not all fights occur on battlefields, and not all warriors carry weapons. But if anything proves the adage about the pen being mightier than the sword, then the story of these two female abolitionists, who fought as hard as any soldier, deserves some attention. Angelina Grimké (born February 20, 1805–1879) and Sarah Moore Grimké (born November 26, 1792–1873) in Charleston, South Carolina, were the privileged daughters of The Honorable John Faucheraud Grimké, judge of the Supreme Court of South Carolina, and Mary Smith who descended from Irish and English Puritan stock. John had been a colonel in the Revolutionary War and fought with distinction at the battle of Yorktown with Lafayette's brigade. His position and wealth placed his family in the higher echelons of the very exclusive society of Charleston. His children were accustomed to luxury and the family-owned slaves.

Sarah and Angelina were the very first women from a southern slave owning family to publicly denounce slavery. They both became extremely popular for their public lectures in the northern states.

Most young children of Southern planters didn't see a difference between their white and African American playmates. They would have had little or no concept of racism in the contemporary sense, until their parents or teachers informed them. Sarah Grimké felt a profound abhorrence toward the whole institution of slavery from a very early age, and her sentiments were reciprocated by several of her brothers and sisters.

Judge Grimké and his family, along with many members of the community, were devout High Church Episcopalians who clung stoically to biblical teachings and chastised those who neglected to adhere to their stringent practices of church or household worship. It must have been quite confusing for the Grimké children, who were forced to physically witness slave punishments and then compelled to listen to contradictory scripture advocating brotherly love and forgiveness.

When youngest sister Angelina Emily was born, Sarah was about twelve years old. She established an immediate affinity with the baby of the house. It was an affinity that would endure for the rest of their lives. Sarah's devotion and affection for Angelina could have been due to their mother Mary, who despite being a very devout woman, was quite undemonstrative in her affections for her children. She was, however, intelligent and had a taste for reading, especially theological works.

Sarah and Angelina notched up quite a few notable "firsts." They were the first women from a southern slave owning family to publicly denounce slavery, the first women to act as agents of the American Anti-Slavery Society, the first women in the antislavery movement to address audiences composed of both men and women, and the first women abolitionists to defend the rights of women to move outside their traditional roles. Together, the Grimké sisters helped to transform women's activism in the United States. When they were at the height of their popularity, Angelina usually received the majority of the public's attention. This was probably because she was better at public speaking and was married to Theodore Dwight Weld, one of the most prominent abolitionists of the day.

As Sarah matured, her intense dissatisfaction with slavery resulted not only from her disgust over the abuse slaves received, but also from the opportunities that they so were cruelly denied. She could not understand why slaves were not allowed to learn to read or write. Each Sunday afternoon during her teenage years, Sarah surreptitiously taught Bible classes to the slave children. This was in direct contravention of the Alabama Slave Code of 1833 that included the following law: Any person who shall attempt to teach any free person of color, or slave, to spell, read, or write, shall upon conviction thereof by indictment, be fined in a sum of not less than two hundred fifty dollars, nor more than five hundred dollars.[33]

When Sarah's father discovered that she was teaching a slave girl, he threatened the girl with a whipping and sternly lectured his daughter on the precarious implications of her actions. It's entirely possible that this incident, among many others, reminded Sarah that her affinity with the slaves was because she was also denied chances to enact her educational aspirations purely because she was a woman.

As a young woman, Sarah left her established church and became a Quaker, attending meetings soon after. It was at this juncture that she became convinced that she had experienced a divine call to become a minister.

At the age of twenty-nine, she left Charleston and moved to Philadelphia, where she faithfully attended the Fourth and Arch Street Quaker meetings in an attempt to pursue her calling. Many of her fellow Quakers became highly critical about the content and delivery of her speeches, which culminated in Sarah severing all ties with the Quaker movement and focusing almost exclusively on the abolition of slavery.

In 1829, Sarah's younger sister, Angelina, who had also embraced the Quaker religion, moved to Philadelphia. Angelina wasn't as demure as her older sister and refused to quietly accept the imposed restrictions on her ambitions. Eventually, she also completely severed her connections to the Quakers and became involved in the abolition movement, a movement that had been denounced by many Quaker leaders as being too overtly political.

In October 1836, the Grimké sisters left Philadelphia and traveled together to New York where they met with members of the American Anti-Slavery Society. Then in November of that same year, they formed a National Female Anti-Slavery Society and set out on a tour of New England, where they addressed groups of women and distributed pamphlets.

---

33   Frazine K. Taylor, *Researching African American Genealogy in Alabama: A Resource Guide* (Montgomery, AL: NewSouth Books, 2008).

At the outset, the Grimké sisters began meeting in private homes for the purpose of informing and involving women in the cause of abolition. In didn't take long for the word to get around and eventually they discovered that no parlor in any city that they visited was capacious enough to accommodate all the women who wanted to attend. It should be added that public entertainment was scant in those days, so piling into someone's living room and crushing their petticoats was regarded as a suitable alternative. Their insight and their experiences of living in a slave-owning family were both authentic and informative, which contributed greatly to their personal rise in popularity. Despite social prejudices against women speaking in public places, their growing number of followers and devotees meant that they were compelled to hold their meetings in churches. The Grimkés's first lecture tour lasted approximately six months. In that time, they personally visited sixty-seven New England towns and addressed around 40,500 people. An ensuing stadium tour was never considered due to the lack of stadiums.

Congregational ministers in Massachusetts appointed pious Reverend Nehemiah Adams to publish a pastoral letter attacking women abolitionists. While no names were mentioned in the communiqué, it was abundantly clear that it was written with Sarah and Angelina Grimké in mind.

Angelina's ambitions eventually elevated to address the role of women in American society. She was, in many ways, a staunch feminist who openly compared white women to slaves when she said, "If women have no means of making their political desires known, then they are no more than slaves to their husbands, fathers, and brothers."[34] Go girlfriend. She went on to compare white women to the revolutionary fathers, who rebelled against having no representation in the English Parliament, yet were still held accountable to the jurisdiction of intractable English laws imposed on the colonies. "If the American colonists had a right to speak against the King and Parliament, then women certainly have a right to speak against the men who now govern the American political system."[35] She was

---

34   Katherine Dupre Lumpkin, *Emancipation of Angelina Grimke* (The University Of North Carolina Press, 2011).
35   Ibid.

clearly establishing a political argument and defending women's right to petition Congress as they saw fit. Angelina was on a roll.

Sarah's contributions as an active abolitionist and defender of women's rights are remarkable. She had been openly denied educational and vocational opportunities and was rejected by her church. But her writings and reform work were greatly influential. The battle they fought was to attempt to change minds at a time when women were considered the weaker members of an extremely male-dominated society. They succeeded to some extent. Sarah's ultimate goal was to be recognized as useful member of society. Her lifelong struggle to meet that goal was often beset by misogyny and prejudice, but through her accomplishments she did indeed become a useful and highly respected citizen.

The injustice that Angelina confronted and addressed during her lifetime threatened the young nation. The battle for the very soul of America was at stake. This is why her story is so inspirational because she reasserted the power of the human spirit. She was a remarkable woman indeed and deserves every conceivable accolade.

When the sisters were verbally attacked on occasion for their opinions and their public speaking, they were forced to develop rhetoric that defended their womanhood and their right to be involved in political affairs. The sisters quickly developed a political identity, an identity that allowed them to confidently take the rostrum and extoll their stance concerning antislavery and women's rights. They were the first American women to become advocates for the antislavery movement, which in time led to women developing conscious political identities.

The abolitionist movement in the United States of America, which the Grimké sisters fervently extolled and believed in, was part of a concerted effort to end slavery in a nation that valued personal freedom and believed "all men are created equal," even though this equality hypocritically depended largely on the hue of one's skin. As the abolitionists grew more vociferous in their demands, slave owners became more intransigent in their responses, which eventually fueled regional divisiveness and would ultimately culminate in a devastating civil war.

The lesser protagonists of history have always engrossed me. I grew up around very strong women, my mother among them. Living in a community that didn't even see color televisions until the mid-70s, we relied on great storytellers to keep us entertained—and my village had some legends in this department. They would relate stories of hardship, heroism, and depravation that would often bring a tear to my eye. My mother always said that "it wasn't only the men that did the fighting you know, the women suffered as well." She was right. This made me want to know more about women's roles during conflict. I love folklore because it's where one can find the heart of the people. Whether the stories were embellished or not is beside the point. A good local story can reveal so much about the character and nature of people, as I hope that the stories in this chapter have.

CHAPTER ELEVEN:

IF JOHNNY COMES MARCHING HOME.

Stories of brothers fighting together and against each other in the American Civil War tend to induce historians to wax lyrical and hang on overused clichés. Brother against brother and family against family naturally occur during such conflicts and yet there are few other instances of warfare that provoke people to display such emotive reactions. Hopefully, this chapter can focus on a few lesser-known instances of fraternal and domestic involvement in this most devastating of fights.

In 1861, the secessionist south was unprepared for war. Only eleven million of the United States' population of thirty-two million lived in the South. Four million slaves that wouldn't be armed for obvious reasons augmented this number. It wasn't a poor region by any means. Its wealth depended on products such as cotton, tobacco, rice, and sugar, while 94 percent of America's manufactured goods emanated from the northern states. Raw products like iron, steel, and coal gave the North a further marked advantage. This is why one of the North's first hostile moves was to attack the southern economy by blockading sea access to the southern ports. The South would endure the deficiencies imposed by economic isolation and remain resolute in its assertion that they wanted to preserve states' rights, and therein lay the seeds of conflict that erupted into all-out war between the two sides.

Innumerable stories of heroism and courage have emerged from this period in history over the years, but one of the most fascinating tales of the Civil War recounts the experiences of two unmarried brothers, who had distinctly opposing ideas regarding their loyalties. Clifton Kennedy Prentiss was born in 1835 and William Scollay Prentiss came into the world in 1839. Both were born somewhere near Baltimore, Maryland, where they lived. Clifton and William first became disaffected in 1857 when they vehemently disagreed with each other regarding the slavery question. In time the arguments escalated, became more vociferous, and eventually they both left the family domicile in anger vowing never to speak to each other again. When the Civil War broke out, Clifton went north to join the Union army while William headed south to fight for the Confederacy.

Baltimore native Clifton died for his country. So did brother William Prentiss. Same country, just different aspirations. They were briefly reunited and made amends. Walt Whitman wrote, "each died for his cause."

April 14, 1861, was the fateful date that Fort Sumter surrendered to Confederate forces, beginning what would become a long and punishing civil war. President Abraham Lincoln sent out a call for all troops to rush to defend the nation's capital, Washington, DC. Two short days after, Clifton first enlisted in the Seventh New York State Militia and served thirty days before he transferred to the Fifth Maryland Infantry (Union) on March 30, 1862. After his promotion to second lieutenant on July 31,

1862, he joined the Sixth Maryland Infantry. As the Civil War laboriously dragged on, Clifton rose steadily through the ranks and was eventually promoted to captain, then major, brevet lieutenant colonel, and finally brevet colonel. On the basis of this information, it's reasonable to assume that he had a relatively successful military career.

Younger brother William decided that he would take a different path entirely, enlisting first as a private in company D of the First Maryland Infantry and then on August 27, 1862, transferring to company A of the Second Maryland Infantry. Stories of fraternal ties lapsing into fratricidal hatred were ubiquitous in border states such as Maryland, where many families harbored divided loyalties. There were doubtless other instances of domestic disharmony, but the story of the Prentiss brothers is worthy of note. During the Civil War, Maryland was regarded as a slave state, but it never seceded from the Union. The majority of the population living north and west of Baltimore was loyal to the Union, but those citizens living on farms in the southern and eastern areas of the state were largely sympathetic to the Confederacy.

While William fought wherever the Confederate Army of Northern Virginia campaigned, Clifton saw action with the Union Army of the Potomac. As the war progressed and reaped its deathly harvest, Clifton and William would hear sporadic rumors that the other's regiment was camped in proximity, but they wouldn't meet again in person until April 2, 1865. That was the date that Lieutenant General Ulysses S. Grant, general-in-chief of all Union forces, ordered an all-out assault on Robert E. Lee's Confederate positions just south of Petersburg, Virginia, where his army had been entrenched for almost a whole year.

The day that Grant ordered the first assault on the Confederate positions at Petersburg on the morning of April 2 was reminiscent of future World War I assaults. It was preceded by a three-hour "softening up" artillery bombardment before the first wave of infantry launched their attack. The fighting was particularly fierce in the maze of trenches and dugouts south of Petersburg, but by mid-afternoon, stubborn enemy defenders had managed to repel the initial Union onslaught. One Massachusetts soldier wrote, "It was a hard fought battle, but it brought brilliant success, though with a terrible cost."[36]

A unit from the Sixth Maryland Infantry, led by Major Clifton Prentiss, participated in this attack against the Confederate earthworks. Clifton was leading his men forward as they chased routed Southerners from their positions. It was at that moment while ejecting rebel forces from their trenches that a bullet struck him full in the chest, pierced his lung, and ripped out most of his sternum.

Part of the attack on Petersburg was depicted in the movie *Cold Mountain*[37] The main protagonist of the story served with the Confederate army during the Civil War; however, the producers freely admit that they took serious liberties with the real story, which begins with the soldier deserting from a hospital in Raleigh, North Carolina, where he was recovering from a neck wound he received at Petersburg, Virginia, during the last days of the Civil War.

William Prentiss was one of the Confederate soldiers defending the fortifications when he got some shrapnel in his knee. After the battle concluded with a Union victory, some of the Maryland Union soldiers were tending the wounded on the battlefield. It was then that they discovered William Prentiss, who told them that he had a brother in the Sixth Maryland Infantry. The soldiers realized that William's brother was in fact their major who was lying close by, gravely wounded, at the Armory Square Hospital. William timidly asked if he could see his brother. Many historians and admirers have embellished this story with proposed emotional dialogue between the two brothers. No one can know what was really said when they eventually met in their respective hospital beds, but it must have been an emotive occasion. They hadn't spoken civilly to each other for many a long year.

According to one source, when word was brought to Clifton about his brother, he allegedly said, "I want to see no man who fired on my country's flag" and flatly refused to see his Confederate brother. This, again, could be conjecture, but a Union colonel pleaded with Clifton to relent. To facilitate, he ordered William

---

36   A. Wilson Greene, *The Final Battles of the Petersburg Campaign: Breaking the Backbone of the Rebellion* (Knoxville, TN: University of Tennessee Press, 2012).
37   A. Wilson Greene, *Campaign of Giants: The Battle for Petersburg*, vol. 1 (University of North Carolina Press, 2018).

to be brought over to his brother's beside. When Clifton glared at William in disgust, William smiled back. Both men, who had been separated since the onset of the war, were briefly reunited. Within moments, the tears were flowing freely. During their time in the hospital, William had his leg amputated; meanwhile, Clifton's lung became infected.

Clifton and William had fought against each other in their respective armies for four long, painful years, but now as the war reached its climax, they were reunited in Armory Square Hospital. Sadly, neither soldier would survive the wounds they received in the same battle. William died at Armory Square on June 24, 1865. His mortal remains were then interred at Green-Wood Cemetery in west Brooklyn, New York City. Clifton returned to his home at 35 Livingston Street in Brooklyn where he died on August 18, 1865, less than two months after his brother. In life they had fought against each other on the battlefield, but in death they were united and buried side by side, where they have remained ever since.

At the Armory Square Hospital, a man who described himself as an "army hospital visitor" was helping out where he could. Walt Whitman became one of America's greatest poets. Poets have an innate capacity to exaggerate (otherwise they wouldn't be poets), but Walt Whitman modestly estimated that during his three years as a volunteer nurse, he assisted around one hundred thousand sick or wounded soldiers. He only wrote about fifty or so of the patients that he tended to, and specifically remembered the Prentiss brothers because the diary entry for May 28–29, 1865, is titled "Two Brothers, One South, One North."

The story of the Prentiss brothers exemplifies the Civil War slogan "brother against brother" to a large extent, but they were not the only brothers to choose opposing sides in that heart-wrenching conflict. Two brothers, born in Scotland and building new lives in America, found themselves fighting each other for their adoptive country at the Civil War battle of Secessionville in 1862. Although they both held different views on the future of their adopted country, fraternal affections between them remained firmly intact throughout.

The Campbell brothers immigrated to America sometime in the 1850s. James Campbell settled in Charleston where he worked as a drayman and clerk, joining a Confederate militia company known somewhat paradoxically as the Union Light Infantry, sometimes referred to in jest as the Forty-Second Highlanders (probably because of its predominately Scottish ethnicity). His brother Alexander settled in New York but had spent time in Charleston working as a stonemason shortly before the war began. While in Charleston, he also enlisted in a militia company later identified in letters from his brother as "the H.G.s," which was probably the Home Guard, composed primarily of the foreign-born residents of Charleston.

As preparations for war began on both sides, the brother's exchanged correspondence. In early June 1862, Alex's unit was transferred to Charleston where it occupied parts of James Island, placing him in sight of the city where he and his brother had once lived. Alex learned of his Confederate brother's service in the vicinity of Secessionville from Henry Walker, a prisoner captured in a skirmish on June 3, 1862. He relayed the information home in a letter to his wife on June 10. "We are not far from each other now." This was in essence another notable case of brother against brother.

At the time neither brother was initially aware that they were fighting in proximity to each other's units at Secessionville. As the first and most successful attack against Fort Lamar reached its zenith, Alexander, now a color sergeant in the Seventy-Ninth Highland Regiment, planted the flag of the United States before the parapet of Fort Lamar. In the face of massed musketry and canon fire, he stoically held it there until ordered to withdraw. In the midst of the fighting, when Confederate resistance began to buckle, James (now a lieutenant in the Confederate army) mounted the parapet unarmed, rolled a log down into the mass of advancing Union troops, seized a Union musket, and continued fighting.

A newspaper in Charleston wrote about the exploits of the Campbell brothers referring to them as "another illustration of the deplorable consequences of this fratricidal war."[38] It further stated that Alexander Campbell, "fought gallantly in the late action" and "displayed...a heroism worthy of his regiment and a better cause." James Campbell "was conspicuous and has been honorably mentioned on our side."

Shortly after the battle, James wrote his brother, "I was aston- ished to hear from the prisoners that you was color Bearer of the Regmt [sic] that assaulted the Battery at this point the other day. I was in the Brest work during the whole engagement doing my Best to Beat you(.) but I hope you and I will never again meet face to face bitter enemies on the Battlefield(.) but if such should be the case You have but to discharge your duty for your cause for I can assure you I will strive to discharge my duty to my country and my cause."[39]

The letter from brother to brother was conveyed across the battlefield under a flag of truce. Shortly after the battle, Confederate James attempted to pay a visit to his brother by going to the Union lines and asking if the Seventy-Ninth Regiment was on picket duty. The officer in charge of the Union troops flatly refused permission for James to cross the lines and seek his brother. He also refused to send for Alex, so he could be brought out for a fraternal meeting.

Alexander wrote his wife in New York, including a copy of James' letter. "It is rather bad to think that we should be fighting him on the one side and me on the other for he says he was in the fort during the whole engagement(.) I hope to god that he and I will get safe through it all and he will have his story to tell about his side and I will have my story to tell about my side."[40]

After Secessionville, the war continued for these two brothers. Alexander was wounded in the foot carrying the US colors in the aftermath of the Union defeat at the battle of Second Manassas (the Second Battle of Bull Run). He was one of five Highlander color bearers wounded during that battle. Alexander never fully recovered from his wound but was promoted to second lieutenant and eventu- ally resigned his commission and left the army in May 1863.

James continued to fight for the Confederacy, helping to defend Charleston. In the famous attack on Battery Wagner on July 18, 1863, James was in the fort, having endured a terrible artillery barrage. When Union troops overran part of the fort, James volun-

39   Ibid.
40   *Him on the One Side and Me on the Other: The Civil War Letters of Alexander...* By Alexander Campbell, James Campbell, Terry A. Johnston

teered to investigate. Suddenly two Union soldiers charged at him with their bayonets. He managed to push them from the parapet, then he ordered the other Union soldiers there to surrender. They grabbed him by the leg and dragged him into the ditch below. When they withdrew from the fort, they took James as one of their five prisoners. While incarcerated in a Union prison, he was promoted to first lieutenant. He still managed to remain in contact with his brother Alexander, and was eventually freed on June 12, 1865, whereupon he returned home to Charleston.

After the war, James managed a plantation and eventually bought land on the Ashepoo River south of Charleston. He was active in Charleston's St. Andrew's Society and the United Confederate Veterans. Alexander moved to Connecticut and established a business manufacturing artistic monuments. The brothers corresponded with each other and remained on good terms for many years after that devastating war had concluded. After enjoying long productive lives, James died in 1907 and Alexander passed in 1909.

The Civil War inflicted more than six hundred thousand casualties on that young nation. Even one of the highest profile families of the 1800s couldn't agree on a side. First Lady Mary Todd Lincoln had six relatives that fought for the Confederates. In the border state of Maryland, as already noted, potential secession deeply divided the state's residents.

The story of the Prentiss brothers accentuates the deep divisions than ran throughout that state. Almost sixty thousand Maryland men fought for the Union while twenty thousand took up arms for the Confederate cause. The Goldsborough family is another example of brother fighting brother. The decidedly Anglo-Saxon family was considered landed gentry before the Norman Conquest of 1066. They lived at Goldsborough Hall, or Chase, near the town of Knaresborough in Yorkshire. In 1669, Nicholas Goldsborough left England for America. Many generations later, Leander Worthington Goldsborough was married. The sons Charles, William, and Eugene found themselves on opposite sides of the north-south divide during the Civil War. While brother William became a major for the South, the other brother, Dr. Charles, became a surgeon in the Union army. Eugene is listed as being a private in the First Maryland Infantry Regiment, but there aren't many additional details about him.

At the battle of Front Royal on May 23, 1862, William actually took Charles prisoner, which wouldn't have exactly nurtured their fraternal bonds. Amid the smoke and chaos of the fighting, Captain William Goldsborough knew that he was fighting against fellow Marylanders. At a certain moment, William spotted a Union soldier standing few yards away and demanded his surrender. When the soldier turned toward him, his jaw dropped to somewhere around his waistline. It was his brother Charles, who obediently did as instructed and surrendered to his brother. The battle was the only time in United States military history that two regiments from the same state with the same numerical designation took the field against each other. The fight was between First Maryland Regiment (Confederate) and First Maryland Regiment (Union), which on that occasion resulted in a victory for the southern forces.

Shortly after his capture, Charles was sent to the infamous Libby Prison in Richmond, Virginia. During the Civil War it earned a grim reputation. Prisoners from the Union army were subjected to terrible overcrowding and abominably harsh conditions, which resulted in many of them suffering from disease, malnutrition, and a high mortality rate. On the basis of this, it's safe to assume that Charles couldn't thank his brother enough. After he was later paroled and returned to the Union army, Charles was assigned duty at a Union prison in Delaware, and that's where things became even stranger.

During the famous Gettysburg campaign, brother William was seriously injured and subsequently captured by Union forces. He was eventually held prisoner at Fort Delaware. The boot was now on the other foot when, to his surprise, Charles discovered that William and their other brother, Eugene, were both languishing in the prison as captured Confederate soldiers. According to records in the National Archives, it is estimated that 215 Confederate prisoners died at Fort Delaware as a result of typhoid and malaria. William and Eugene were not among them, so there must have been some fraternal affection between these brothers at war.

African American brothers Baldy Guy (1841–1911, possibly follicularly challenged) and George Guy (1845–1928), with their cousin Henry Guy (1827-1902), fought in the Battle of Brice's Cross Roads on June 10, 1864, in Guntown, Mississippi, during the Civil War. Baldy Guy was wounded on the first day of battle by suffering a gunshot in the left shoulder. Henry Guy was a prisoner of war on two occasions. The Battle of Brice's Cross Roads—also known as the Battle of Tishomingo Creek or the Battle of Guntown—was between 4,787 troops led by Confederate Major General Nathan Bedford Forrest (who became the first pointy-hatted, white-bed-sheet-wearing grand wizard of the Ku Klux Klan) and an 8,100-strong Union force led by Brigadier General Samuel D. Sturgis. The battle concluded with a resounding defeat for the Union forces.

All three relatives served in the Fifty-Fifth Regiment, United States Colored Volunteer Infantry between May 22, 1863, and December 31, 1865. Baldy was in company B, George in company H, and Henry in company A. Of the 223 Union soldiers killed during the Battle of Brice's Cross Roads, half of them were African Americans. They were called the United States Colored Troops (USCT), composed primarily of African American soldiers, although members of other minority groups also served within the units. By the end of the Civil War, roughly 179,000 black men (10 percent of the Union army) had served as soldiers in the US Army, among whom were eighty black commissioned officers, and another 19,000 served in the navy. During the course of the war, almost forty thousand black soldiers died while thirty thousand of men succumbed to infection and disease. There is no existing documentation regarding black Confederate combat units in service during the war, nor any evidence of a black man being paid or pensioned as a Confederate soldier, although some did receive pensions for their work as laborers.

Another famous border state with divided loyalties during the Civil War was Kentucky. Senator John J. Crittenden attempted to induce a compromise on the slavery issue. His efforts failed. His

sons, George Bibb and Thomas Leonidas, went on to fight for opposite sides in the Civil War. George became a brigadier general for the
South. Thomas was a Union general. These family members never
fought against each other directly, and they all survived the war.

George Bibb attended the United States Military Academy
at West Point, where he graduated in 1832. He became a career
soldier who served with distinction in the Mexican-American
War and earned a brevet promotion to major for his actions at
the battles of Contreras and Churubusco. By 1856, he was a
lieutenant colonel in the regular army. During the secession crisis
of early 1861, George accepted a commission as colonel in the
Confederate States Army. He was promoted to brigadier general
on August 15 and briefly commanded a brigade in the short-lived
Confederate Army of the Potomac before he received another
promotion in November and was assigned the district of East
Tennessee. On January 18, 1862, his forces were defeated at the
Battle of Mill Springs, which greatly weakened the Confederate
hold on eastern Kentucky.

George Bibb briefly commanded the Army of Central Kentucky's
Second Division but was relieved of duty and arrested for drunken-
ness on March 31, 1862. He was restored little more than two weeks
later, but a court of inquiry was ordered that summer. In October,
George resigned his commission, so he could serve out the remainder
of the war in relative peace and inebriation. After the war, he became
the Kentucky state librarian until 1871, which wouldn't have necessarily deterred his inclination for imbibing his beloved "falling
down" water. He died in Danville, Kentucky, on November 27, 1880,
and is buried in the state cemetery at Frankfort beside his brother
Thomas Leonidas.

Thomas Leonidas didn't attend West Point and probably
had no intention of doing so. Instead, he chose to study law with
his illustrious father at a time when the United States actually
needed lawyers. He began his law practice in Kentucky in 1840
and was elected state attorney in 1842 for his district. Thomas
had also fought in the Mexican-American War as a colonel of the

Third Kentucky Volunteer Infantry and aide to General Zachary Taylor. His military career would have its ups and downs, but with the onset of the Civil War, he accepted a commission as the commander of the Fifth Division, Army of the Ohio, where he fought at the battle of Shiloh in July 1862. After Shiloh, he was promoted to major general on July 17, 1862, and commanded the II Corps in the Army of the Ohio during the Perryville campaign. He then led the XXI Corps through the Tullahoma campaign and at the Battle of Chickamauga. When it came time to point fingers, Thomas and fellow corps commander Alexander McDowell McCook were blamed for the defeat and subsequently relieved of command, but both were later exonerated and acquitted of any charges.

So after Thomas was removed from command of XXI Corps in 1863 and with his military career not looking too great, he transferred to the Union's Army of the Potomac in 1864. That same year, he assumed command of the First Division, IX Corps, and led it in the eastern theater during the battles of Spotsylvania Court House and Cold Harbor. On December 13, 1864, he resigned his commission.

After the war in January 1866, George was appointed to the Kentucky State Treasury, but only remained there for a few months. In July 28, 1866, at the request of US President Andrew Johnson, he returned to US Army service as colonel for the Thirty-Second Infantry. He received a brevet promotion as brigadier general on March 2, 1867. He then transferred to the Seventeenth Infantry in 1869, where he served until he resigned his commission in 1881. He died on October 23, 1893, at Annadale, Staten Island, New York, and is buried in the Frankfort Cemetery in Kentucky.

I was once told that one of my notable ancestors fought in the American Civil War. I needed to know more. I have always loved American literature. I read my first book on the Civil War when I was just eleven years old. It was *The Red Badge of Courage* by Stephen Crane. Twelve years ago I began visiting the United States for the purpose of promoting my books, but this was a dual mission. I dearly wanted to meet Civil War experts and battlefield guides and visit as many battlefield sites as possible, beginning with Gettysburg. What really got my interest was first, the abolitionist movement, and second, the number of emigrant families who became directly affected by this tragic conflict. Historically whenever there's been a big fight, there's a strong possibility that the Scottish or the Irish have been involved to some extent or another, and this chapter proves my point. So if Johnny came marching home, was it to his new home or his old one?

required for enlistment in the UK was, at face value, quite strin-gent—but many exceptions were made, specifically among young teenagers who were perfectly prepared to lie about their real age.

The following list extracted from the British War Office's instructions issued with army orders on August 1, 1914, states that the examining doctor would require the following:

- The recruit is sufficiently intelligent

- Vision, with either eye, is up to the required standard

- Hearing is good

- Speech is without impediment

- There are no glandular swellings

- A well-formed capacious chest, along with sound lungs and heart

- The recruit is not ruptured in any degree or form

- Fully-developed and well-formed limbs

- Free and perfect motion of all the joints

- Well-formed feet and toes

- The recruit doesn't have any congenital malformation or defects

- The recruit doesn't have any traces of previous acute or chronic disease that point to an impaired consti-tution

- The recruit possesses a sufficient number of teeth suitable for eating[41]

---

41   "Instructions for the Physical Examination of Recruits," The Long, Long Trail, July 23, 2017, https://www.longlongtrail.co.uk/soldiers/a-soldiers-life-1914-1918/enlisting-into-the-army/instructions-for-the-physical-examination-of-recruits/.

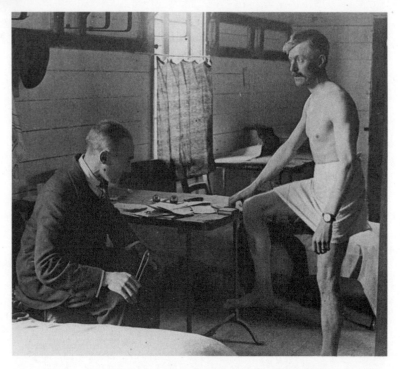

The criteria for joining the British Army during the early years of World War I were a little sluggish. "How old are you, son?" asked the recruiting sergeant. "I'm fifteen, sir," replied the young lad. "Well, go outside, add on a few years until you're nineteen, then reapply today. I'll get you in, son."

Those were the recommended requirements, but most doctors would check teeth and scrotum, place a tick on their list, and that was it. According to records of the day, any of the following maladies could prevent induction:

- Presence of tubercular disease

- Constitutional syphilis (nothing to do with political aspirations)

- Bronchial or laryngeal disease (most would be smokers)

- Palpitation or other heart diseases

- Generally impaired health

- Vision that fell below the standard

- Vocal or hearing defects

- Pronounced stammering (a problem easily overcome by pointing and nodding)

- Loss or decay of teeth to such an extent that they interfered with eating (dental requirements were largely neglected by the working class)

- Contraction or deformity of chest or joints

- Abnormal spine curvature

- Defective intelligence (should have been in the first list)

- Hernia

- Hemorrhoids (most northern men had them)

- Varicose veins or varicocele, if severe

- Inveterate cutaneous disease (Scrofula and other glandular afflictions)

- Chronic ulcers (most northern Englishmen had them too)

- Fistula

- Any disease or physical defect causing the recruit to be unfit for the duties of a soldier[42]

The problems with this list is that it would have exempted a significant percentage of the male population in most of the bellig-

---

42   Ibid.

erent countries. Either way, the die was cast and the war was on. Across the UK and mainland Europe, mothers and fathers waved a tearful farewell to their sons, never knowing if they would ever see them alive again.

"My Boy Jack," by Rudyard Kipling

"Have you news of my boy Jack?"

Not this tide.

"When d'you think that he'll come back?"
Not with this wind blowing, and this tide.[43]

John Kipling was the only son of British author Rudyard Kipling. In World War I, his father used his masonic connections and his influence to get John an army commission, despite his having been decisively rejected for having desperately poor eyesight. Rudyard Kipling maintained a lifelong hatred of the Germans, but in time but he would eventually come to terms with his own folly when he wrote:

"If any question why we died,

Tell them, because our fathers lied."

It is ironic that Kipling was the person to select the phrase "Known unto God" for the gravestones of all unknown soldiers when he had no idea what had happened to his own son.[44]

There was no greater tragedy in World War I than the callous, multitudinous sacrifice of almost a whole generation of healthy young men on the Western Front and in other theaters. There couldn't have been a more petrifying prospect than waiting for the whistle to blow in those godforsaken trenches in preparation to go over the top. That damnable whistle could signal one's almost inevitable demise by machine-gun bullet or shrapnel. Many of

43 Rudyard Kipling, "My Boy Jack," Poetry By Heart, https://www.poetrybyheart.org.uk/poems/my-boy-jack/.
44 Amanda Ameen, "The Truth behind a Poem," The Contemporary Poem, October 22, 2016, https://cpoem.sunygeneseoenglish.org/2016/10/22/the-truth-behind-a-poem/.

the men would, in effect, be waiting to die in the vain hope that it would be a quick and painless death. Heads would cower and flinch at the percussive blasts of enemy artillery shaking one's soul to the core. Stomach muscles would tighten and contract before they obediently ascended the trench ladders and launched themselves into no-man's-land, an undulating, skeletal terrain, pockmarked with shell holes, laced with barbed wire, and steeped with the gut-wrenching stench of the shattered remnants of bodies and almost unimaginable horror. Their eyes would be compelled to absorb an apocalyptic scene of unequivocal destruction and death.

To a large extent the women of Europe and America were swept up in the same all-consuming wave that inspired their husbands, sons, and other male relatives. Failure to join up in the United Kingdom could result in being handed a white feather by a woman. The purpose of this gesture was to shame "every young 'slacker' found loafing" and to remind those "deaf or indifferent to his or her country's needs that British soldiers are fighting and dying across the channel."[45] The power of these women was incalculable. The recipients of the white feather were warned in no uncertain terms that "there is a danger awaiting them far more terrible than anything they can meet in battle," for if they were found "idling and loafing [46] they would be publicly humiliated by a lady. For many, the social ignominy was unbearable.

But there were those who simply didn't make the grade due to medical or moral reasons. This would not exempt them from receiving the white feather. The criteria for acceptance weren't necessarily observed in their entirety and many managed to slip through the net. One of the youngest recruits was only fourteen years old.

---

45   Anne-Marie Kilday and David S. Nash, *Shame and Modernity in Britain: 1890 to the Present* (London: Palgrave Macmillan, 2017).
46   Nicoletta Gullace, "White Feathers and Wounded Men," Library of Social Science, January 13, 2015, https://www.libraryofsocialscience.com/newsletter/posts/2015/2015-01-13-Gullace.html.

One Irish family saw six of their sons go off to war. Four died, a fifth went missing, only one returned home. The problem was, they weren't unique.

Of the six sons that Agnes and Thomas Collins from Waterford, Ireland, waved off to Europe, only one to made it home safely. Four died in Flanders and at the Somme while the fifth was missing, presumed dead until he was found badly injured and repatriated after the war ended.

William Collins was a career soldier who enlisted in the Eighth King's Royal Irish Hussars (a cavalry regiment stationed in India) in 1909. Few details are known about his service, and like most World War I soldiers, he wasn't inclined to divulge his experiences to his family. William's recollections to his children were limited to anecdotes, such as one about his warhorse, Stanford, who he had won in a dice game at Abbeville. He never mentioned the death and destruction and never mentioned his fallen brothers and friends.

Along with William, the other elder Collins brother, Patrick, was a career soldier; however, the four younger brothers signed up once war broke out in 1914. But like countless hundreds of thousands who did the same, they were completely naïve and would have had little or no idea about what they were getting into. Some even believed that they would be home by Christmas and joined on the premise that it was a good way to get work and to see the world.

The first brother to fall was Stephen, who was only sixteen at the time of his death and consequently one of an estimated 250,000 underage boys who fought in the war. The army's statutory age limit for serving overseas was nineteen. Less than a month after the outbreak of war, Stephen was deployed to France as a private with the Second Battalion of the Royal Irish Regiment. Just two months later he died in Flanders on October 19, 1914, and is commemorated on the Le Touret War Memorial in Pas-de-Calais in France.

His brother Michael joined the same battalion of the Royal Irish Regiment and was deployed to the Western Front. He fell in May 1915 at the beginning of an offensive at Aubers Ridge in Flanders, aged twenty-four. It was May 9, 1915, when the first wave of the British attack on Aubers Ridge went over the top in support of the French Artois offensive against Vimy Ridge. Owing to the severe shortage of shells, the preliminary bombardment was limited to a mere forty minutes. They were sitting ducks as they moved out over flat ground intersected by wide drainage ditches. The front lines were only one to two hundred yards apart at this point, and the attackers were supported by the explosion of two small mines under the German lines. The British captured three lines of German trenches, but only two hundred or so surviving Royal Irish were withdrawn from their position, all efforts to reinforce them having been repulsed. An ammunitions shortage and problems with trench layout and communications contributed to a disastrous result for the allies, incurring eleven thousand British casualties for absolutely no material gain whatsoever.

Michael's body was never recovered. His name is among the names of more than fifty-four thousand officers and men commemorated in Ypres on the Menin Gate Memorial, which is dedicated to those whose graves are not known. This is a polite way of saying they were blown to pieces or drowned in the mud and never found.

John Collins was at the battle of the Somme that began on the morning of July 1, 1916, and petered out on November 18, 1916. It is estimated that around one million allied soldiers were injured or killed during this battle. John was twenty-two and a private with the First Battalion of the Royal Munster Fusiliers when he died near Thiepval in Belgium on September 9, 1916. He is commemorated on the Thiepval Memorial to the Missing of the Somme in France.

Joseph Collins was badly injured on the eastern front in Salonika. An exploding shell lodged large amounts of shrapnel in his body. Although the British force at Salonika was maintained on the basis that it would be used only for defensive purposes, offensives were initiated by the French in conjunction with Serbian and, later, Russian forces, with the British playing a supporting role only. A telegram was sent home to inform his mother Agnes that Joseph was missing, presumed dead; however, after a period in a convent, after the war, and to the surprise of his family, he was found alive and repatriated to Waterford. His shrapnel injuries never fully healed, and he spent the rest of his life in debilitating pain.

Patrick Collins was the eldest son and last to die in the war. He was aged thirty and a second corporal in the 173rd Tunneling Company of the Royal Engineers when he was killed on March 29, 1918. He had endured and survived nearly four years of war to be killed just before the allies' advance to victory. As with his brothers, his grave is unknown, but he is commemorated on the Pozieres Memorial at the Somme.

Following Patrick's death, William was released on compassionate grounds. There was no *Saving Private Ryan* movie-star rescue, no fanfare to welcome him home. In the nine years since he had enlisted, Ireland had changed dramatically and support for Irish men fighting with the British army had waned considerably. He arrived home to a grieving mother who had lost four of her sons. She had been abandoned by the boys' father midway through the war and left alone to raise the two youngest boys, Richard and Thomas.

In the small town of Barnard Castle, County Durham, are the names of five out of six brothers who died in World War I, one after another. The brothers were Robert (twenty-two), George Henry (twenty-six), Frederick (twenty-one), John William (thirty-seven), and Alfred (thirty). They all lost their lives on the battlefields of northern France and Belgium in a period of just twenty-two months between September 1916 and July 1918. Four are commemorated in cemeteries near where they fell while Frederick is remembered on the Menin Gate in Ypres, along with the other soldiers whose bodies were never recovered.

In the small town of Barnard Castle, County Durham, are the names of five brothers who died in the First World War, one after another.

It's beyond comprehension to imagine the boys' mother, Margaret Smith, receiving five tragic telegrams from the War Office informing her that her sons had given their lives for king and country. As news of the deaths of successive brothers spread around the town, such was the outpouring of sympathy for the Smiths that some could not bear the thought that even worse might come. One of those most deeply affected was the wife of the local vicar, a Mrs. Bircham, who took it upon herself to write to Queen Mary, George V's wife, to ask for the sixth, Wilfred, to be returned home to ensure at least one brother survived.

Soon after that intervention, Margaret Smith received a letter from Edward Wallington, private secretary to the queen, and this time it bore good news. He wrote that the queen "has caused Mr. and Mrs. Smith's request concerning their youngest son to be forwarded for consideration of the war authorities." Wilfred was duly afforded the necessary official discharge and came back to Barnard Castle to be with his mother in the early autumn of 1918. Despite suffering for years from the effects of respiratory disease caused by a mustard gas attack on the Western Front, he worked as a stonemason and chimney sweep before dying in 1968 at the age of sixty-nine.

Mrs. Smith wasn't unique. Of the six sons born to Julia "Annie" Souls and her husband William, five were killed in World War I. Twins Alfred and Arthur came into the world an hour apart, and they died five days apart. Alfred died on April 20, 1918 and Arthur died on April 25, 1918, both thirty-one years old. According to a family legend, Arthur, who had been promoted to the rank of lance corporal attached to the Seventh Royal West Kents, lost all will to live when he heard of his twin brother's passing.

Their brothers Albert, Frederick (Fred), and Walter Souls were all killed in the summer of 1916, with Frederick perishing in the Battle of the Somme and Albert and Walter losing their lives at Bully-Grenay and Rouen, respectively.

Walter was not killed outright but was transferred to hospital at Rouen in a cheery mood after suffering a leg wound, from which his mother received this letter: "Dear Mrs. Souls, I much regret to have to tell you that your son died very suddenly about nine o'clock yesterday evening. He came to us with a wound in the upper part of his left leg, and on Tuesday he had to undergo an operation, but he rallied from that all right and he seemed to be better. In fact he was quite cheery, and then in the evening on the next day he quite suddenly collapsed and died instantly from an embolism (or clot of blood) in the heart. This will be a dreadful blow to you and you have our deepest sympathy in your great loss. Signed, M. Phillips, Matron, 25 Stationary Hospital, BEF, Rouen."[47]

Annie was granted one shilling per week for each death, which was dismal compensation for the loss of her beloved sons (and with five boys dead, her suffering was doubtlessly immeasurable). Yet there were some in the village who considered that the bereaved Mrs. Souls had received a generous allowance from the government, and by some accounts Annie was viewed with suspicion by certain irascible gossips that lived in their small community.

After the death of the third brother, Prime Minister Herbert Asquith sent her a letter conveying the sympathy of the King and Queen for Mrs. Souls in her great sorrow. She kept a candle burning in a small window overlooking the road in memory of Fred, whose body was never recovered. He disappeared shortly after going over the top during the Battle of the Somme.

A 101-year-old local resident by the name of Maud Pill described the brothers as "'nice-looking' but 'not very tall.'" (Fred, Alfred, and Arthur joined a Bantam force for short-statured soldiers.) All were unmarried. Arthur won the Military Medal, but the details of his act of valor have been lost to posterity.

Thomas and Eliza Everton watched with hearts full of fear and trepidation as all eight of their sons went off to fight, and they were all volunteers. Thirteen months into the war, tragedy struck when the second eldest brother, Thomas William, was killed in action September 25, 1915, during the Battle of Loos at the age of thirty-eight. He served in the Royal Warwickshire Regiment as lance corporal and had previously been listed in North Africa in 1897, for which he received five war medals. The only one of the Everton's boys who failed to return home, he is buried at the Commonwealth War Graves cemetery in Loos, France. Loos was also the battle that consumed the life of young John "Jack" Kipling, who had turned eighteen just before the attacks began.

The remarkable human donation made by the Everton family prompted the Privy Council to send a letter on behalf of King George V in 1915 thanking the parents for their sons' contribution to the war. It read: "I am commanded to express to you The King's

---

47   Michael Walsh, *Brothers in War* (Ebury Press, 2011).

congratulations and to assure you that His Majesty much appreci-
ates the spirit of patriotism which prompted this example, in one
family, of loyalty and devotion to their Sovereign and Empire."

A few months later, in June 1916, Frederick Everton was given
fourteen days' leave from battle to return to his wife after the death
of their daughter Lillian, who was twenty-one months old. Frederick served in the Royal Garrison Artillery. He was discharged in
February 1919 and was awarded three war medals. He died in June
1949. As the war came to an end, the rest of the Everton brothers
came home as heroes to their families, each one wearing numerous
military decorations for their service to their country.

A plaque and memorial bench unveiled in May 2019 was dedicated to a Lincoln family that lost five sons in World War I. Five of
the eight Beechey brothers who fought were killed in the conflict.
Barnard (thirty-eight), Charles (thirty-nine), Leonard (thirty-six),
Frank (thirty), and Harold (twenty-six). Another son, Christopher,
was badly injured. In April 1918 when Queen Mary thanked Mrs.
Amy Beechey for her sacrifice, the mother replied: "It was no sacrifice, ma'am. I did not give them willingly."[48]

Mr. and Mrs. Beechey lost five sons in the First World War. When Queen Mary thanked
Mrs. Beechey for her sacrifice, mother Amy Beechey replied, "It was no sacrifice,
ma'am. I did not give them willingly."

48 Jacqueline Larson Carmichael, *Heard amid the Guns: True Stories from the Western Front, 1914-1918* (Victoria: Heritage House Publishing, 2020).

The country that brought the United Kingdom into the war was Belgium and the violation of Belgian neutrality by the Germans. It's often overlooked that the people suffered greatly at the hands of invading German forces and many assume that the Germans only committed atrocities in World War II. There's no doubt that allied propaganda exaggerated some of the details, but it's an unassailable fact that Belgian civilians were massacred on a number of occasions. In the small riverside town of Dinant, German soldiers murdered 674 victims and destroyed 1,100 buildings. In the village of Tamines, they slaughtered 384 innocent civilians and destroyed 240 buildings.

The devastation and havoc inflicted on Belgium in World War I would, in some cases, take up to seventy years to repair. But as soon as masses of German troops broached the Belgian border in August 1914, many young men signed up to join the fight. That was the case of the three Fabry brothers from Les Avins, in the Liége region of Belgium.

The three brothers, Paul, Jean, and Louis, came from a large family. The eldest, born in 1884, was Louis. He joined a religious order in 1907 and was ordained as a priest in 1913, just before the start of the conflict. Throughout the war, he meticulously kept a diary to record the events as they unfolded. When the war began, the other brothers, Paul and Jean, joined as volunteers. Louis joined them in early 1915 after following a circuitous route through the Netherlands to join the Belgian army.

After a brief spell in training, Louis was thrown into the thick of it as a chaplain and litter bearer. His diaries carefully describe his life in the trenches, his assignments, the bombs falling all around him, and the day-to-day lives of the soldiers alongside him. When he joined the Belgian Thirteenth Regiment, he was briefly arrested on suspicion of espionage but quickly exonerated thanks to his domestic servant who confirmed his identity.

Louis expertly described the condition of the trenches and the gnawing fatigue, along with the material and moral difficulties that his fellow troops faced. He also described the surrounding landscape, such as destroyed farms and the devastated owners who lost absolutely everything to World War I.

Louis never forgot his initial calling and frequently replaced his colleagues by providing an open-air mass, often under extreme conditions. He wrote, "Sunday August 1, 1915, I celebrated the holy mass out in the windy open for the company." On May 17, 1917, he celebrated the Feast of the Ascension bent double in a bomb shelter. His faith was his constant companion throughout. He assisted numerous soldiers in their final moments without trepidation, which eventually caught the attention of his superiors. On October 1916, Louis is mentioned in army dispatches for "having twice, in broad daylight and under enemy fire, gone to the forward trenches in order to comfort the injured."

Despite their different postings and assignments, the Fabry brothers remained in contact for the duration of the war and tried to visit each other as often as possible. In July 1915, Louis found brother Paul serving at an outpost near the Belgian coast. On December 26, 1915, after one particular offensive, Louis received a letter from brother Paul, proving that he was still alive. He even took measures to get his brother transferred to his own regiment and provided material support for them both in the form of small financial donations. A soldier's pay wasn't much in World War I. Meanwhile, the rest of his family were languishing in the German-occupied zone.

In late May 1917, Louis was wounded while attempting to provide support to the soldiers during an all-out attack. In his own words, he got "a big lump of Hun iron in the left shoulder. It was like receiving a big punch." He was first evacuated to the rear for first aid, then to the Ocean Hospital in the Belgian coastal resort area of De Panne where he was x-rayed and operated on for his wound. His brothers both visited him while he was recuperating. At the end of June 1917, he left the hospital and, after a brief convalescent sojourn, he returned to the front.

Louis was full of praise for the "leading role played by the Americans" but didn't forget the "famished, chilled and fatigued" men for whom he retained such warm affection. As the war neared its conclusion, Louis's diary entries become less informative and are frequently reduced to one line and in some cases one-word descriptions. On November 10, 1918, he wrote

"Abdication of the Kaiser?" and then the following day, "Armistice! Victory! Our company has been harshly tested."

Apart from the wound Louis suffered in 1917, all three brothers survived the war relatively unharmed. Louis remained faithful to his religious order and after the war he became the parish priest in a small town where his memory endures today because a street was named after him. He was the only brother to receive such an accolade.

The Fabry brothers were French-speaking[49] Belgians. An interesting story about some Dutch-speaking Belgian siblings came to light recently. Eight of nine children hailing from the same family served on the Western Front, four as Belgians and four as Americans—and all eight of them survived the war. Some of them joined the American Expeditionary Forces (AEF). The family of clog maker Jan Van den Broeck all came from the town of Sint-Niklaas. They had nine children in the family. Five boys and two girls immigrated to the United States shortly before World War I. When war broke out, the two boys who had stayed in Belgium, Leon and Frans, were mobilized. Shortly later, probably in September 1914, brothers Emiel and Jozef left Chicago to return to Europe and became Belgian volunteers. When the United States declared war on the Central Powers on April 6, 1917, brothers Henri, Charles, and August, and sister Henriette joined the AEF. Henriette was a multilingual telephone operator.

While British men marched away to a very uncertain future in 1914, the women who weren't handing out white feathers also wanted to do their part. Kate and Margaret Carruthers were born in Partick, Glasgow, in May 1887, with Kate being the elder by five minutes. As their English father was a ship's surveyor and marine engineer for the Board of Trade, the family frequently moved around the country due to his work commitments. Both she and her sister Margaret became nurses and in 1913 enrolled in the Territorial Force Nursing Service. Kate and Margaret were both called up on August 13, 1914, and put to work at the Fourth Scottish General Hospital, Stobhill in Glasgow. Kate was sent to France on Christmas Day 1914, while Margaret was sent over in May 1915.

---

49   Story provided by dear friend Marie Cappaert. https://www.rtbf.be/ww1/topics/detail_the-fabry-family-three-brothers-at-war?id=8356078

On November 15, 1916, Kate was working at No. 56 Casualty Clearing Station when German aircraft bombed it. Many patients were killed, but Kate stayed on duty for a further twenty-four hours, although she herself had head and leg wounds. Her exemplary courage led to her be among the first women to receive a Military Medal. After she was awarded the medal, the *British Journal of Nursing* offered "hearty congratulations" and described how she attended to surviving patients despite "suffering much."

British King George V had previously decided that women deserved recognition for acts of courage, and a courtier had noted, "at present we have absolutely nothing to give." The Military Medal was extended to women for devotion to duty under fire.

The *British Journal of Nursing* proudly recorded: "Hearty congratulations to Miss Kate Carruthers...awarded the Military Medal, a decoration highly prized by nurses [for] devotion to duty under fire. Now that the Royal Red Cross is awarded to clerical workers and others on active service, it has largely lost the significance it bore [in the 19th century] when it was given to nurses but rarely. On November 15th [1916] [Miss Carruthers] was working at a [CCS (Casualty Clearing Station)] when it was bombed... one bomb struck the camp...Most of [her patients] were instantly killed, and she herself was wounded in the head and legs; nevertheless, though suffering much, she remained on duty until relieved twenty-four hours later, attending to the surviving patients...She was mentioned in dispatches [25 Nov 1916] by the Commander in Chief [Gen Haig] for her bravery."[50]

Confusion over the twins' identity led to three different medal records being created for Kate. She also received the Royal Red Cross in 1919, by which time several thousand Military Medals had been awarded to men. Only 135 women received them during the war; fifty-five of the recipients were military nurses.

After the war, Kate and Margaret continued to work as nurses, eventually retiring together. One of their brothers had died from a brain tumor in 1907, aged twenty-two. Their remaining brother, Lieutenant William Carruthers of the 154th Field Company in

---

50   *The British Journal of Nursing*, 1916, Vol. 57, 58 & 59: With Which Is Incorporated the Nursing Record (Classic Reprint) Mrs Bedford Fenwick. FB&C Limited, 26 Apr 2018

the Royal Engineers, was also twenty-two when he died during the Battle of Arras. The twin sisters died in the same year, 1969, within months of each other.

It's well known that families were considerably bigger in the first part of the twentieth century. It wasn't unusual for a mother, whose womb resembled an inverted potato sack, to give birth to up to ten or eleven children and in some cases even more. The general consensus is that parents had lots of children to ensure that at least some of them survived.

One mother in Yorkshire, England, had ten sons. They all signed up to fight in World War I. The Calpin brothers, aged between eighteen and thirty-seven at the time, are thought to be the biggest "real" band of brothers to have fought in the war. The Calpin's extraordinary contribution to the war effort earned public thanks and personal congratulation from King George V and Lloyd George, the prime minister of the day. Their names were used in a recruiting drive at the time and even broadcast in local cinemas in their home city of York.

One mother in Yorkshire, England, had ten sons and they all signed up to fight in the Great War. The Calpin brothers, aged between eighteen and thirty-seven at the time, are thought to be the biggest "real" band of brothers to have fought in the Great War.

Their story had been more or less forgotten until one of their grandsons did some research and discovered how many of his great uncles, along with his grandfather, had served in the British army: reservist John, age thirty-seven; soldier Patrick, age thirty-six;

infantryman James, age thirty-three; infantryman William, age thirty-two; infantryman Martin, age twenty-nine; infantryman Thomas, age twenty-seven; infantryman Arthur, age twenty-four; gunner Henry, age twenty-two; sailor Ernest, age twenty-one; and sailor David, age eighteen. The family's only fatality was the eldest, John, who was gassed in the trenches in France and brought back to York. He succumbed to his injuries a few weeks later in 1916 after being transferred to a UK hospital. With just one brother lost, the family mirrored the fatality rate among serving British soldiers at the time, which was just over one in ten (11 percent).

It's a sad but tragic fact that after returning to a life of struggle and abject poverty, when the rest of the Calpin brothers passed away, they were buried in unmarked graves because the family could not afford the expense of headstones. This was the fate that awaited many of those who had made the ultimate sacrifice for the country that had promised a return to a home fit for heroes.[51]

The year 1917 was one of the most tumultuous in World War I. The British had launched a punishing offensive toward the Ypres Salient. After some nominal initial successes there, it quickly began to dissipate in the glutinous, putrid yellow-brown mud of Flanders, where hardly anything grew anymore, let alone poppies. The previous year had witnessed the blackest day in British military history at the Battle of the Somme. Earlier in 1916, both French and German forces suffered massive losses of life at Verdun where an estimated 143,000 Germans died out of 337,000 casualties, and France suffered 162,440 deaths out of 377,231 casualties. The battle would eventually lead to mutiny along the French line and would come to symbolize, more than any other battle, the bloody, inhumane nature of trench warfare on the Western Front.

As the war progressed and devolved even further into a pure war of attrition, with neither side making any significant gains, the fire of youthful exuberance was gradually extinguished to such an extent that it became little more than a flickering pilot light. But there was a light, a panacea for the flagging spirits on the Allied side at least. America had declared war on Germany.

---

51   Mark Swenarton, *Homes Fit for Heroes: The Politics and Architecture of Early State Housing in Britain* (Routledge, 2018).

Per capita, more men from the north of England and Scotland volunteered to fight in World War I than any other place in the world at the time. I was extremely fortunate to meet and talk with veterans from my village when I was a kid. I still have cassettes of some of the interviews I recorded for my sociology project when I was sixteen years old. Every town and village in Scotland and England has a cenotaph, or a memorial to those who lost their lives in this terrible sacrifice of a generation of young men. We often heard about the mother from York who waved off ten sons. It's relatively safe to say that almost every family in my part of the world lost someone, and my family was no exception.

CHAPTER THIRTEEN:

OVER WHERE?

Newly appointed German foreign minister Arthur Zimmer-
mann dispatched a telegram on January 16 to his Washington
ambassador, Count Johann von Bernstorff, for the purpose
of forwarding it to Heinrich von Eckardt, the German minister
in Mexico City. The telegram stated in no uncertain terms that
if the United States entered the war, Eckardt was authorized to
offer Mexico an alliance in which the two countries would fight
side by side, with Germany providing financial aid and consenting
to Mexico regaining the territory it had lost to the United States
after the Mexican-American War in 1846–1848. Eckardt was also
told to encourage the Mexican president, Venustiano Carranza, to
invite Japan to change sides.

Soon after the damning telegram was published, Germany
launched a sequence of provocative acts of war against the United
States. On March 16, 1917, the American vessel *Vigilancia* was
sunk without warning, costing the lives of fifteen merchant seamen.
Other ships soon followed as German naval aggression persisted
and increased. Berlin and Washington were now heading for an
unavoidable collision. Increasing xenophobia and animosity toward
Germans, along with a growing fervor among American citizens to
get physically involved in the European war, added further fire to

the flames. From April 16, 1917 on, all males older than the age of fourteen who were still regarded as natives, citizens, denizens, or subjects of the German Empire became ostensibly regarded as "alien enemies."

On April 2, 1917, President Woodrow Wilson addressed Congress and requested, in no uncertain terms, a solid declaration of war against Germany with these words: "We have no selfish ends to serve. We desire no conquest, no dominion. We seek no indemnities for ourselves, no material compensation for the sacrifices we shall freely make. We are but one of the champions of the rights of mankind....We enter this war only where we are clearly forced into it, because there are no other means of defending our rights....The world must be made safe for democracy. Its peace must be planted upon the tested foundations of political liberty.... We shall be satisfied when those rights have been made as secure as the faith and the freedom of nations can make them. Just because we fight without rancor and without selfish object, seeking nothing for ourselves but what we shall wish to share with all free peoples, we shall, I feel confident, conduct our operations as belligerents without passion and ourselves observe with proud punctilio the principles of right and of fair play we profess to be fighting for."[52] Only fifty-six of 531 congressmen and senators objected to the motion, which was subsequently passed, and from then on it was game on for America.

Meanwhile, the prime factor that unified the British and French in 1917, apart from fighting a common enemy, was the fact that America could—and would—make a substantial difference and hopefully tip the balance in favor of the Allied cause. But first America had to mobilize for war before it could effectively participate, in what President Wilson would famously describe as "the war to end all wars."[53] Nevertheless, all the rhetorical speeches couldn't detract from the undeniable fact that America simply wasn't prepared for war.

---

52 *Woodrow Wilson: The Essential Political Writings*: By Woodrow Wilson, Ronald J. Pestritto

53 Thomas J. Knock, *To End All Wars, New Edition: Woodrow Wilson and the Quest for a New World Order* (Princeton, NJ: Princeton University Press, 2019).

Despite being woefully underprepared, Wilson appointed General John Joseph "Black Jack" Pershing to lead the AEF. Pershing was a close ally and supporter of Wilson's presidency and was therefore the natural choice. The General Organization Plan of the AEF was an essential part of Pershing's strategy to build and train an independent American army in France. He flatly rejected French and British demands to amalgamate his troops into their depleted armies and insisted on forming an independent American army before committing any US troops to the front lines. Wilson therefore gave Pershing a written order before his departure for Europe, forbidding him from amalgamating American forces. Pershing stubbornly maintained the stance that American forces would only fight under a completely American chain of command on a distinctly American section of the Western Front.

Pershing was born on September 13, 1860. He passed an entrance examination for West Point. Although at that time he had no designs on honing a military career, he liked the idea of getting a West Point education.

He became an exemplary cadet and even a member of the West Point Honor Guard that escorted the funeral procession of President Ulysses S. Grant. After graduation, Pershing served in the Sixth Cavalry in a number of minor military engagements against the Apache's led by Geronimo. In the Spanish-American War he commanded the African American Tenth Cavalry and was later awarded the Silver Star. Pershing had earned the nickname "Black Jack" for his service with the African American Tenth Cavalry unit when they led the charge in the battle at San Juan Hill, but the name also came to signify his harsh demeanor and rigorous, almost callous implementation of military discipline.

By late 1917, both French and British forces were applying new tactics in an attempt to lessen casualties. They would get a serious lesson from the Germans on precisely how to do this the following year. The jaded blow-the-whistle-and-charge strategy had inflicted far too many deaths and wounded on all sides. It was time to implement new ideas and methods.

Pershing wrote: "It was my opinion that the victory could not be won by the costly process of attrition, but it must be won by driving the enemy out into the open and engaging him in a war of movement. Instruction in this kind of warfare was based upon individual and group initiative, resourcefulness, and tactical judgment, which were also of great advantage in trench warfare. Therefore, we took decided issue with the Allies and, without neglecting thorough preparation for trench fighting, undertook to train mainly for open combat, with the object from the start of vigorously forcing the offensive."[54]

These young American soldiers may have been lacking in some areas of training, but they brought a vigor and zeal to the Allies that had long since evaporated in the ranks of their war-weary armies. They brought enthusiasm, courage, and spontaneity to a conflict that had sapped the will from almost every combatant. In the summer and fall of 1918, the AEF encouraged independent thinking and actively expanded on certain tactics, such as advances by rushes or by infiltration of small units, which previously only officers had directed. Skirmish lines, for example, were to cross open, fire-swept areas by advance of individuals or squads, with platoon leaders resuming command only after some predetermined terrain feature had been reached. All of these measures reflected a tactical decentralization and encouragement for initiative undreamed of in other Allied armies.

Consequently, the American military cemetery at Meuse-Argonne covers 130.5 acres and contains the remains of 14,246 American military from World War I. It is considered to be the largest United States Army Materiel Command (USAMC) in Europe.

"Listen to your parents" is an age-old adage, but there were surely exceptions, such as Rudyard Kipling. Well here is another potential contender. All four sons and one daughter of former President Theodore Roosevelt served in World War I. Among those Roosevelts was daughter Ethel, who was serving as a Red Cross nurse in France, where her husband, Richard Derby, was a surgeon. She was actually the first member of the Roosevelt clan that was active in a World War I war zone.

---

54   Marc K. Blackburn, *Interpreting American Military History at Museums and Historic Sites* (Lanham, MD: Rowman & Littlefield, 2016).

Ethel served as a Red Cross nurse in France, where her husband Richard Derby was a surgeon. She was actually the first member of the Roosevelt clan active in a World War I zone, but her brothers would follow.>

Two famous Roosevelt brothers died in different wars but are buried together in Normandy. Theodore died shortly after the Normandy landings of June 1944. He was commanding the Fourth Infantry Division at the time. In the little town of Chamery in France there's a water fountain dedicated to the memory of young Lieutenant Quentin Roosevelt, which was presented to the towns-people by his family. During World War I when indoor water taps weren't a domestic feature, most of the village used the fountain to obtain clean drinking water. In July 1918 when the Allies attacked, the French village of Chamery was well behind the frontlines. At that time the Germans were dispatching reinforcements, including aviation units, to the front. The importance and significance of mili-tary aviation had evolved as the war had progressed. It was used for bombing, vital reconnaissance, and of course the iconic aerial dogfights against German aces such as the Red Baron and Hermann Göring, who (by the time he became one of Hitler's henchmen) probably couldn't even fit into a Fokker Triplane World War I fighter because he had gained so much weight.

These aircraft may have appeared cumbersome and fragile on the ground but a trained pilot could transpose these canvas and plywood contraptions into swift, maneuverable, and well-armed aircraft. This inevitably made some of those illustrious pilots quite famous, and for some that fame has endured. The pilots of these colorful biplanes and triplanes that clashed above the trenches or in no-mans-land were often compared to the chivalric knights of the Middle Ages and bound by a similar code based on mutual admiration and deep respect. World War I saw the advent of air traffic control when the US Army installed the first operational two-way radios in planes. In 1917, a human voice was first transmitted by radio from a plane in flight to an operator on the ground. It also gave birth to the fighter pilot. Airplanes were deployed en masse for the first time in both air-to-air combat and reconnaissance missions.

On July 14, Quentin Roosevelt, the youngest son of Theodore Roosevelt, was flying a Nieuport 28 fighter when he was tragically killed in action. From the age of four years old, Quentin had been a public figure and a darling of the American people. When his father became the president of the United States, he spent many years being raised in the White House.

At the young age of twenty, he didn't have a great deal of experience and had only been flying in combat for nine days, which was paradoxically the life expectancy for a World War I pilot fighting over the frontlines. He had been missing since July 14, 1918, when he and four other pilots from the US Army Air Service's Ninety-Fifth Aero Squadron were ambushed by at least seven German aircraft near the village of Chamery.

Quentin had died behind enemy lines a mere 915 meters east of the Chamery fountain. On July 15, the German army at the site of his crash afforded him a burial with full military honors. Three German pilots took credit for bringing down Quentin's biplane but most historians accredit this to Sergeant Carl-Emil Graper, who said that Quentin had fought courageously. The Germans were naturally shocked when they discovered that they had killed the son of an American president. According to one American prisoner of war who watched the ceremony, around one thousand German soldiers paid their respects. On the cross they erected, the soldiers wrote: "Lieutenant Roosevelt, buried by the Germans."[55]

---

55   *Flight & the Aircraft Engineer*, 1918, p. 923.

His father was inconsolable when he was duly notified on July 17 that Quentin had been reported missing and presumed dead.

Quentin Roosevelt was a flight leader in the Ninety-Fifth and despite his famous family, he was considered by his comrades to be a regular guy. Captain Eddie Rickenbacker, the top World War I American ace wrote, "Everyone who met him for the first time expected him to have the airs and superciliousness of a spoiled boy. This notion was quickly lost after the first glimpse one had of Quentin."[56]

Quentin Roosevelt was the fifth child of Teddy and Edith Roosevelt and undeniably his father's favorite. He was the golden boy, the hilarious juvenile terror of the White House, funny, fearless, academically gifted, mechanically brilliant, and personally charming. When the United States entered World War I, Quentin Roosevelt was studying at Harvard University. His father had argued for American entry into the war, so it was only natural for Quentin and the other three Roosevelt sons to join the military. Consequently, Quentin dropped out of Harvard and joined the First Aero Company of the New York National Guard. The unit trained at a local airfield on Long Island, which was later renamed Roosevelt Field in Quentin Roosevelt's honor.

The First Aero Company was federalized in June 1917 as the First Reserve Aero Squadron and was sent to France. Roosevelt went along and was assigned as a supply officer at a training base. He learned to fly the Nieuport 28 fighter, a light biplane fighter armed with two Vickers machine guns, which the French had provided for the American pilots. In June 1918, Roosevelt joined the Ninety-Fifth. Quentin was generally regarded as a good pilot but gained a reputation for being a risk-taker. With only four weeks of training under his belt, he got into the fight in early July 1918 and by July 5, 1918, he had been in combat on two occasions. On his first mission, the engine of Roosevelt's Nieuport malfunctioned. A German fighter shot at him but missed. Later that day he took up another plane and found himself in a terrible situation when both machine guns jammed.

---

56   Neville Duke and Edward Lanchbery, *The Saga of Flight: From Leonardo Da Vinci to the Guided Missile, an Anthology* (New York, NY: John Day Co, 1961).

According to After Action Reports, on July 9 he shot down a German plane and may have got another. It was July 14, Bastille Day, when American pilots were ordered into the air as part of the American effort to halt the German advance during what became known as the second battle of the Marne. The German army was attacking toward Paris and the AEF was in their way.

In World War I, observation planes that spotted targets for the artillery were a serious threat to both sides. The job for Roosevelt and the other American pilots was to escort vital observation planes over German lines. They had accomplished their mission and were heading home when they were ambushed by at least seven German planes. The weather was overcast, so Lieutenant Edward Buford, the flight leader, decided to break off and retreat. At that juncture he saw an American plane engaging three German aircraft.

Buford later said, "I shook the two I was maneuvering with, and tried to get over to him but before I could reach him his machine turned over on its back and plunged down and out of control. At the time of the fight I did not know who the pilot was I'd seen go down. But as Quentin did not come back, it must have been him. His loss was one of the severest blows we have ever had in the squadron. He certainly died fighting."[57]

When the Germans retreated and the Allies retook Chamery, Quentin Roosevelt's grave became a regular tourist attraction. Soldiers visited his grave, had their photograph taken there, and took pieces of his Nieuport as souvenirs.

The commander of New York's Sixty-Ninth Infantry, Colonel Frank McCoy, had served as President Roosevelt's military aide and had known Quentin when he was a boy. At McCoy's direction, the regiment's chaplain Father (Captain) Francis Duffy had a cross made and put it in place at the grave. "The plot had already been ornamented with a rustic fence by the Soldiers of the Thirty-Second Division. We erected our own little monument without molesting the one that had been left by the Germans,"[58] he wrote in his memoirs. "It is fitting that enemy and friend alike

57   Earle Looker and Arthur Hayne Mitchell, *Colonel Roosevelt and the White House Gang* (Balboa Press, 2016).

58   Francis Patrick Duffy, *Father Duffy's Story; A Tale of Humor and Heroism, of Life and Death with the Fighting Sixty-Ninth (Illustrated Edition)* (Pickle Partners Publishing, 2014).

should pay tribute to his heroism." An Army Signal Corps photographer and movie cameraman recorded the event. After the war, the temporary gravestone was replaced with a permanent one and Edith Roosevelt donated a new fountain to the village of Chamery in memory of her son. Quentin Roosevelt's body remained where he fell until 1955. Then, at the request of the Roosevelt family, Quentin's remains were exhumed.

He was laid to rest next to his brother, Brigadier General Theodore Roosevelt, Jr. They had both served the AEF during the war. Five days after Quentin was killed, Theodore was wounded near Soissons. He would later die in World War II during the Normandy campaign in July 1944. Theodore Roosevelt Jr., or Ted as he was called, was a brigadier general in the army who led the men of the Fourth Infantry Division ashore on Utah Beach on D-Day before dying of a heart attack on July 12, 1944. Both men are buried in the Normandy American Cemetery in Colleville-sur-Mer, on the site of the temporary American St. Laurent Cemetery, which was established by the US First Army on June 8, 1944, as the first American cemetery on European soil in World War II.

When the US declared war in April 1917, former president Roosevelt attempted to don his army uniform again but was prevented by the order of President Wilson—though every one of Roosevelt's sons accepted a commission. Theodore Jr. was a successful businessman and married with three children when he was commissioned a major. Archibald ("Archie"), who married shortly after the declaration of war, was commissioned a first lieutenant. They were on the first troop transport to France. Kermit, thinking that it would take too long for American troops to go into action, used his father's influence to secure a commission in the British army where he commanded a British light-armored motor battery in Iraq. This later earned him the British Military Cross for gallantry. In 1918, after the American Expeditionary Force arrived in Europe, Kermit joined their ranks as a captain in the Seventh Field Artillery of the First Division. Unlike his three brothers, Captain Kermit Roosevelt emerged from World War I without sustaining any serious injuries.

Kermit was a well-read man. He could read or speak Greek, French, Portuguese, Swahili, Arabic, Hindustani, Urdu, and Romany. A prolific writer, he authored a score of books mainly related to hunting and exploration, including two that were coauthored by his oldest brother, Ted. Kermit's book, *War in the Garden of Eden* (1919), recounted his service with the British armed forces during World War I.

Archibald "Archie" Roosevelt was born on April 9, 1894, the second youngest of the Roosevelt children. During World War I, Archie served with distinction as a decorated captain with the Twenty-Sixth Infantry of the AEF in France. He was awarded the Silver Star for gallantry and being "an officer of great coolness whose conduct has been exemplary." He also received France's Croix de Guerre. Archie was given a full disability discharge from the army after suffering a severe leg wound during an artillery bombardment.

After the Pearl Harbor attack of 1941, Archie lobbied his cousin, President Franklin Roosevelt, for a commission in the US Army. His request was granted, and he was commissioned as a lieutenant colonel and battalion commander with the 162nd Infantry in New Guinea for two years. During his time in the army during World War II, Archie was seriously wounded again in the same leg, this time by an enemy grenade. He was awarded second and third oak leaf clusters for his Silver Star from World War I and was once again given a full disability discharge from the army. Archie has the distinction of being the only American ever to be medically discharged twice for the same wound in two different wars.

Theodore "Ted" Roosevelt Jr. was shot in the leg and almost blinded by a German gas attack in World War I. Ted, who had a reserve commission in the army, was called up shortly after World War I broke out. When the US declared war on Germany, Ted volunteered to be one of the first soldiers to go to France. Once there he distinguished himself as the best battalion commander in his division. According to the division commander, "He braved hostile fire and gas and led his battalion in combat. So concerned was he for his men's welfare that he even purchased combat boots for the entire battalion with his own money."

Ted eventually took command of the US Army's Twenty-Sixth Regiment of First Division as lieutenant colonel. He fought in several major battles and was gassed and wounded at Soissons during the summer of 1918. He received the Distinguished Service Cross for his action during the war. France conferred upon him the chevalier degree of the *Légion d'Honneur* (Legion of Honor) on March 16, 1919. Before the troops even came home from France, Ted was one of the originators and founders of the soldiers' organization that would become known as the American Legion. When the American Legion met for the first time in New York City and Ted was nominated to become the Legion's first national commander, he politely refused the nomination because he didn't want his acceptance to be misconstrued as a mere political machination.

President Teddy Roosevelt was no stranger to tragedy. He had fought childhood asthma, coped with the deaths of his first wife and mother on the same day, stared down rustlers as a rancher in the Dakotas, faced enemy fire in the Spanish-American War, survived an assassination attempt in 1912, and survived tropical illness and exhaustion during a 1914 expedition to the Amazon. Six months after Quentin's death, on January 6, 1919, he died suddenly of a heart attack in his sleep at the age of sixty.

It would be a heart attack that took a much younger Mr. Elisha Whittlesey. He was the first of his family to enlist in the ambulance service on May 19, 1917, in Boston, Massachusetts, as a private in the Harvard Ambulance Unit of the American Field Service. This organization immediately proceeded overseas and served with the French army. Elisha displayed exceptional daring and courage that were characteristics indubitably present in this illustrious family. One veteran friend said that Elisha was absolutely fearless and often rushed on for wounded comrades amid an over-whelming storm of shells where few others would venture.

Entered military service on May 19, 1917, as a private in the Harvard Ambulance Unit of the American Field Service, which served in the French Army. He served gallantly until the U.S. Army took over and he failed a physical exam due to a heart ailment. He worked in the Portsmouth, New Hampshire, Navy Yard for the rest of the war.

When the army requisitioned the ambulance service on October 9, 1917, Elisha was subjected to a physical examination but failed to pass the test due to his bad heart. He returned home feeling terribly dejected and declared to his friends he would join a Canadian regiment, feeling sure he would be accepted there. He was so anxious to serve his country that finally he went to the Portsmouth, New Hampshire, navy yard where they gave him a rough position at first in handling steel plates. He stuck it out at Portsmouth until the war ended, then he returned to Harvard and finished his courses. Elisha had a remarkably keen and receptive mind just like his brother, Colonel Charles Whittlesey. Charles was very modest, unassuming, and would never talk of his war experiences.

Elisha was noted for his courage and gallantry under fire and was honored by the French government for his service. He then returned to Harvard and in 1920 graduated from the School of Business Administration. On March 4, 1922, Elisha tragically died of a heart attack at his home in Pittsfield, Massachusetts. His remains are buried in the Pittsfield Cemetery.

Melzar Merrick Whittlesey desperately wanted to emulate his brothers and do his part. He joined the coast guard on May 14, 1917, and attended Officer's Training Candidacy at Plattsburgh, New York, and Fort Monroe, Virginia. Then he served as a second lieutenant in the Coast Artillery Corps in Boston until August 27, 1917. After this he decided he'd had enough of the raging seas and on March 10, 1918, he opted for training as a pilot at Austin and San Antonio where he was promoted to first lieutenant in August 1918. He never saw service overseas but had he been given the chance, there's no doubt that he would have gone.

The third Whittelsey brother was Charles, mentioned earlier. For the lesser informed, the name might not ring a bell, but most will have heard of the famous Lost Battalion. The Lost Battalion is the name attributed to the nine companies of the Seventy-Seventh Division that comprised of roughly 554 men who became isolated by German forces during World War I after an American attack in the Argonne Forest in October 1918.

Major Charles was a successful New York lawyer, who had recently graduated from Williams College. He enlisted in the first Plattsburgh officers' training camp. After receiving his commission, he was sent to Camp Upton. He sailed for France in April 1918 and participated in quite possibly the heaviest AEF engagement on the Western Front, the Battle of the Meuse-Argonne.

The battle in the region of the Meuse-Argonne would come to represent the zenith of the AEF's contribution to World War I. It would be the place where legends were cemented and heroes were made. It was a remarkably intricate operation that entailed involving AEF ground forces fighting through rough, hilly terrain, which the German army had spent four years fortifying. The purpose and objective of the offensive was the capture of the railroad hub at Sedan. Seizure of this location had the potential to completely dislocate the rail network supporting the German army in France and Flanders, and to force their withdrawal from the occupied territories.

One of the great logistical accomplishments of World War I was the transference of American troops from the Saint-Mihiel salient to the new section of the front that extended thirty miles east to west and was situated to the north and northwest of Verdun.

The AEF needed to relocate forty miles to a location along the west bank of the Meuse River. Throughout the next two weeks, a massive movement of troops, artillery, and supplies took place, syphoned along three roads into the area that would become the new battleground. This movement was completed over only three roads. To avoid unwelcome enemy attention, most of the transportation occurred during the hours of darkness. These logistics were expertly organized and coordinated by Colonel George C. Marshall, who would eventually become secretary of state and orchestrate the famous Marshall Plan after World War II. In September 1918, Marshall was on the staff of the AEF and had been a significant planner of American operations on the Western Front.

The operations at the attacks would constitute part of French Army commander Marshal Ferdinand Foch's larger offensive against the Germans. The AEF would be launched simultaneously along with concentric attacks of the British toward Mons while the French would attack in the center and provide support for the Allies in their operations.

By September 1918, after sustaining heavy losses, the Germans had committed all of their available reserves. Meanwhile, the Allies were still receiving a steady stream of reinforcements. If a breakthrough on both flanks of the enormous salient held by the German armies in the north of France could be achieved, this offensive had the potential to effectively end the war.

An excerpt from the Seventy-Seventh Infantry's After Action Report from the National Archives reveals details about what transpired during this fateful battle:

> *During the first phase of the World War the French made an attempt to clear the "Forest of Argonne" of the enemy, and had lost many men in the endeavor. Thereafter further attempt was made, until the Allied Offensive, which was launched September 26, 1918. It had remained unmolested for nearly four years in the hands of*

the enemy, who had early in the war occupied it, and had skillfully developed its natural features into one vast impregnable fortress.

The "Forest of Argonne" was an area of densely wooded hills and slopes with many ravines, gullies, and swamps, all of which were covered with tangled underbrush; consequently the Germans were able to place their machine guns to command all roads and paths traversing it, and had located them in positions which enabled the gunners to place a series of interlocking bands of fire between trees and along systems of barbed wire, which they had cleverly constructed and concealed, during their unmolested occupation. All of this, combined with his cleverly concealed artillery positions, his hidden observation posts, and infantry with supporting weapons, rendered the "Forest of Argonne" most inaccessible to direct attack and hostile penetration.

The most impossible task of clearing the "Forest of Argonne" by direct attack was recognized by the Allied Command, and during the discussion of the Meuse-Argonne Offensive, plans were discussed as to how it could be taken without a heavy attack in that difficult region. It was decided that the right of the Fourth French Army, which was the 39th French Corps, operating on the west of the forest, and the American divisions, operating on the east of the Forest, would advance, simultaneously, launching a scalloping movement on the east and west outskirts of the Forest, thus creating and developing a pocket from which the enemy would be obliged to withdraw in order to avoid capture.

As a result of this plan, a speedy with-drawal of the enemy from their Forest strong-hold was anticipated, and very little resistance was expected. For the above reasons was the 77th Division assigned such a wide zone of action, with the mission of mopping up the forest as the enemy withdrew. Information has also been obtained that the enemy troops occupying the "Forest of the Argonne" were organizations of the "Landwehr Reservers"—"old fellows," they called them—and it was thought that they had lived lives of ease and comfort for nearly four years, while unmolested and secure in their forest fastness, consequently would not offer a great deal of resistance. Contrary of supposition, these troops were determined and stubborn in the conduct of their defense and resistance, and proved to be among Germany's best troops. It is very true that they had remained in the Forest for a long period, but they had not remained idle, nor were they so elderly, for they had perfected and developed a system of defense which was most difficult to overcome. The "Landwehr" divisions were reinforced by the 76th German Reserve Division, which greatly strengthened the enemy resistance. Both the "Landwehr" and the 76th Reserves were fresh troops, unworn by long service at the Front, and they fought coura-geously, contesting every foot of ground after falling back upon their main line of resistance. From the morning of September 27th, their resistance commenced in earnest, and from then on new enemy divisions appeared on the Front.

Returning to the plan of attack, the Amer-ican divisions operating on the east of the "Forest" advanced rapidly, as planned, but the *right of the Fourth French Army, operating on the west of the "Forest, was unable to advance, owing to the organization and defense of the enemy territory to its front, which consisted of well-constructed trench systems organized in depth, surrounded by solid masses of barbed wire, and covered with second-growth brush. Also, the strong enemy defensive positions at La Palette Pavilion, and those extending west, dominated all of the ground in front of the right of the Fourth French Army.*

The liaison mission between the right of the Fourth French Army and the left of the 77th Division, charged to a Franco-American liaison group, composed of American colored troops and a like number of French troops, and operating under the 38th French Corps, was not accomplished, owing to the unforeseen and determined opposition by the enemy on the left of the Forest, and at all times during the operation the right of the Fourth French Army remained to the left rear of the left of the American line. Consequently, the contemplated pocket was not formed, and the enemy did not withdraw.

Thus we find that the 77th Division faced the "Forest of Argonne" and its occupied defenses with the left flank exposed to the enemy territory to the left and left front, and holding a seven-kilometer zone of action. Due to the combination of circumstances, as stated above, the 77th Division became much involved in the Forest, and many times during those memorable days, regiments, battalions, and even companies were obliged to settle their own disputes with the enemy. Is it so astonishing, then, that the

organizations of the 77th Division should have
found themselves engaged on various occasions
with both flanks open? It was the indomitable
courage, optimism, and determination of the
personnel of the division, from its commander,
whose efficient leadership and will carried the
division forward, to its last private soldier,
which enabled it to realize upon emerging from
the Forest before Grandpré, eighteen days after
it entered, that success had crowned its efforts.[59]

Major Whittlesey could read a map like a book; he was intelligent, astute, and exceptionally cool under fire. He bore the same hardships as his officers and men, and they stood with him to the last. He conducted his command to the objective designated for him by the division commander, occupied the position assigned him, and organized and held that position until the remainder of the division, on the right, and the French, on the left, were able to move up on his flanks five days later.

The story of the Lost Battalion and its ice-cool leader Charles Whittlesey became the stuff of legend and was widely reported by the domestic press in the United States and internationally. He was an American hero, who was consequently awarded the Medal of Honor for his role in the Argonne Forest.

So, to separate the man from the legend, it's important to take a closer look. First of all the Lost Battalion is a misnomer because it was not a battalion but was composed of seven companies of infantry and one machine-gun company. It consisted of companies A, B, C, E, G, and H of the 308th Infantry, company K of the 307th Infantry, and company C of the 306th Machine Gun Battalion. A battalion is composed of only four companies. Second, it was not "lost." Major Whittlesey knew exactly where he was and had advanced to the exact position to which he had been ordered.

Charles Whittlesey was a deeply troubled man who displayed some symptoms of PTSD when he struggled to make sense of his experiences. Outwardly he maintained the stance of a stoic war

---

59   *Lost Voices: The Untold Stories of America's World War I Veterans and their Families*
Hardcover – Illustrated, June 1, 2018 by Martin King (Author), Michael Collins (Author).

hero, but inwardly he was battling some serious demons. There is some contemporary speculation that points to the fact that he never married, never had a girlfriend, and spoke frequently about feeling out of place in society. According to one academic, who shall remain unnamed, there is every possibility that he may have secretly been gay, but maybe that's a specious conclusion. More than likely, he was just a deeply sensitive person who, like untold millions of veterans, could neither process nor externalize his horrific experiences. Like so many others, his story would end tragically.

On November 24, 1921, just three short years after the end of World War I, Whittlesey booked passage from New York to Havana aboard a steamship called the USS *Toloa*. On November 26, the first night out from New York, Whittlesey dined with the captain and then retired for the evening, around 11:15 p.m. It was noted that he was in high spirits. Whittlesey was never seen again. He was reported missing the next morning. It is presumed that he committed suicide by jumping overboard, although no one had seen him jump, and his body was never recovered.

Trained in Plattsburgh, New York, starting in July, 1916, where he rose up through the officer ranks to be a Major in the 308th Infantry regiment, 76th Infantry Division. He led the 308th and K company of the 307th known as "Lost Battalion" in the Argonne Forest, France, from October 2-7, 1918. For his courage and leadership, Whittlesey was awarded the Congressional Medal of Honor on December 2, 1918.

Several theories existed at the time as to what had pushed Whittlesey to such depths of depression. Those close to him believed that his death could be counted among war casualties inasmuch as it was his sensitivity to the constant reminders of the destruction of the war that drove him to eventual suicide. Some believed that his suicide was caused by feelings of guilt while others believed that it was his modesty and inability to adjust to the life of a hero that caused the crippling depression that eventually ended his life. Whatever the exact reason may have been, it is clear that Whittlesey's death was indirectly related to the unhappiness that befell him after his experiences in the war. His friends and comrades never forgot him.

This chapter was inspired by my own book *Lost Voices, The Untold Stories of America's World War I Veterans and Their Families* by me and Michael Collins. The archive of information that we assembled for this volume was simply too fascinating to leave alone. I referred to that archive again for this chapter, focusing on some well-known and some lesser-known stories of the doughboys and their families.

CHAPTER FOURTEEN:

NEVER SUCH DEVOTED SISTERS.

The American Red Cross had been assisting Allied wounded since the beginning of World War I in some form or another, but when America officially entered, two particular sisters living a very comfortable life volunteered to do their bit. Dorothea and Gladys Cromwell, actual descendants of British dictator Oliver Cromwell, were both born in Brooklyn in 1885. Educated at private schools in New York City, they studied and traveled abroad extensively, which was largely thanks to their privileged lifestyle. They had both inherited a substantial fortune from their father, who was a trustee of the Mutual Life Insurance Company of New York City. The socialite twins were living together in a spacious Park Avenue apartment when they decided to abandon all previous comfort and volunteer to work for the Red Cross, first in a canteen and then as nurses in France (near the front at Verdun).

World War I nurses pose together at an American Red Cross canteen in Meuse, France, December 23, 1918. Second from left is Gladys Cromwell, and her sister, Dorothy Cromwell, is on the right. On January 26, 1919, the police commissioner of Bordeaux confirmed that they had both committed suicide. Their bodies were discovered a few weeks later on March 20th, 1919. What drove them to it?>

The head of the canteen where they worked described the Cromwell twins as "angels who not only do first-class work on day or night service, but also find time to visit the soldiers in the French hospitals and to befriend the little French refugee children. Everybody loves them and admires their efficiency and courage in real danger."[60]

The Cromwell twins soon became celebrities in France and were happy to continue their work there, even after the armistice of November 11, 1918, had brought all hostilities to an abrupt end. Urged to return to America by their only brother, Seymour, they boarded the SS *La Lorraine* January 19, 1919, at Bordeaux Harbor, for the voyage back to their home in New York City.

An AEF private called Jack Pemberton was on duty on the upper deck of the *La Lorraine* the night it began its pan-Atlantic journey.

---

60   Constance M. Ruzich, ed., *International Poetry of the First World War: An Anthology of Lost Voices* (London, UK: Bloomsbury Academic, 2020).

As he huddled against a blustery, freezing wind and a dank mist, he saw two women, each wearing a black cape, walking arm-in-arm, talking. They then separated, one of the women climbed onto the ship's rail, and then vanished. The second woman followed, also ascending the rail and disappearing into the murky blackness below. Pemberton actually heard two faint splashes, presumably as the bodies of the twins impacted the ocean. He ran to his commanding officer who alerted the bridge, and the alarm was sounded. This process took fifteen minutes, by which time the ship had traveled five miles out of the port and the river channel was too narrow, making it nigh impossible to turn around and look for the sisters.

The Cromwell sisters had endured being bombed by enemy planes. They had heard the continuous hellish clamor of war in close proximity while stoically performing their duties and frequently watched young men breath their last breath of life. They had witnessed the true horror of the Western Front up close, and it must have affected them deeply. These two Park Avenue socialites had enjoyed a privileged life, but nothing could have prepared them for the tragedy of war, and eventually they themselves became a part of that global tragedy.

Maybe they were suffering from PTSD? Maybe, like so many others who witnessed the war, they had seen too much and couldn't physically or mentally digest or process their horrific experiences? Gladys and Dorothea Cromwell received the Croix de Guerre posthumously, and the Médaille de la Reconnaissance française, which is a profound French accolade attributed to civilians. They were buried with full military honors at Suresnes American Cemetery, where they have the company of 1,500 other Americans who died in World War I or World War II. The sisters are also honored with a cenotaph at the Green-Wood Cemetery in Brooklyn, New York City—the place where they were born.

Gladys Cromwell was a remarkably talented poet. Her book, *Poems*, was published late in 1919.

The Mould

No doubt this active will,
So bravely steeped in sun,
This will has vanquished Death
And foiled oblivion.
But this indifferent clay,
This fine experienced hand,
So quiet, and these thoughts
That all unfinished stand,
Feel death as though it were
A shadowy caress;
And win and wear a frail
Archaic wistfulness.[61]

In October 1919, it was reported that each of the Cromwell sisters had left an estate worth $661,748, which is roughly the equivalent of just over $9 million in today's money.

Deep in the mist-covered mountains of southeastern Kentucky, in the small town of Oil Springs, Johnson County, lived the Minnich family. They donated two daughters and one son to the American war effort during World War I. The three children of William W. and Myrain F. (née Long) Minnich were Elizabeth "Lizzie" Eleanor, born November 22, 1883; Margaret Gretchen, born July 30, 1888; and John Bayles, born February 6, 1890. One year to the day after the United States declared war, Elizabeth and Margaret joined the American Red Cross. Five days later on April 11, 1918, their brother John enlisted. At the time of his enlistment, Elizabeth was thirty-four, Margaret was twenty-nine, and John was twenty-eight.

---

61   Glayds Cromwell, *Poems* (Macmillan Company, 1919).

The Minnich family donated two daughters and one son to the American war effort during the Great War. Elizabeth, Margaret, and John Minnich.

On May 28, 1918, Elizabeth and Margaret were ordered to the Holley Hotel in New York City in preparation for overseas deployment. While they waited, they were provided with comfortable quarters at various locations around the city and fitted with Red Cross nursing uniforms. Most afternoons were spent at the armory in New York City where the nurses were drilled and given military instruction.

During their stay in New York, the Red Cross Association looked after them. By July 12, 1918, the Minnich sisters were aboard the famous White Star Line's RMS *Olympic*, which arrived at Southampton, England, on July 19. The *Olympic* was the sister ship of the *Titanic* and *Britannic*. The latter had, at that time, been converted into a troop transport in support of the war effort. The former was deep below the north Atlantic. Getting on a ship with a sister that had a dubious safety record must have taken quite a lot of nerve. At least they wouldn't have to listen to Celine Dion.

Their brother John didn't make it overseas. During his military service, Private First Class John Bayles Minnich served at the Edgewood Arsenal in Maryland. According to his service record, he served with the newly organized Chemical Warfare Service. He was eventually discharged on December 8, 1918. After his service, he went on to live a long and productive life. John Minnich died on April 21, 1977, at the Ormond Beach Hospital in Florida.

In 1936, Lizzie became extremely ill, and, due to her veteran status, she was sent to the veteran's home in Dayton, Ohio, for treatment where she died following a three-year illness on June 16, 1939. Her body was then brought back to Kentucky where she was buried at the Ashland Cemetery with full military honors. Margaret Gretchen Minnich Blain died April 1, 1978, at the Regency Nursing Home in Forestville, Maryland, one year after the death of her brother John.

As a small side note, it was during World War I that sanitary napkins for women were first invented. When America officially entered the war, the Kimberly-Clark Corporation started to mass-produce the padding for the purpose of using it for surgical dressing. Red Cross nurses assigned in the battlefields discovered that this product was remarkably absorbent, so they decided to use it for their own personal hygiene; hence, this seemingly innocent item brought great fortune to the once-small firm. Kimberly-Clark's new invention of sanitary napkins was branded Kotex, which stood for "cotton texture." They became available to the public in October 1920, only two short years after the armistice was signed.

Before America even considered entering the war, Britain was reliant on those indomitable Commonwealth countries that assisted with their extensive war effort. Australian Janet Isobel Gallagher was one of three female members of the Gallagher family who decided to serve overseas with the Australian Army Nursing Service and dodge bullets during World War I as opposed to remaining at home and ducking boomerangs. When she enlisted on June 13, 1916, she was already thirty-five years old and a devout Catholic. Precisely how those two details interconnect is a matter of speculation. Janet and her aunt Evelyn Gallagher enlisted on the same day, and they spent much of the war tending wounded in the same hospitals. All the unmarried Gallagher ladies were of a certain age, which would have qualified them all as spinsters.

Australians were assured that due to the severe Indian climate they would only serve there for six months before being sent to another ANZAC or British medical facilities in France or Mesopotamia.

Janet was among several hundred Australian nurses sent to India at the request of the British government to work in military hospitals. As a result, many were staffed mainly by Australian nurses who cared initially for sick and wounded evacuated from Mesopotamia until facilities could be established near the fighting, and for British troops of the Indian garrison. Mesopotamia was the historical region of Western Asia that occupied the area of present-day Iraq, and parts of Iran, Turkey, Syria, and Kuwait. The Australians were assured that, due to the severe Indian climate, they would only serve there for six months before being sent to other Australian and New Zealand Army Corps (ANZAC) or British medical facility in France or Mesopotamia; however, many ANZAC nurses were all too familiar with searing heat and tropical conditions before they arrived on the subcontinent.

The Gallaghers were perfectly prepared for that eventuality. Many of their patients in India became victims of tropical diseases. Two Australian nurses died of cholera while serving there.

Janet Gallagher sailed on the RMS *Kashgar* and arrived in India on September 27, 1916. Her first posting was at the Gerard Freeman Thomas Hospital in Bombay. In May 1917, she was sent to a 1,500-bed hospital in Poona where she remained for about eighteen months. While at the Deccan War Hospital, she was promoted to Sister, although her promotion did not seem to have been noted officially until late in 1918 after she had left India.

In October 1918, she left Bombay for Egypt where she nursed at the Thirty-Second British General Hospital (BGH) at Abbassia, close by Cairo, until she left for England at the end of the year. In England, she was attached to Second Australian Auxiliary Hospital (AAH) at Southall and very briefly to First Australian General Hospital before being admitted to a hospital herself due to a persistent illness. She was not considered fit to resume nursing for nearly three months after which she joined the 3 AAH at Dartford.

Janet returned to Australia on duty on HMAT *Orsova* arriving in Sydney on September 6, 1919. She was discharged in Sydney on October 23, 1919. After the war and after some long-winded correspondence with the government authorities, she was told that she was only entitled to the British War Medal because India was not regarded as being in a war zone. She is commemorated on the Australian Capital Territory (ACT) Memorial and the City of Queanbeyan's Wall of Remembrance. After the war, Janet continued practicing her métier in Sydney, which included working as a midwife at South Sydney Women's Hospital and later in the northern suburbs of Sydney. She died unmarried in North Sydney on December 30, 1957.

Flora Gallagher was the first of the three female members of the Gallagher family to enlist; she served from 1915 to 1918 as a nurse at military hospitals in Egypt, England, and France. When she signed up to the Australian Army Nursing Service in Sydney in October 1915, she fibbed a little when she gave her age as thirty-three years of age. Records prove that she would have been closer to forty—but outside certain circles, it wasn't polite to ask.

Flora Gallagher was the first of the three female members of the Gallagher family to enlist; she served from 1915 to 1918 as a nurse at military hospitals in Egypt, England, and France. She was one of many angels of the Anzac's.

Less than a month after enlisting, Flora traveled to Egypt on HMAT *Orsova* as reinforcement for Second Australian General Hospital (AGH) at Ghezireh Palace Hotel, which had been taken over to accommodate the overwhelming numbers of wounded and sick patients from Gallipoli. She spent all of 1916 nursing in Egypt. The disastrous Gallipoli campaign began with an attempt to force the Dardanelles by naval power alone, but early bombardments on the coastal ports failed, and three Allied battleships were lost to Turkish mines. On March 18, 1915, British Secretary of State for War, Lord Kitchener (he of "Your Country Needs You" fame), appointed General Sir Ian Hamilton to command a seventy thousand strong Mediterranean Expeditionary Force. It consisted of the

British Twenty-Ninth Division, a Newfoundland battalion, Indian troops, two divisions of the new and untried ANZAC, a Royal Naval Division, and a French colonial division.

By October, the campaign had completely stalled, and Hamilton was relieved of command. Sir Charles Monro, who had the common sense to recommend that the Allies should immediately evacuate their positions in the Dardanelles, replaced Hamilton. The actual evacuation proved to be the most successful part of the entire campaign. Anzac Cove and Suvla Bay were evacuated in December 1915 and by January 9, 1916, the Helles area had been cleared of Allied troops.

In January 1917, Flora was sent to England where she was briefly attached to the Second Australian Auxiliary Hospital (AAH) at Southall and the 3 AAH at Dartford before being sent to France in February to nurse Western Front casualties. There she was attached to the Fourteenth British General Hospital (BGH) near Boulogne. In the middle of the year, she spent three weeks in a hospital in England suffering from a mysterious illness, which wasn't actually that mysterious at all. For the next year, she alternated between nursing at the two hospitals but became increasingly ill.

Late in August 1918, after more than eighteen months nursing in France, she returned to England and was then sent back to Australia. Once she was home, she was operated on for acute appendicitis.

Early in November 1918 while Flora was recovering from her appendix operation, her hometown held an official public ceremony for her, whereupon she was presented with a special-ly-minted gold medal. In early 1919, her army appointment was terminated for medical reasons. Flora died in the hospital in Sydney on January 20, 1938.

Australia and New Zealand had contributed a significant percentage of their populations to World War I. Australia incurred 215,585 casualties from the 331,781 that initially enlisted, and New Zealand suffered 58,526 casualties from the 98,950 that enlisted. In total 416,809 Australians enlisted for service in the World War I, which effectively represented 38.7 percent of the total male popula-tion between the ages of eighteen to forty-four. The total population of New Zealand in 1914 was just over one million. In all, more than 120,000 New Zealanders enlisted, and around 100,000 served overseas. Most were young men, and nearly one in five who served abroad never returned. The total number of military and civilian casualties in World War I was around forty million. From that number there were twenty million deaths and twenty-one million wounded. The total number of deaths includes 9.7 million military personnel and about 10 million civilians. The Allies lost about 5.7 million soldiers while the Central Powers lost about 4 million. The AEF sustained around 320,000 casualties of which 53,402 died in battle, 63,114 were noncombat deaths, and 204,000 were wounded. The 1918 influenza pandemic (also mistakenly referred to as the Spanish flu) during the fall of 1918 took the lives of more than 25,000 men from the AEF while another 360,000 became gravely ill.

Lest we forget!

I vividly recall hearing the story of two direct descendants of Oliver Cromwell from one of my aunts, who had been a Red Cross nurse in World War II. My mother's sisters were as thick as thieves. There were five of them and no family occasion could proceed without them all being there. I did some research on the Cromwell sisters and some other unlikely candidates for frontline duty for this chapter.

CHAPTER FIFTEEN:

HE STARTED IT.

The tired and jaded Austrian Habsburg Empire provided the delinquent seeds that germinated to become one of the primary causes for World War I, which was inevitable anyway. The assassination of their precious Archduke Franz Ferdinand was the work of a Serbian official called Milan Ciganovic (who was a fully paid-up member of an anti-Austrian terrorist organization known as the Black Hand). He was accidentally-on-purpose allowed to escape by Serbian officials, who also had no affection for the Habsburgs. This begs the question: What precisely was Austria good for? According to some notables, lederhosen isn't a garment, it's a punishment from God. Any country that recognizes the flügelhorn as a national instrument was obviously capable of being the potential harbinger of doom.

Apart from other things, World War I was the result of nationalism and industrialization, which were the two humungous ideologies that were permeating and disseminating throughout the length and breadth of Europe in the nineteenth century. Combine this with German unification, ongoing territorial disputes, and sibling rivalry, particularly between the royal dynasties, and the result was on the cards.

During the previous century, after the Franco-Prussian War (1870–1871), Germany's first chancellor (Otto von Bismarck) had skillfully manipulated alliances, purely to isolate France and maintain peace in Europe. Bismarck was ousted in 1890 by Kaiser Wilhelm II, whose reckless foreign policies were ultimately responsible for the lapse of the prospective alliance with Russia that Bismarck had worked so hard for years to achieve. When Germany failed, France stepped in and seized the chance of making an alliance with Russia. Britain signed up to that one too.

It's too simplistic to claim that World War I started because of a disaffected Serbian with a grudge. The causes ran far deeper than that. During the latter part of the nineteenth century, if you were of royal lineage there's a good chance you might have been related to Queen/Empress Victoria, the baby factory that turned out nine children (who in turn had forty-two grandchildren).

Eventually, seven members of the silver spoon mob would occupy European thrones in Greece, Romania, Britain, Germany, Spain, Norway, and Russia. They would all take sides during World War I with disastrous consequences.

When Victoria's favorite granddaughter Alexandra Feodorovna, or Alix of Hesse, fell in love with Nicholas Romanov, heir apparent to the Russian throne, Victoria was not amused. She regarded the Russians as barbaric and corrupt, and fervently opposed the match. Victoria rejected Nicholas on two consecutive occasions, but Alix eventually procured Victoria's grudging approval and married him just after he became tsar of Russia. How wonderfully convenient was that? During Nicholas's reign, Russia imploded into revolution and war, and his beloved British cousin, George V, whom he resembled greatly, declined to offer any aid at all to the Romanovs because he considered it politically unpalatable at the time. That's a loving cousin then?

Victoria's most contentious grandchild, bar none, and the permanent butt of royal ragging was Kaiser Wilhelm II, the nervous, volatile, Oedipus-complex-afflicted ruler of the German empire. He was the product of what Victoria considered to be one of her most successful matches: the marriage of her eldest daughter Victoria (Vicky) to Prince William of Prussia. Good old Queen Vic was the matchmaker in extremis and took her unofficial calling very seriously. She was very outspoken and had an imposing reputation, which was probably due to her diminutive stature. Standing a mere four foot nine inches in her later years, she was almost as wide as she was tall.

Unlike many of Victoria's other grandchildren, Wilhelm rarely heeded the advice of his illustrious grandma. But deep down he doted on her and craved her attention and that of the rest of her family. Victoria treated Kaiser Wilhelm with relative courtesy and compassion, but his other relatives found him arrogant, tactless, and obnoxious, and frequently refused him admission to their little royal "in crowd." George and Nicholas were the worst conspiratorial offenders who grasped every opportunity to ridicule the future Kaiser Wilhelm and frequently bullied him. This, among other things, left the lad with some profound emotional scars, some of which would never heal.

Wilhelm was a deeply troubled individual who had survived a traumatic breech birth. Ineptitude, clumsiness, and brute force used by the English and German doctors had injured Wilhelm's head and neck, severing some nerves leading to his left arm. It resulted in a condition known Erb's palsy that left him with a withered left arm about six inches (fifteen centimeters) shorter than his right. As a result of his disability, he was unable to cut up his own food or even dress himself. He attempted to conceal this deformity and consequently many photographs display him holding a pair of white gloves in his left hand to make the arm seem longer than it actually was.

There ensued a series of excruciating and humiliating attempts to cure the boy's physical impairment. These included the use of electric currents, the application of a prosthetic iron arm, and hugely uncomfortable body braces. On occasion, the court physicians would strap Wilhelm's healthy arm to his body to force him to use the paralyzed one. Another potential remedy was forcing the prince, as he was then, to endure regular "animal baths," which involved wrapping a freshly slaughtered hare around the damaged arm for half an hour. Precisely what medicinal benefits this had is not recorded. Wilhelm endured all the pain and misery because his mother approved of these quack remedies, and he loved his mother dearly (a little too much, in fact). By the time he reached puberty, he was attending boarding school and writing some very disconcerting letters in English to his mother. Vicky never reciprocated or addressed his pubescent problems, choosing instead to correct his grammatical mistakes. Their relationship had deteriorated through the years, and it had all started so well.

When he was born, Wilhelm's English mother Vicky was smitten, but when it became obvious that there was no cure for his disability, she coldly took a distance from her half-English son. The loving affection that she had lathered on him as a small child dissipated until it was completely extinct. Vicky became cold and unresponsive, and this troubled Wilhelm to distraction. He would grow up feeling deeply inferior to his other royal siblings and actively sought other ways to aggrandize his position in society. This manifested itself in various ways. When his father died and he inherited the throne, he set about commissioning the building of warships to compete with the British navy. He was insanely jealous of his English relatives.

Vicky had harbored high aspirations for her first-born son. She hoped he would be just like his grandfather, Prince Albert (Victoria's consort). When she eventually digested the extent of his disability, she made little effort to conceal her bitter disappointment, which her son was all too aware of. He knew that he was considered totally inadequate in her eyes, and it broke his heart.

It has often been observed that his strained relationship with his English mother later caused him to develop an equally uncomfortable relationship with England itself. From the 1890s onward until 1914, Wilhelm made regular visits to England and made a point of being present for Cowes Week on the Isle of Wight, where he often competed against his uncle in the yacht races. Among other things, Wilhelm was an honorary admiral of the British navy. The Danish-born Alexandra, who served the British monarchy first as Princess of Wales and later as queen, also disliked Wilhelm—probably because she never forgave the Prussians for seizing the region of Schleswig-Holstein from Denmark in the 1860s.

There was one occasion when Wilhelm was escorted to Queen Victoria's summer residence by a squadron of imperial German warships and arrived in Cowes on his personal steam yacht, *Hohenzollern*. Since Queen Victoria had made her other grandson an admiral of the British fleet earlier that year, it appeared that the emperor arrived in an exact replica of the uniform associated with that position. This was an unambiguous slight against the British monarchy. In a letter to British diplomat Sir Edward Mallet, the kaiser observed, "Fancy wearing the same uniform as St. Vincent and Nelson. It is enough to make one quite giddy."[62] It was glaringly apparent to all who knew Kaiser Wilhelm that he was a few sandwiches short of a good picnic, but he was the emperor of Germany, so it didn't matter how far he'd slipped off the trolley.

Despite his dismally poor associations with his English relatives, when he received news that Queen Victoria was dying in January 1901, Wilhelm urgently traveled to England to be at her bedside. When she died, he remained there for the funeral. He had an especially poor relationship with his Uncle Bertie, the flamboyant and ever-so-slightly naughty Prince of Wales (later King Edward VII). Edward strongly resented Wilhelm and treated him not as the emperor of Germany but merely as another errant nephew unworthy of his royal attention. In turn, Wilhelm often snubbed his uncle, whom he referred to as "the old peacock" and lorded his position as emperor over him, but he was present at King Edward VII's funeral in 1910. Of course he was.

In 1913, Wilhelm hosted a lavish wedding ceremony in Berlin for his only daughter, Victoria Louise. Among the notable guests at the wedding were his cousins Tsar Nicholas, who disliked Wilhelm intensely, and King George V, who attended with his wife Queen Mary.

Wilhelm has been described by some as mentally unstable, immature, narcissistic, and a megalomaniac, wholly unsuitable for any kind of leadership. He actively pursued an aggressive foreign policy, which created the perfect storm that made the outbreak of a major European war inevitable. It was just a matter of time

---

62   Ian Lloyd, *An Audience with Queen Victoria: The Royal Opinion on 30 Famous Victorians* (Stroud: The History Press, 2019).

and opportunity. During his tumultuous thirty-year reign, the kaiser antagonized both relatives and allies alik, and was widely blamed for launching the disastrous World War I, which would cause unparalleled devastation. Despite being half English, his deep resentment and jealousy of the British fueled his hatred. So there you go. He started the war, and he wanted it, but it would inevitably lead to his downfall.

He was the supreme commander of the armed forces, with an unquestionable right to make all-important appointments in the civil service and the military. Officers, courtiers, and diplomats inevitably became tongue-lolling sycophants. Embarrassed by his physical weakness, Wilhelm had a powerful desire to prove himself. He sought to compensate for his shortcomings by retreating into his own fantasy world of the army. Wilhelm was obsessed to the point of mental instability with militarism, and he was never more content than when he was surrounded by his military friends. He aspired to be a second Frederick the Great and openly relished all the pomp of the Prussian military while passionately believing in increasing the strength of Germany's armed forces. Where else was it going to lead?

The day before the armistice was signed, Wilhelm and his family escaped to the Netherlands and remained in exile. They were bitterly disappointed and overwhelmingly frustrated until June 4, 1941, when he died of a pulmonary embolism at age eighty-two. It's ironic that he lived such a long life when he shortened the lives of so many millions. The only consolation to be gained from that is the fact that he was wracked with hatred and bitterness until he expired, so it wouldn't have been much of a life. At least he didn't suffer the fate of his Russian relatives the Romanovs.

World War I formally ended with an Allied victory on November 11, 1918. This bloodthirsty "Game of Thrones" witnessed centuries-old empirical dynasties vanishing from the map. These included the Ottoman, Habsburg, and Romanov empires. A fourth, the German Hohenzollern Empire, which had expanded during the last year of the war by occupying sizeable territories in East-Central Europe, was significantly reduced in size, deprived of its overseas colonies, and transformed into a parliamentary democracy that eventually became hugely unpopular with the German people.

Magnanimous Western European empires didn't escape the catastrophe of World War I either. Most of Ireland gained independence after a determined bloody resistance against regular and irregular British forces. The legacy of the British Empire, in countries such as Egypt, India, Iraq, Afghanistan, and Burma, responded to unrest with considerable force. France staunchly resisted any attempts to curb its imperial ambitions in Algeria, Syria, Indo-China, and Morocco. Even further afield from the main theaters of World War I, Japan was severely beating up Korea. Although the United States never claimed to harbor empirical ambitions, once it was catapulted into a position of unparalleled prominence and influence, it struggled hard to delineate its role in the world and reconcile its republican traditions with its growing power and expanding imperial domain.

The mobilization of millions of imperial subjects proved essential for nearly all of the incumbent combatant states, from Germany to the Ottoman, Habsburg, and Romanov empires and, of course, the Allied powers. Hundreds of thousands of Indian, African, Canadian, and Australian soldiers (among others) fought and died on the Western Front, as well as in a range of auxiliary theaters. Laborers from China proved vital to the conduct of the war, as did the involvement of the Japanese Empire, which used the war as an opportunity not only to try to expand further into China but also to stage an extensive occupation of Siberia that lasted until 1922. There can be no doubt whatsoever that AEF was the deciding factor that compelled the Germans to sue for peace. They ended the war a defeated and economically ravaged country with a chip on its shoulder bigger than the rock of Gibraltar.

World War I should indeed have been the war to end all wars—but it wasn't. How could it be? German nationalism would rise again, only this time there wouldn't be a disturbed emperor at the helm. This time it would be someone and something inherently more sinister, more malicious, and more hateful than anything or anyone that had gone before. The situation would inevitably culminate in a downward spiral that would lead to another world war, and this time killing innocent citizens would become part of the evil equation.

This chapter is about the seriously disaffected monarch Kaiser Wilhelm. We were always told as kids that Kaiser Bill started World War I. He was one of three principal monarchs of the age, who were as follows: Kaiser Wilhelm II of Germany, King George V of England, and Tsar Nicholas II of Russia. In fact, they were all cousins: Wilhelm and George were first cousins, George and Nicholas were also first cousins, and Wilhelm and Nicholas were third cousins. Wilhelm's mother was the sister of George's father; George's mother and Nicholas's mother were sisters from the Danish royal family. All three men were also fifth cousins, being equal descendants of King George II of England. Eventual conflict between these inbred pedigrees was inevitable. As you have read, this chapter has shown the roots of the animosity between these competitive and highly dysfunctional royal households.

CHAPTER SIXTEEN:

SETTING SUN, RISING STAR.

Every head of state throughout the civilized world should have seen this one coming, and indeed some did, but most remained in denial that it could never happen again. Some even had the bad manners to look shocked and surprised when it happened. As the League of Nations floundered and ultimately failed, it was inevitable that someone was going to have to pay for the years of ignominy and subjugation that had been inflicted on the German people as a direct result of the desperately flawed and punitive Treaty of Versailles.

Simmering discontent had been easily transposed to seething hatred for the injustice that afflicted the Germans for well over a decade. They had endured the corrupt and mismanaged Weimar Republic, which kowtowed to the victors of World War I and actively enhanced the status quo. The country was ripe for a transformation, and now they had a focal point for all this discontent provided by a charismatic, resentful former corporal who had taken defeat very personally.

In his epic about the Roman Empire, *I, Claudius*, Robert Graves had written, "Let all the poison that lurks in the mud, hatch out."[63] There was still a lot of poison after the mud of the trenches

---

63   Robert Graves, *I, Claudius* (Camberwell, Vic: Penguin Books, 2011).

had dried, and most of it was on the boots of disaffected German soldiers. The 1920s had been a tumultuous decade for nigh on everyone. The stock markets had crashed, abject poverty was rife, and the conditions for a perfect storm were prevailing yet again. In Germany, all it needed was a spark to ignite the simmering detestation that had permeated almost all levels of society by the end of the decade.

It's an inalienable fact that nothing draws two people closer than a mutual dislike of a third party. In the case of Germany, it was the allocation of blame that stoked the imaginations and satiated the seething vitriol, which now manifested in the newly appointed führer and *Reichskanzler* (Imperial Chancellor), Adolf Hitler. During the years that followed his ignominious usurping of power, Hitler managed to annex all the territories that had been previously taken from Germany by the Treaty of Versailles. By 1940, Japan had officially recognized the leadership of Germany and Italy in the establishment of a new order in Europe by signing a document that was known as the Three-Power Pact. The three countries agreed to cooperate and assist one another with "all political, economic, and available military means."[64]

On December 7, 1941, all bets were off as Japan bombed Pearl Harbor and Germany declared war on America. It would soon be time to call on the young men and women of all Allied nations to step up to the plate again.

Meanwhile in Washington DC, it was generally acknowledged that reorganization within the US Army was long overdue. When Germany had invaded Poland in 1939, the US Army was ranked in strength only seventeenth in the world, marginally behind Romania. At that time there were only three effective divisions within the whole United States. It's remarkable to reflect that only six years later they would number over six million personnel. But this time it was going to be different. This time all incumbents would also cynically target innocent civilians.

Hitler had aptly demonstrated his propensity to initiate invasions of neighboring countries when on March 12, 1938, he

---

64　The Editors of Encyclopaedia Britannica, "Tripartite Pact: World War II," Encyclopaedia Britannica (Encyclopaedia Britannica, inc.), https://www.britannica.com/topic/Tripartite-Pact.

ordered the Anschluss (connection-union). It was the green light for his troops to waltz unopposed into Austria to annex the German-speaking nation for the Third Reich and actively prevent the von Trapp family from inflicting further musical purgatory on an unsuspecting nation.

Then, on the premise that he wanted to free the subjugated German-speaking peoples of the Sudetenland, he marched into Czechoslovakia. Believing that he was on a roll, his next target was Poland—but his first priority was to negotiate with the despised Communist regime to neutralize the possibility that they would resist the full-scale invasion. August 23–24, 1939, saw the signing of the German-Soviet Nonaggression Pact in Moscow. In a surreptitious protocol, the Germans and the Soviets nefariously agreed that Poland should be divided between them, with the western third of the country going to Germany and Soviet forces occupying the eastern two-thirds.

Having made this deeply cynical agreement, Hitler assumed that Germany would be able to attack Poland without Soviet or British intervention. He gave orders for the invasion to commence on August 26, 1939. On August 25, news about the signing of a formal treaty of mutual assistance between Great Britain and Poland caused Hitler to temporarily postpone the start of hostilities. But he remained determined to ignore the diplomatic efforts of western powers to restrain him. Finally, at 12:40 p.m. on August 31, 1939, Hitler ordered the invasion of Poland to start at 4:45 the next morning. In response to this unprovoked act of aggression, Great Britain and France declared war on Germany on September 3, 11:00 a.m. and 5:00 p.m., respectively. World War II had kicked off.

During the ensuing years, Britain would stand alone and endure the retreat from Dunkirk, the Blitz, and various other conundrums in the western desert, before America stepped up to the plate to dramatically help ease the burden and level the playing field in favor of the Allied cause.

World War II also saw the advent of organized counterintelligence. There had been spies long before that, but never on a scale envisaged by Winston Churchill in 1940. That's when the cigar-chomping bulldog had commissioned the formation of the Special

Operations Executive (SOE) to, in his words, "set Europe ablaze"[65] with sabotage and intelligence gathering. It soon became obvious to all concerned that women would become an imperative aspect of this highly clandestine organization.

When researching poignant stories of brothers and sisters who went to war, there were some stories that simply grabbed the attention and beggared belief. This is one of them. To the locals in Torquay, on the south coast of England, she was known as the "crazy old cat lady." But this quiet, dignified lady guarded a well-kept secret. She was a bona fide hero. Back before World War II, she was one of two young English sisters, Eileen and Jacqueline Nearne, who wanted to do their part for their country.

The Nearne family had four children: a son called Francis, another called Frederick, and two daughters, Jacqueline and Eileen. Jacqueline was born on May 27, 1916, in Brighton, England, and her younger sister Eileen was born in London on March 16, 1921. Their father was English and their mother Spanish. They lived in England until 1923 when the family moved to France, where all the Nearnes became fluent in French. At the time ominous storm clouds were congregating on the horizon. Following the German invasion in 1940, they made their way back to England traveling a circuitous route via Portugal and Gibraltar, finally arriving in London in early 1942. Two years previous, Frederick had made his way to England to volunteer for active service, and just over a year later, his sisters made the momentous decision to follow him.

They expected to find it relatively easy to procure work as translators, but considering their linguistic abilities, the War Office had distinctly other ideas on the subject. Jacqueline was first recruited into the SOE under the cover of being a member of the First Aid Nursing Yeomanry (FANY) on the condition that she was strictly forbidden to disclose her true métier to anyone; however, she couldn't keep it a secret from Eileen, who immediately launched a successful bid to get herself accepted into the secret service.

---

65   E. H. Cookridge, *Set Europe Ablaze: The inside Story of Special Operations Executive-Churchill's Daring Plan to Defeat Germany Though Sabotage, Espionage, and Subversion* (New York, NY: Thomas Y. Crowell Co., 1967).

Eileen was initially offered a position in the Women's Auxiliary Air Force (WAAF) but respectfully declined. She probably considered her extensive knowledge of French could be used for a more important purpose, and it didn't take long before this came to the attention of the Special Operations Executive, in which her brother, Francis, also served.

Jacqueline was taught how to make Morse code transmissions with a suitcase radio. In 1943, she was dropped into France to act as a courier, carrying vital spare parts for radio transmitters inside her makeup bag, which she did for fifteen months. While there, she adeptly formed the link between several clandestine SOE groups covering a large area in and around Paris. Jacqueline, though willing to risk her own life, was completely against allowing her little sister to do the same. So when she was flown to France to work as a courier, she made her SOE bosses promise to keep Eileen, then in her early twenties, safely in Britain where she was working as a London-based signals operator who handled communications from undercover field agents in Nazi-occupied France. Eventually during the war, three of the four members of the Nearne family would be gainfully employed by SOE as undercover agents in Nazi-occupied France. Eileen could have easily done her bit and sat out the war in relative safety but that wasn't in her DNA.

In March 1944, she was parachuted into occupied France and using the codename Rose, her mission was to help set up and maintain a Paris-intelligence network called Wizard. The sole purpose of Wizard was to seek out and secure funds for the French Resistance. Eileen's role was to initiate and maintain a wireless network between Paris and London, which allowed potential financiers to check that they were dealing with genuine SOE agents as opposed to Nazi infiltrators.

It almost goes without saying that it was an extremely precarious vocation, fraught with danger, along with the possibility of imminent arrest and subsequent torture by the Gestapo. With her colleague Jean Savy, they would devise a phrase of their own choosing to confirm the agents' legitimacy. Eileen would send it to operatives in London, and when the prospective backers heard their "message personnel" repeated during broadcasts of the BBC European Service, they could be sure their contacts were authentic.

For a while Eileen was successful, but with the Gestapo becoming increasingly more vigilant, she was compelled to frequently change her location. On July 21, 1944, while operating from a deserted house on the outskirts of Paris, she was arrested. Thankfully, she had managed to destroy her notebooks and hide her equipment before she was taken to their HQ, but her radio was found and seized.

At the Gestapo HQ, she was subjected to an extensive, degrading, and brutal interrogation. Nevertheless, she refused to divulge information and stuck resolutely to her story that she was simply a Frenchwoman in need of employment who had been asked to send some messages on behalf of an English businessman. The Nazis were smart as well as evil; they didn't buy it.

In August 1944, Eileen was sent to the infamous women's concentration camp Ravensbrück (where another SOE operative, Violette Szabo, had been summarily executed). Eileen was also threatened with execution and further tortured, but she stoically refused to deviate from her cover story despite enduring unimaginable brutality. Her courageous non-compliance ensured the safety of her SOE colleagues stationed in France and the continuation of their work.

During the following months, Eileen was moved around several different labor camps until she finally ended up in Markkleeberg concentration camp near Leipzig. In April 1945, when American troops were in proximity, the inmates were sent on a forced night-time march. Eileen seized her opportunity to escape and, together with two Frenchwomen, fled the march and sought cover in a forest. Enduring several days without food, the women headed west to Leipzig and took refuge in a church. The Roman Catholic priest there hid them in a bell tower until the city was liberated by American troops on April 15.

Eileen had lapsed into unconsciousness and was revived just as American soldiers were storming the bell tower. She identified herself as a British intelligence agent, but they assumed she was delirious or lying and would not believe her. Luckily, Eileen's colleagues in London confirmed her story, and she was back in England just a few weeks later.

In recognition of her wartime service, Eileen was awarded the Croix de Guerre and received the Member of the Order of the British

Empire (MBE). After the war, she struggled with the psychological damage that she had incurred from being tortured and incarcerated in the most inhumane conditions. She lived with Jacqueline in London until moving to Torquay after her sister's death in 1982. Eileen desired a life of privacy and seclusion, rejecting any and all opportunities to celebrate her wartime heroism. She just wanted the company of her beloved felines until one day she peacefully left this life with her secrets intact. The death of an aging eccentric recluse is rarely an event to be given more than a few lines in a local newspaper, but some accurately suspected that there was more to it than that.

After her death in 2010, the truth of Eileen's remarkable life came to light, and she was buried with full military honors befitting her service and achievements. In keeping with her wishes, her ashes were scattered at sea. She was one of many unsung heroes who were quite happy to remain anonymous, but some deeds refuse anonymity. Now we know.

Fighting and suffering for one's country is one thing, but what if that country regards you and your family as enemy aliens? It makes no difference that you were born and raised there; you and your kind are not welcome. Offering up your life to fight for a country that disseminates hatred against your people wouldn't be the first consideration.

One Japanese American family's home life was seriously disrupted when the parents and other family members of three brothers, Victor, Johnny, and Ted Akimoto, were forced into an internment camp. In the United States, after Pearl Harbor, there was a nationwide fear of the Nisei, the first generation of Japanese children born in the United States who were American citizens. Despite all this humiliation the Akimoto family had suffered, the brothers still went ahead and pledged their loyalty to the country that regarded them as a potential threat, along with more than 1,400 American-born Japanese.

On February 19, 1942, President Franklin Delano Roosevelt issued Executive Order 9066, which changed the lives of hundreds of thousands of Japanese Americans living along the west coast of America. Within weeks, many Japanese Americans would be incarcerated. Thousands of Japanese were compelled to sell their homes.

Despite all this adversity, Victor Akimoto was the first to enlist. He wanted to be a role model for his brothers, and his example also motivated other Nisei men and women who would eventually volunteer for military service during World War II.

The Akimotos went out on the premise that if Japanese Americans could courageously serve in the US Armed Forces, then perhaps America would finally move beyond seeing these people of Asian descent as a different people, a different race, and just regard them as what they were: patriotic Americans prepared to fight and die for their country.

The interment naturally afflicted Victor's family who sold their home, household furnishings, and family heirlooms at ridiculously low prices. The American authorities in the assembly and internment camps strictly prohibited items such as cameras and short-wave radios, along with ceremonial Japanese *katana*, *wakizashi*, and *tanto* swords. In mid-1943, the Akimoto family reported to the Granada War Relocation Center in Colorado, known commonly as Camp Amache.

Then on June 12, 1942, President Roosevelt authorized the activation of a segregated US Army combat unit, which became known as the 442nd Regimental Combat Team (RCT), comprised of Japanese Americans from Hawaii and the camps. On January 31, 1943, Roosevelt said, "The principle on which this country was founded and by which it has always been governed is that Americanism is a matter of mind and heart. Americanism is not, and never was, a matter of race or ancestry." He went on to say, "Every loyal American citizen should be given the opportunity to serve this country."[66] The Akimoto boys became a part the 442nd RCT.

The 442nd RCT combined with the all-Japanese American 100th Infantry Battalion, which was already fighting in Europe. While in Europe, the combined 442nd-100th became the most decorated military unit for its size and length of service in US history. Their remarkable success on the battlefields of Europe and the Pacific

---

66   "Americanism Is Not, and Never Was, a Matter of Race or Ancestry," WSU Libraries Digital Collections (Washington State University), https://content.libraries.wsu.edu/digital/collection/propaganda/id/221.

went a long way to changing the negative attitudes of many Americans toward the Japanese Americans in the United States.

The three Akimoto brothers who served America in the 442nd endured very different fates. In March 1944, Johnny, the youngest of the brothers, received his orders to ship out to Italy. Victor and Ted's orders were to remain in the states and train new recruits. The news of Johnny's orders to ship out infuriated Victor. He had promised his folks to keep Johnny and Ted safe. Victor approached the company chaplain who, like most serving clergy in the US military, had a great deal influence, and he then spoke to the company commander on Victor's behalf, in an attempt to seek alternate solutions.

Victor wanted to take Johnny's place on the front line, but the commander explained that qualified sergeants, like Victor and his brother Ted, were needed stateside to train new recruits that were arriving at the army camp daily. Therefore, Victor's request was vehemently denied. The only feasible solution available to him at the time was to request a demotion to private. Because of the urgent need for trained frontline combat soldiers in Europe, this request was reluctantly granted.

Meanwhile in late 1943, Johnny was preparing to land on the beaches near Anzio, Italy. This was going to be a vital element of the southern European campaign for the Allies due to its close proximity to Rome. The primary objective was to capitalize on the resounding victories in North Africa by continuing to pressure the Axis in southern Europe and hopefully relieve pressure on the Soviet forces on the eastern front.

The battle for Anzio began January 22, 1944, and lasted until June 5, 1944. The Allies soon discovered that the mountainous terrain was definitely not conducive to infantry tactics, and they soon became wedged in an extensive mud-inundated marshland surrounded by German and Italian troops who occupied the high ground and rained hell on the Allied lines. The battle inflicted nearly forty thousand Allied casualties, including seven thousand killed and thirty-three thousand wounded or missing in action. While in combat, Private First Class Johnny Akimoto contracted hepatitis and became seriously ill. He died on August 2, 1944. For his service he was awarded the Bronze Star Medal, the European-African-Middle Eastern Campaign Medal, the Good Conduct Medal, the Victory Medal, and the Combat Infantryman Badge.

Victor also served with the 442nd RCT-100th Battalion in Italy during the Rome to Arno campaign. While fighting in Italy, he was cited for taking on four German soldiers single `handedly without a weapon. Technical Sergeant Victor also served in the Vosges Mountains of France and saw action in Belmont, Biffontaine, and participated in the Lost Battalion rescue. (Not to be confused with Charles Whittlesey's World War I Lost Battalion.)

Victor was badly wounded during the fierce battle to rescue this particular Lost Battalion, the First Battalion of the 141st Regiment of the Thirty-Sixth Division, a Texas unit, which was surrounded by the enemy and isolated for almost a week. This punishing four-day battle was one of the bloodiest fighting experienced by the 442nd. He was taken as a prisoner of war (POW) on October 24, 1944, by the Germans and died of his injuries on December 14, 1944, at German POW camp, Stalag 1X-B (Bad Orb) hospital in Germany.

Ted's war was entirely different. While his brothers were fighting the enemy and the elements in Italy, Ted remained stateside and worked for the army as a training sergeant. Although assigned to the Infantry Training Center at Fort McClellan, Alabama, after training at Fort Benning, Georgia, Ted enquired about being sent overseas to fight alongside his brothers in the 442nd.

When a company clerk reliably informed Ted he had new orders, he leapt at the opportunity to get away from Fort Benning. Ironically, Ted, who wasn't a fluent Japanese-language speaker, took command of 120 Nisei translators and interpreters in preparation for his next assignment; he was being deployed to Japan in preparation for a possible invasion.

On August 6 and August 9, all bets were off when atomic bombs were unleashed on Hiroshima and Nagasaki. Days before Ted was due to be deployed, imperial Japan surrendered on August 14, 1945. The war in the Pacific was well and truly over.

Despite the invasion being cancelled, Ted's unit still shipped out and docked in Yokohama. When he saw the desultory state of the Japanese people, along with other GIs, they grabbed whatever they could carry from the ship, including candy, food, clothing, and medical supplies for them. Sometime later, Ted heard that the Army Signal Corps needed a photographer, so he applied for the position and was appointed as one of General Douglas MacArthur's photographers, but surprisingly it was for the purpose of taking well-posed photographs of the man himself.

Using MacArthur's personal plane, Ted took some of the very first photos depicting the horrific effects of the devastation and radiation poisoning in Hiroshima. As the only brother to survive World War II, Ted assumed that he had intentionally been kept away from combat because the US Army did not want his parents to lose another son. This may have indeed been the case. After four years of noncombat service, Ted received an honorary medical discharge from the army after the removal of one of his kidneys.

Many years later, Ted discovered that Victor had struck a bargain with the chaplain to prevent Ted from being deployed to the frontlines in Europe. Ted never forgot the sacrifice that his brothers made for their country, which had initially berated and humiliated both him and his family, and he never forgot what Victor had done for him. In 1988, President Ronald Reagan signed the Civil Liberties Act that publicly apologized for the incarceration of Japanese.

Americans and offered each survivor $20,000 in restitution. During the signing of the law, President Reagan stated, "Here we admit a wrong. Here we affirm our commitment as a nation to equal justice under the law."[67] Took a while though, didn't it?

Some years ago, I met a proud veteran, of the 442nd Regimental Combat Team. Despite terrible odds, the 442nd's actions distinguished them as the most decorated unit for its size and length of service in the history of the US military. As you've read, this chapter has some stories of Japanese brothers who fought together and apart in World War II. It also contained a story that I heard from a journalist friend of mine some years ago concerning the covert lives of two ex-SOE operatives.

---

67   Steven Johnston, *The Truth about Patriotism* (Durham, NC: Duke University Press, 2007).

CHAPTER SEVENTEEN:

SAVING PRIVATE WHO?

Unless one has been living under a rock in Wyoming for the past twenty or so years, there's every possibility that the magnificent movie *Saving Private Ryan* may have come to your attention at some point or another. As Ted Akimoto discovered, there was a sole-surviving son rule, and being the last surviving son was usually a ticket home (or a pass-combat-and-do-something-less-dangerous card). This is the whole premise on which the movie is based. But it is highly unlikely, to the point of ridiculous, that a staff officer at the Pentagon, much less the chief of staff, would have taken the time to stop everything and personally intervene to protect the last surviving son from potential harm. It was, however, a noteworthy gesture from the military that did actually spare some parents from further agonizing grief.

This small observation doesn't detract from this volume's acknowledgment that those first twenty-five minutes of *Saving Private Ryan* are quite possibly the most powerful depictions of the Normandy invasion's brutality ever filmed.

The most prolific responses gained from searching for the truth behind the movie usually brings up the Niland brothers, but there were others too. There's every possibility that attention was drawn to the Nilands from Tonawanda, New York, because one of them had served with the famed 101st Airborne Division, which was the subject of the famous TV epic *Band of Brothers*. Some of the actors who were in this magnificent series went on to better things while a significant number of the lesser known were reduced to participating in overpriced, cheesy *Band of Brothers* tours. Another detrimental effect was that the series paved the way for every shaved-headed, cerebrally-challenged moron from Normandy to Eindhoven to watch it, then claim to be World War II experts, and even have the audacity to provide guided tours.

According to Steven Spielberg, the core subject matter for *Saving Private Ryan* was very loosely gained from the wartime experiences of Sergeant Frederick "Fritz" Niland (1920–1983) of company H in the 501st Parachute Infantry Regiment of the 101st Airborne Division. He was friends with Warren "Skip" Muck and Donald Malarkey, two of the *Band of Brothers* series' key characters who served with company E ("Easy Company") in the 506th Parachute Infantry Regiment of the 101st Airborne Division.

Fritz was stationed at Aldbourne—a small village roughly six miles northeast of Marlborough—in Wiltshire, England, with US Army paratroopers of Easy Company, Second Battalion of the 506th Parachute Infantry Regiment, 101st Airborne Division. They were based there from late 1943 to mid-1944.

One weekend, Fritz was in the company of Donald, Warren, Chuck Grant, and Joe Toye when they procured passes to London. Once there, they had the occasion to meet up with Fritz's brother, Bob, who was a squad leader in the Eighty-Second Airborne and had seen action in both North Africa and Sicily. They spent the evening in a city pub listening to Bob talk about his combat experiences.

It's a well-documented fact that Fritz fought courageously during those first tumultuous days of the Normandy campaign. He had been forced to jump early after his plane was hit by enemy flak. He landed miles away from his target and struggled behind enemy lines for nine days. He eventually, with some help from the French Resistance, rejoined his unit in time for a key battle to secure the town of Carentan and link Allied forces at the designated Omaha and Utah beaches.

A few days following his return to his unit, Fritz ventured over to the Eighty-Second Airborne Division to see how his brother had faired. On his arrival at the Eighty-Second HQ, he was regretfully informed that Bob had been killed on D-Day. He was told that Bob's platoon had been surrounded, and he manned a machine-gun, hitting the Germans with harassing fire until his platoon retreated through the encirclement. He had used up several boxes of ammunition before being tragically killed.

Before having time to digest the news of Bob, Fritz decided to visit the Fourth Infantry Division position to see another brother, Preston, who was a platoon leader with these "Ivy Men." Sadly, Second Lieutenant and Platoon Leader Preston in company C, First Battalion of the Twenty-Second Infantry, Fourth Infantry Division had been killed just a day after Bob. He died during heavy fighting to take the German-held Crisbecq Battery, just north of Utah Beach, where the Fourth should have landed. The Fourth Infantry Division had experienced a relatively unopposed landing on Utah Beach and had actually landed a good four miles south of their objective. It was at the juncture of the Tare Green and Uncle Red sectors that General Theodore Roosevelt Jr. furrowed his brow and abruptly pointed his cane to the ground as he uttered, "We'll start the war from right here. Go inland any way you can, we'll worry about those bastards another day!"[68]

Downcast and utterly disheartened, Fritz returned to his unit where he heard that the company chaplain, Father Francis Sampson, was looking for him. He wanted to inform Fritz that his third brother, Edward, a pilot in the China-Burma-India theater, was assumed to have been killed that same week.

A check of a nearby cemetery in Normandy revealed Bob's grave. So, believing Fritz to be his family's only surviving son, Father Sampson notified the War Department and initiated the paperwork to have him brought home. Shortly after, the army authorities agreed to remove him from the combat zone as soon as it was feasibly possible. Father Sampson escorted Fritz to Utah Beach and a

68   Martin King, Mike Collins, and Jason Nulton, *To War with the 4th: A Century of Frontline Combat with the US 4th Infantry Division, from the Argonne to the Ardennes to Afghanistan* (Philadelphia, PA: Casemate, 2016).

plane flew him to London on the first leg of his return to the States, where Fritz spent the rest of war working as an Military Policeman in New York.

Fritz's parents, Michael and Augusta, had received all three telegrams from the War Department on the same day. But despite their unimaginable heartache, they still had two surviving sons: Fritz and his brother Edward who, despite reports to the contrary, hadn't been killed in Burma. He had parachuted from his B-25 Mitchell and roamed dolefully around the Burmese jungle before being captured on May 16, 1944. He survived the horrors of a Japanese POW camp and was found about a year later on May 4, 1945, when the camp was liberated. Just for the record, in his book *D-Day: June 6, 1944*, Stephen Ambrose had incorrectly stated that Edward had died in Burma.

On the flipside of the coin is the story of four American brothers who all served and returned from World War II. One of those brothers was William Hannigan who said, "I was a member of H Company, 504 Parachute Infantry Regiment [82nd Airborne Division], and we had come off the line for rest and kind of repair. We were in [*sic*] Ramerville in France when the Germans invaded the forest. And we were pulled out on trucks; inadequately armed and given, you know, clothes. We were just pulled out in necessity in this thing. Wasn't well thought out, but we did get up on these trucks and were taken right up to Bastogne. My brother was at Bastogne, and I always told him that we saved his skinny little butt, but maybe we shouldn't have. And he later on, you know, being a paratrooper and in the 101st and me in the competitive Eighty-Second, whenever he asked how many jumps I'd made, whatever I said, he would add one. Whatever he said, I would add one. And we bought it so many years that we kind of don't know."[69]

Bill's brother Gordon E. Hannigan served with the 501st Parachute Infantry Regiment, 101st Airborne Division. Unfortunately, there isn't a great deal of information about the remaining two brothers. But it's an established fact that John "Jack" Burton Hannigan served in the US Navy throughout the war and Arnold

69   Michael Collins and Martin King, *Voices of the Bulge: Untold Stories from Veterans of the Battle of the Bulge*. Zenith Press, 2011.

Alfred Hannigan was in the US Army. They all did their part, and they all survived.

Those indomitable fighting Irish stepped up to the plate yet again in World War II. When war reached the United States in 1941, six sons of an Irish American family living in Sledge, Mississippi, all dutifully signed up and went to war. Their parents back home in Mississippi, William Dudley O'Neal and Mary Etta Peeples O'Neal, were inevitably distraught but respected their sons' wishes and dutifully waved them off one by one. They would have had no idea that their beloved boys were going to witness some of the biggest and most violent encounters by US forces in World War II. From the battles of Midway, Guadalcanal, and Okinawa to the Normandy campaign and the Battle of the Bulge, there would be a member of the O'Neal clan present. But would they all make it home?

The youngest O'Neal, Iven (known as "Bruce" to his friends and family), served as part of the Ninety-Seventh US Infantry Division in Le Havre, France, and the Rhineland. He would see service with General George Patton's invincible Third Army. The Ninety-Seventh arrived at the ETO (European Theater of Operations) on March 3, 1945—quite late in the war, but they would still see some hard fighting. It was the last of the Organized Reserve infantry division to enter active duty. They were sent to Europe due to the high number of American casualties that had been incurred as a direct result of the Battle of the Bulge and were prepared to participate in the final assault on Germany. Later on in his military career, after Japan had surrendered, Bruce participated in the occupation. Bruce's brother Harl also served in Europe under Patton. But he got there sooner, landed in Normandy just days after D-Day, and took part in the Battle of the Bulge. Stanford White O'Neal served as part of the Sixth Air Force.

One newspaper article claims that Harl was based in England, but according to military sources, the US Sixth Air Force served primarily in defense of the Panama Canal. They were also engaged in antisubmarine operations in and around the Caribbean. Harl "Bud" O'Neal passed away at age ninety-seven, on Saturday afternoon, January 6, 2018, at Oxford Health and Rehab in Oxford, MS.

Robert Glenn O'Neal served in the South Pacific as a Navy Seabee, but the most harrowing story to emerge from the saga of these six brothers concerns Ralph O'Neal, who certainly had the most dramatic escape from the war. He served in the navy aboard the ill-fated USS *Vincennes*.

On August 8, when Captain Frederick L. Riefkohl (commander of the *Vincennes*) decided to turn in at 12:50 a.m. after a long shift. On August 9, he left his ship in the hands of the executive officer, Commander W.E.A. Mullan. Around an hour later, lookouts registered flares and a star shell accompanied by the low intimidating growl of gunfire. Six Japanese cruisers and one destroyer, under the command of Japanese Vice Admiral Gunichi Mikawa, had turned north and were steaming with great haste directly toward the *Vincennes*.

The first Japanese searchlight beams had zeroed on the *Vincennes*, and at roughly 1:55 a.m., the American cruiser opened fire with her main battery turrets. Shortly after, the *Vincennes* shook and shuddered under the impact of Japanese shells raining in from an ominous coal black sky.

On hearing this unexpected pounding that his ship was taking, Commander Riefkohl leapt out of his bed and charged up to the bridge where he rang down to the engine room with orders to increase speed. Unfortunately, owing to the thunderous roar of naval combat, internal communications were disrupted. It is doubtful that the order was ever received. Still, moving at 19.5 knots, the heavy cruiser reeled again under the withering impact of another series of direct hits.

At 2:00 a.m., the *Vincennes* veered starboard in an attempt to evade enemy fire, but Japanese gunners had no intention of allowing the already-disabled American vessel to escape intact. The coup de grace was delivered by a couple of torpedoes that tore into the ship's number one fireroom and rendered the *Vincennes* useless. She had been hit at least fifty-seven times by enemy shells and was gradually beginning to capsize, when at 2:10 a.m. the Japanese mercifully ceased fire and retired. At 2:30 a.m., Riefkohl reluctantly gave the order to abandon ship. Serviceable life jackets and rafts were issued, and the crew began the sorrowful task of complying with their commander's order. Struck from the navy list on November 2, 1942, the *Vincennes* was awarded two battle stars for her participation in the Battle of Midway in 1942 and the invasion of Guadalcanal.

This would have been little comfort for Ralph's parents. They had heard news reports on the radio and now sadly presumed their son was dead. With six sons dispersed in various theaters around the world, the trepidation of losing another son became too much for the O'Neal parents to bear. William O'Neal sought help from Governor Theodore G. Bilbo to retrieve his youngest son Bruce from the war.

What they didn't know was that Ralph had dove from the precipitous deck of the *Vincennes* as it listed to port and aimlessly bobbed around in shark-infested waters, praying to be rescued. As luck or divine intervention would have it, his prayers were eventually answered. Deeply affected by this terrible ordeal, Ralph returned home a mere shadow of his former self.

Unfortunately, the tedium of military communications took a great deal longer in the 1940s than they do today. The senior O'Neal's message eventually arrived as the war in Europe was winding down. When it reached Bruce, he decided that he wanted to remain with his comrades and stay fighting for his country like his brothers.

The war also took its toll on the last brother Jack. He served as part of the Sixth Marine Division in the Pacific and Alaska. After the battles of Saipan and Tinian, they were stationed at a rest area in Saipan. The Sixth Marine Division (and reinforcing units) earned a Presidential Unit Citation. The citation reads: "For extraordinary heroism in action against enemy Japanese forces during the assault and capture of Okinawa, April 1 to June 21, 1945."[70] It took Jack years to come to terms with the numbing post-traumatic stress disorder as a result of the terrible Battle of Okinawa (April 1, 1945–June 21, 1945). It was the last major battle of World War II, and one of the bloodiest. Incessant rain, kamikaze fighters, and fierce fighting on land, sea, and air resulted in a terrible harvest of death on both sides.

---

70   Benis M Frank and Henry I Shaw, Jr., *Victory and Occupation* (Washington, DC: Historical Branch, US Marine Corps, 1968).

Six brothers went to war and six returned, but they were all deeply affected in some way or another. In 2010, Bruce decided that it was time to open his story of his family's wartime experiences to the world.

The fate of the Sullivan brothers was referred to in *Saving Private Ryan*. Now here's the rest of the story.

ACTION REPORT *479 Serial 03719. Loss of USS Juneau, November 13, 1942. Lieutenant Commander H. E. Schonland. On November 13, 1942, the USS Juneau was struck on the port side, probably in the vicinity of the ship's bridge, by a torpedo fired by a Japanese submarine. The entire ship exploded in a column of brown and white smoke and flame that rose over a thousand feet in the air. The Juneau literally disintegrated with the loss of all aboard. This report of the incident was filed by the commander of the USS San Francisco, which was accompanying the Juneau at the time of its destruction. The Japanese submarine was not intercepted.* [71]

It was a lucky St. Patrick's Day when explorers in the South Pacific discovered the wreck of USS *Juneau*, a World War II light cruiser that was sunk after being torpedoed. The wreckage was about 2.6 miles below the surface of the Pacific Ocean, just off the coast of

---

71   National Archives Washington DC.

the Solomon Islands. More than six hundred American servicemen were killed in the attack. Among the dead were five sons from the same family from Waterloo, Iowa: the Sullivans. This was the highest price that any one single American family paid in the whole of World War II.

Considering the life they had lived with their dysfunctional parents back in Waterloo, it's hardly surprising that they escaped to join the US Navy. Their father, Tom, was a physically abusive, chronic alcoholic who went off on serious liver-wrenching benders whenever he had a couple days off from his job as a freight conductor on the Illinois Central Railroad. Alleta, their mother, suffered from bouts of deep depression during the Great Depression, which wasn't particularly original but could render her immobile for days on end. Barely completing junior high, all five boys had left school early and were frequently unemployed. They had a sister called Genevieve "Gen" who doesn't feature much in the story but lived to tell the tale.

Collectively, the Sullivan brothers were regarded as local troublemakers who enjoyed nothing more than knocking back cheap liquor and raising hell in the neighborhood. They were literally Hells Angels before the term had even been coined. As members of an early motorcycle gang known as the Harley Club, they attended rallies and meetings at a biker bar and charged around Waterloo terrorizing the more genteel folks there (who naturally felt intimidated by this reckless rabble of errant youths). So it's not surprising that local residents breathed a collective audible sigh of relief when George and Frank enlisted in the US Navy in 1937 at peacetime. They served together for four years before returning home in May 1941, whereupon they found work with their brothers at the local meatpacking plant.

All bets were off after the Japanese attack on Pearl Harbor, which galvanized the five Sullivans to want to sign up and join the navy. It isn't documented if the locals were relieved at this prospect, but in all likelihood they probably were. Even the youngest brother Al—who although being only seventeen at the time was already married and had a twenty-one-month-old son—was so desperate to get away from the tethers of his premature domestic situation, he would have even joined the French Foreign Legion. His brother George wrote to the Department of the Navy in late December asking that the Sullivans and two friends from their motorcycle club be allowed to serve together.

The local church was filled to capacity when this news got around, and their prayers were answered. The navy somewhat reluctantly acquiesced to the Sullivan's request that they all serve on the same ship. This is despite the fact that although the service didn't actively encourage family members to serve together, they needed recruits, so didn't discourage the practice either.

It was a momentous day when the brothers were assigned to the light cruiser *Juneau*, which was commissioned on February 14, 1942. A local press photographer took a shot of the five smiling Sullivans on board the vessel, and the local residents in Waterloo rejoiced. They could now take out the trash without the prospect of being mugged and towed down the street attached to a Harley. The well-disseminated publicity photo would later become a familiar emblem of American sacrifice. The family now became local celebrities and regularly made the front pages in Waterloo. Tom and Alleta's offspring became known as "the Navy's five Sullivans."[72]

The *Juneau* spent its first months in service on the fringes of naval combat against German U-boat wolf packs in the Caribbean and both North and South Atlantic before heading out to the southwestern Pacific theater on August 22, 1942. Armed with its specialized array of antiaircraft guns, the rapid Atlanta-class light cruiser had the potential to protect naval forces from enemy planes. Although it was swift in the water, the only downside was that its insubstantial armor also made the light cruiser dangerously vulnerable to torpedoes and surface attacks from enemy vessels.

On November 12, 1942, these shortcomings were highlighted when the vessel became engaged in a fierce night battle not far from Guadalcanal. During that action, a Japanese torpedo severely damaged the ship, and the following morning, the crippled light cruiser retired from the battle area. As she floundered and struggled to make eighteen knots on a looking-glass ocean, she presented a tempting target for nearby Japanese submarine *I-26*. The following

---

72   James Sullivan, *Unsinkable: Five Men and the Indomitable Run of the USS Plunkett* (New York, NY: Scribner, 2020).

day, accompanied by the USS *San Francisco*, the USS *Juneau* was struck on its port side by a torpedo. The hit was probably in proximity to the ship's bridge, which caused her magazines to detonate. Then within seconds a violent explosion blew the entire ship to smithereens, and the vast column of brown and white smoke and flame rose over a thousand feet in the air. The *Juneau* literally disintegrated and sank in just forty-two seconds with the presumed loss of all aboard. The commander of the USS *San Francisco* filed a comprehensive report of the incident.

Four of the Sullivans, Coxswain Francis Sullivan, Second Class Seamen Joseph, Madison, and Abel failed to make it to the deck in time to abandon their doomed ship. Gunner's Mate Second Class George Sullivan, who had been wounded during the November 12 night action, managed to dive over the side into shark-infested waters and drag his limp body onto a nearby raft.

Within a half hour of the sinking, an American B-17 bomber soaring overhead spotted men in the sea. There were, by the pilot's estimate, between one hundred and two hundred sailors clinging to debris from the cruiser. In retrospect, this could have been an exaggeration of the actual numbers who managed to get off the *Juneau* in time.

The B-17 pilot radioed Captain Gilbert Hoover of the light cruiser *Helena* and commander of the flotilla, who, possibly fearing the loss of more men, decided not to deviate from his course. Then the aircraft circled again to drop supplies, but for several vital days the navy did nothing to rescue the stricken sailors. Desperate time passed, as one by one the meager survivors of the *Juneau* succumbed to their injuries, dehydration, or shark attack. When South Pacific Area Commander Admiral William F. Halsey was informed of what had transpired in the exchange between the pilot and Captain Hoover, he immediately stripped Hoover of his command. Nevertheless, a full week passed after the sinking before only ten survivors of the estimated 140 thought to have survived were fished out of the ocean. They were not in a good way.

It was assumed that at least one, or maybe even two, of the Sullivans had survived. Two survivors who did make it alive vividly recounted death of eldest brother George Sullivan. He had scrambled on to one of the small life rafts but after three or four days, he was growing weak and hallucinating. One night, Gunner's Mate Second Class Allen Heyn told a naval interrogator "George declared that he was going to take a bath. He removed his uniform and jumped into the water. A little way from his raft, 'a shark came and grabbed him and that was the end of him. I never seen him again.'" [73]

Sometime later in early 1943, there were stories circulating in Waterloo alluding to the fates of the Sullivan brothers. This prompted Alleta Sullivan to write a poignant letter to the Department of the Navy: "I am writing you in regard to a rumor going around that my five sons have been killed in action in November. A friend from here came and told me she got a letter from her son and he heard my five sons were killed. I am to christen the U.S.S. TAWASA Feb. 12th at Portland, Oregon. If anything has happened to my five sons, I will still christen the ship as it was their wish that I do so. I hated to bother you, but it has worried me so that I wanted to know if it was true. So please tell me."[74]

On Monday morning, January 11, she received the reply that bowled her over from Lieutenant Commander Truman Jones, who delivered the news in person. With Tom and Alleta and Al's wife, Keena, assembled in the family's living room, Jones read from a carefully prepared script, "I'm afraid I'm bringing you very bad news. The Navy Department deeply regrets to inform you that your sons Albert, Francis, George, Joseph, and Madison Sullivan are missing in action in the South Pacific."

The formal announcement made no absolutely mention of the terrible debacle that exacerbated the final act of this tragic naval drama. Adding salt to the wounds, local people in Waterloo who had also lost sons in the war began complaining vociferously about the preferential treatment the Sullivan family was receiving. How perfectly petty and small-minded. No other family had lost five sons. The Sullivans deserved preferential treatment for the sacrifice their boys had made in defense of their country.

---

73   "One Who Survived." American Heritage, February 1, 2022. https://www.americanheritage.com/one-who-survived

74   Kathleen Sullivan Weishaar, *The Sullivan Brothers History during the War Years, July 1942-July 1948* (Nortonville, KS: Kathleen S. Weishaar, 2013).

At the behest of the navy, President Franklin D. Roosevelt wrote Alleta a personal letter of condolence: "As Commander in Chief of the Army and the Navy, I want you to know the entire nation shares your sorrow. I offer you the condolence and gratitude of our country. We, who remain to carry on the fight, must maintain the spirit in the knowledge that such sacrifice is not in vain."[75] Naval authorities then encouraged the parents to visit Washington DC, where First Lady Eleanor Roosevelt and Vice President Henry A. Wallace personally met with the parents.

The Sullivan's surviving sister Genevieve enlisted in the US Naval Reserve as a specialist (recruiter) third class, and, along with her parents, they personally visited over two hundred shipyards and manufacturing plants to encourage the workers there.

In conclusion, *Saving Private Ryan*, was ultimately about *Saving Private Ryan*, but it was a metaphor, an excellent example of the thousands of heartbroken families who willingly or reluctantly sent their sons off to a precariously uncertain future. Many would survive and return *corpus intactum*, but they wouldn't be the same boys who left those cities and farmsteads across the United States to answer the call.

After the movie was released, many enthusiasts asked me if it was based on real events and real people. (I had the same problem with *The Da Vinci Code*.) I discovered that there are numerous candidates on whom it could have been based. Some of the events depicted in the movie were real enough, and it was obviously inspired by these; however, what transpired was that many families sent all their sons to war. Some made it back, but a significant number didn't. In this chapter there are some well-known contenders for the "Private Ryan" title, and there are some lesser known too. My dear departed friend veteran William "Bill" Hannigan told me about his service with the Eighty-Second Airborne during the Battle of the Bulge and how all his brothers signed up too.

75   Holly S. Fenelon, *That Knock at the Door: The History of Gold Star Mothers in America* (Bloomington, IN: iUniverse, Inc, 2012).

CHAPTER EIGHTEEN:

MORE DEVOTED SISTERS.

As the title for this chapter indicates, here are more stories of courage and heroism of truly devoted sisters. It is estimated (these estimates have an inane tendency to vary) that in the course of World War II around 350,000 women served in the US Armed Forces, not forgetting the more than six million vital munitions workers who pulled long hours in grimy factories from coast to coast. Who can forget the rousing image of Rosie the Riveter? Then there were over three million who volunteered for the Red Cross. Some were killed in combat or captured as prisoners of war. Over sixteen hundred female nurses received various decorations for courage under fire.

Women's duties in the military were wide and varied but mainly included working as nurses, driving trucks, repairing airplanes, and performing clerical work. The Women Airforce Service Pilots (WASP) flew planes from the factories to military bases. Other branches of the military that recruited women included the Women's Army Corps (WAC), the Navy Women's Reserve (WAVES), the Marine Corps Women's Reserve, and the Coast Guard Women's Reserve (SPARS)—not forgetting the thousands of female chemists and engineers who were recruited to work on the Manhattan Project, developing the atomic bomb.

Adolf Hitler scathingly derided Americans as degenerate for putting their women to work. The role of German women, he said, "was to be good wives and mothers and to have more babies for the Third Reich." So what about those vicious women concentration camp guards like the despicable Irma Grese who worked at Auschwitz? After the liberation of the camps, Grese was convicted of crimes involving murder and ill treatment of prisoners. At the age of twenty-two she was consequently sentenced to death. One of her lovers was reputed to have been Josef Mengele, the "Angel of Death." It's very doubtful that their relationship was established for the purpose of procreation as prescribed by Hitler, who deigned from personally indulging the practice by all accounts. Which brings us to a popular song that was sung during the war regarding the Führer and his horrible clique. Sung to the tune of "Colonel Bogey" (the tune the prisoners whistled in *Bridge on the River Kwai*), it goes like this:

> *Hitler has only got one ball*
>
> *The other is in the Albert Hall*
>
> . . . .
>
> *Himmler is someone sim'lar*
>
> *But poor Goebbels has no balls at all.*

In America when war broke out, quickie marriages became standard practice, as teenagers married their sweethearts before their men went overseas. In fact quickies, in some form or another, were ubiquitous. Although fettered by an entirely misogynistic male-dominated society, American women were considered integral to the war effort. They served in uniform, both at home and abroad. General Dwight D. Eisenhower felt that he could not win the war without the aid of the women in uniform.

The following story is about four wonderful ladies who joined different branches of the military to do their part. Moreover, they were sisters from a family that had recently moved to Boulder, Colorado. Their extremely attractive photo came to the nation's attention when it appeared on a recruitment poster bearing the rousing inscription "Dad had no boys." America understood the power of public relations back then too.

The family patriarch, Charles Gahm, was a Swedish immigrant who had moved to Boston, Massachusetts, in 1911 at the tender age of sixteen. His name Gahm is actually of German origin and refers to someone from Gahme near Pössneck in Thuringia, Germany. Charles was eager to extol his love and loyalty to his adopted country. A mere six years later, he registered for the draft and went on to serve as a private first class in the US Army during World War I.

It was while he was serving in the army that Charles went home on leave. While in New York, he had the good fortune to meet his friend's cousin, Eleanor Sheideberg, the daughter of German immigrants. According to the family, when their eyes met, they were both immediately smitten (a classic case of love at first sight). He married Eleanor Scheideberg on April 14, 1919, in North Platte, Nebraska.

The four Gahm daughters were Florence, Evelyn, Ellen, and Dorothy. Ellen and Dorothy were born in Nebraska in 1920 and 1922, respectively. They were born before the family's move to a cattle ranch thirty miles north of Sterling, Colorado. Florence was born on the ranch in 1923 and Evelyn in 1927.

The oldest two daughters had left home and were serving their country in 1943 when their parents and the two youngest sisters moved to Boulder. Ellen, the oldest at age twenty-four, was a private first class in the Women's Army Corps, stationed at the Cushing General Hospital in Framingham, Massachusetts.

Dorothy, a year younger, had been a teacher in Sterling before joining the Marine Corps at Cherry Point, North Carolina. Florence, twenty-one, was an aviation machinist's mate, second class in the WAVES. Her thirty-three months of duty included a six-month tour in Hawaii.

Closer to home, eighteen-year-old Evelyn attended the University of Colorado, and then received training at Colorado General Hospital as a cadet nurse.

After the war, all of the sisters had families of their own and went their separate ways. Evelyn Patrick died in Lander, Wyoming, in 1995; Florence Wall died in Montrose, Colorado, in 1998; and

Ellen Peterson died in 1999 in Victor, Idaho. Dorothy Ellison and her husband Claude moved to a ranch in Kremmling, Colorado, after longtime ownership of a gas station at 28th St. and Valmont Rd. in Boulder. Dorothy died in 2003. She and her parents are buried in Boulder's Green Mountain Cemetery.

By the end of World War II, a majority of women wanted to keep their jobs, but many were inevitably forced to quit because of the men returning home and the greatly-reduced demand for war materials. Women veterans who had served their country with distinction were vehemently discouraged when they tried to take advantage of benefit programs for veterans, such as the GI Bill. It transpired that a nation that desperately needed their help in a time of crisis was neither ready nor receptive of the greater social equality, which would slowly evolve during the ensuing decades after the war. During the war GI calendar girls looked fabulous, but they had a lot to answer for.

Another one of the vital components that helped the Allies on their way to victory was good intelligence. Much of which was provided by those who were employed at Bletchley Park, where the German Enigma machine had been decrypted by the sublime, inimitable genius Alan Turing and his remarkable team.

All employees were compelled to sign the Official Secrets Act, hence many of their stories didn't emerge until the 1970s when a shocked nation, which wasn't particularly difficult to shock, began reading published memoirs of former SOE and intelligence operatives. This brings us to the tale of two more British sisters, Pat Davies and Jean Argles, who both worked as highly secretive codebreakers for British intelligence during World War II. Moreover, they didn't even tell their parents, who remained happily oblivious throughout the war and long after it had elapsed.

Due to the highly sensitive nature of their work, the Owtram sisters never told either parent what they were doing for the war effort.

In 1941, their father Cary Owtram, a distinguished World War I veteran and senior major, was attached to the British 137th Field Regiment, Royal Artillery, which was originally based in the seaside town of Blackpool, Lancashire, in the north of England. In that same year, his regiment sailed out from Liverpool onboard the *Dominion Monarch*. This was a former luxury cruise liner that had been requisitioned as a troop carrier. She sailed on September 22, 1941, to a top-secret destination in Singapore, where he was honorably promoted to the rank of colonel. He was there when Britain signed an unconditional surrender to Japanese forces on February 15, 1942. It was a humiliating and fateful day when the colonel reluctantly became one of around eighty thousand British, Indian, and Australian prisoners captured by the Imperial Japanese Army. When he was initially interned at Chungkai POW camp, his seniority saw him appointed as the British commander. Chungkai was the largest of dozens of camps that were strung out along 260 miles of the Siam-Burma (Thailand-Myanmar) railway. Back in dear old "Blighty" (a British colloquial expression for home), the colonel's family had heard the terrible news of the dramatic fall of Singapore but had no idea what had become of him.

They had to wait until April 1942 to know he had survived, and it was a whole year later that they received his first postcard. The entire family was absolutely devastated, but their devoted mother, Bunty, kept the family and the home running like clockwork, regardless of the terrible strain of not knowing if her husband would make it through his internment. Bunty also worked as an air raid warden.

Thousands of miles away in Thailand, the colonel led an overpopulated camp that housed around eight thousand prisoners, many of whom were in a pitiful physical condition. They were injured, desperate, starving, sick, and subjected to the most inhumane treatment imaginable by their Japanese captors and the dreaded *Kempeitai*, the Imperial Japanese Army's equivalent of the Nazi's Gestapo.

Despite all the adversity, the colonel did what he could to help raise morale among the prisoners, even to the point of risking immediate execution with the razor-sharp blade of a samurai sword. He established a police force, a hospital, a theater, and even went as far as establishing a news-sharing network system that sourced its highly dangerous information from a clandestine wireless. In true British don't-let-the-bastards-grind-you-down style, the colonel, a talented tenor, also helped organize theatrical productions and concerts, which surreptitiously poked fun at the despicable Japanese guards and their ruthless commander.

Meanwhile in England, Pat and Jean were keeping themselves busy. In August 1942, a year after their father had left, Pat had joined the Wrens (WRNS, or the Women's Royal Naval Service) as an interceptor, and thanks to her German-language skills, she was sent for training as a special duties linguist. She was eventually set to work at secret naval listening stations.

When she was asked to sign the Official Secrets Act, she hesitated but understood entirely that she wouldn't be able to reveal anything about her occupation. The potential consequences were dire indeed and punishments for breaching the act could result in execution. She listened to German Enigma code transmissions, passed these along to Bletchley Park, and reported German operational messages right up until the German fleet capitulated. Then she did translation work at General Eisenhower's HQ.

Her sister Jean signed up with the First Aid Nursing Yeomanry (those FANY's were everywhere, which has already been established in this volume). She later expanded her talents into code and cipher work for the intelligence services.

The sisters and their mother had absolutely no idea that their father—along with other unfortunate prisoners—was suffering the most devastating conditions when they were put to work on the infamous Siam-Burma railway, as depicted in the movie *Bridge over the River Kwai*. Beset by amoebic dysentery, beriberi, malaria, tropical ulcers, and malnutrition, it is estimated that one-fifth of all the POWs who worked on the railway during its sixteen-month construction between 1942 and 1943 died in the most squalid conditions. Others were murdered by their guards or succumbed to exhaustion.

By the time the war in the Far East had ended, 61,811 POWs (30,131 of them British) and 177,900 Asian laborers had worked on the railway. A small number of US troops who survived the sinking of the USS *Houston* during the Battle of the Java Sea also worked on this railway.

After it had been completed, all officers, along with Colonel Owtram, were transferred to the brutal Kanchanaburi POW camp in Thailand. Surrounded by dense forested hills and glistening paddy fields, this was also the location of the infamous bridge.

Due to the highly sensitive nature of their work, the sisters never told either parent what they were doing for the war effort.

In 1945 while sailing home from the Far East, Colonel Cary Owtram trembled with anticipation at the prospect of being reunited with his beloved family. Thoughts of his wife Bunty, son Bobby, and daughters Pat and Jean had sustained him and helped him endure those abominable three years of captivity. He found it peculiar to say the least when a Red Cross nurse on his troopship insisted she had met his youngest daughter in Italy a few months previous. The colonel told the nurse that she must be mistaken.

In their father's mind, Pat and Jean were still young girls safe at home in Lancashire, but the nurse insisted that she had tended a certain Jean Owtram, who had fallen off a cliff into the sea in Italy. The nurse then asked if this person was any relation. The colonel insisted that it must have been a different person.

Keeping secrets wasn't the sole preserve of the sisters. They later discovered that during his time in captivity, the colonel had secretly kept a diary. He wrote his memoirs and sent them to multiple publishers but was extremely depressed when he received only rejection letters. Most of them said that military history wasn't a particularly interesting subject. Colonel Owtram died in 1993, aged ninety-three, having received an Order of the British Empire (OBE). In 2017, his book, *1000 Days on the River Kwai*, was finally published and rightfully received a lot of praise. Shame that this didn't happen while the dear man was alive.

After the war, Pat attended university before becoming the first female reporter on the staff of the *Daily Mail* in Manchester. She later moved to the BBC where she met her future husband, Ray Davies. Jean became a social worker and later the careers officer at the new Lancaster University where she met Michael Argles, fell in love, and got married, simply because that's how they did it in those days. During an interview on May 3, 2020, both sisters revealed their true occupations during World War II, and then set about visiting numerous schools throughout the United Kingdom relating their stories. At the time of writing, Pat Davies is a sprightly ninety-seven, and Jean Argles is ninety-five. Bless them.

Now imagine the scene. Two young, pretty, blond-haired, blue-eyed Dutch girls on bicycles laughingly approach a handsome SS officer and begin to flatter him. They flirt and pander to the man and eventually talk him into taking a little walk into the nearby woods for some fun and games. The SS officer is easily tempted by the prospect of some illicit sex, so he obediently follows them. The canopy in the woods reduces visibility. As the SS officer enthusiastically begins to remove his trousers, a hand reaches from behind, covers his mouth, and then as quick as a flash, a razor-sharp blade is gruesomely drawn across his throat. Blood spurts and runs down the victim's collar drenching the surrounding foliage. The murder is fast, silent, and bloody. Another enemy has been eliminated, and absolutely nobody suspects those two young girls, who stealthily remove the dead SS officer's luger (a type of pistol) and wallet before returning to their bicycles as if nothing happened.

It's a widely accepted fact that many British SOE operatives, both male and female, worked with various resistance groups in Europe, and many paid for this with their very lives.

Working for the resistance in a Nazi-occupied country was at best precarious, at worst downright fatal. But to some extent, it was even more dangerous for domestic resistance operatives than it was for the SOE. This was because when Nazi authorities arrested a member of the resistance, they would also target family members and friends, innocent or otherwise. In some cases, this practice was used to coerce the captive into providing information, but more often than not, it was just a despicable and heinous act of vengeance.

Their "rule by fear" led to many associates of resistance members being ostracized in their own communities and becoming social pariahs. Another powerful deterrent for even knowing anyone in the underground was the possibility of ending up in a Nazi labor or concentration camp. But this didn't deter two brave young Dutch sisters who had no qualms at all about defying the Nazis.

The Oversteegen (pronounced "overstaygen") sisters Freddie and Truus (pronounced "trues") were noble Dutch resistance fighters who survived to tell the tale. On May 10, 1940, Nazi forces invaded the Netherlands, which in turn eventually became home to one of Europe's most irascible and effective anti-Nazi networks. At the time of the German invasion, the girls were only fourteen and sixteen years old, respectively. Their dear friend and fellow resistance operative, the nineteen-year-old Hannie Schaft, whom the Nazis called "the girl with the red hair," became a revered Dutch national hero, and rightfully so.

When the occupation began in earnest, Freddie and Truus never imagined they would eventually be complicit in the killing of German soldiers and collaborators. They were both raised in the historic Dutch city of Haarlem. After their parents divorced, they gleaned their first lessons in active defiance at home from their staunchly working-class, communist mother. By all accounts, she instilled a sense of commitment and compassion in the girls' minds and actively encouraged them both to join the local resistance— which wasn't necessarily conducive to great parenting, but it fired up the girls.

Leading up to the Nazi occupation, the Oversteegen family had been preoccupied sheltering German Jews, dissidents, and homosexuals who were desperate to flee persecution under the punitive Nazi regime of the 1930s.

After the invasion, Freddie and Truus handed out pamphlets opposing the occupation and daubed the walls in Haarlem with anti-Nazi propaganda posters. In 1941, their actions came to the attention of a local Dutch resistance group, and they were asked to join their ranks. They became the only two females in a clandestine seven-strong team, collectively known as Haarlem Council of Resistance.

Once there, they were taught how to handle explosives and weapons, and most importantly how to avoid detection and deflect attention while on duty. It was remarked that when Freddie wore her hair in braids, she only looked about twelve years old, and who could possibly suspect someone so young and innocent looking? As the two girls meandered around Holland on their bicycles, Nazi occupation forces and collaborators didn't pay any attention. Freddie's first assassination occurred when she approached a Dutch collaborator in a local park who was assembling a list of Jewish people to hand over to the German authorities. Freddie calmly approached the woman and asked her name. When the woman replied, and her identity was confirmed, Freddie sedately whisked out a revolver from her satchel and shot the woman in the forehead point blank.

They would have had no idea that the girls were carrying vital documents and weapons for the resistance. In time, they expanded their activities to include burning down a Nazi warehouse, along with escorting Jewish children and refugees to hiding spots. They also organized false identification papers for them.

As the war and the occupation progressed, the sisters even worked "honey traps" on SS officers and collaborators, luring them into the woods to face inevitable death. Before long, the sisters graduated to eliminating their own targets, physically mowing down these selected targets from their bicycles with concealed machine guns. Other activities entailed acting as vital lookouts while fellow resistance operatives murdered German soldiers, blowing up bridges, and railway tracks.

One day their beloved friend Hannie was captured and executed. This only served to galvanize the sisters' convictions even further. Thankfully, they both survived the war and lived well into their nineties. They died within two years of each other: Truus in 2016 and Freddie in 2018. The trauma that Freddie experienced during the war haunted her for the rest of her life.

In the Netherlands, acts of individual heroism and resistance were not only celebrate, but came to emblematize the Dutch nation as a whole. The notion of collective resistance has become a cornerstone of the founding myth disseminated in contemporary Dutch society. This is a flagrant attempt to deflect from the theory that in the Netherlands, a larger percentage of the population collaborated with the Nazis than in any other Western European country.

It's also important to note that Dutch Jews who returned to the Netherlands after the war returned home to a largely unwelcoming and unsympathetic society. A society that actually expected gratitude from them, for the assistance they received during the war. Furthermore, Dutch society actively suppressed Jews from publicly voicing their experiences. It's also interesting to point out that three-quarters of Dutch Jews residents in the country during the Nazi occupation were murdered. In other Western European countries such as Belgium and France, these percentages were considerably lower. The Dutch government was particularly diligent in prosecuting resistance operatives and assisting the Nazi authorities with their ignominious round-ups of Jews.

There were simply too many stories of sisters who went to war to confine their deeds to one chapter. One particular trio of singing sisters became, for many, the sound of World War II. Another little Dutch duet didn't sing but were an absolute menace to occupying Nazi forces in the Netherlands. The connecting factor here is clandestine operations performed by some of these gallant people during a very dangerous time. I heard about the Dutch sisters from a Dutch historian friend of mine who lives out near the German border, and I thought they earned a mention here.

CHAPTER NINETEEN:

SINS OF THE FATHER.

In 1940, the German children of notorious Nazis such as Heinrich Himmler, Hermann Göring, Rudolf Hess, Hans Frank, Martin Bormann, Albert Speer, and Josef Mengele lived a life of opulence and privilege. They were, in most cases, oblivious of the abominable atrocities perpetuated by their fathers, who all held prominent positions in Adolf Hitler's Third Reich.

When Germany was resoundingly defeated, many of these children would see their domestic arrangements implode. In time, some chose to disown their past, but there were others who most definitely didn't. And while some openly condemned their fathers, others elevated and worshipped them unconditionally to the very end.

Rudolf von Ribbentrop was the son of a leading Nazi. Born on May 11, 1921, in Wiesbaden, he was one of five children from parents Joachim and Anneliese (neé Henkell) von Ribbentrop. His mother was the daughter of a prominent sparkling wine producer, and his father was a company wines and spirits salesman before Hitler appointed him as foreign-policy advisor in 1936. Precisely what qualifications Joachim had for the position apart from being a leering sycophant is unclear. While daddy Joachim worked as Hitler's ambassador to Britain from 1936 to 1938, Rudolf attended the exclusive Westminster School and learned to speak fluent English. One of his classmates, Peter Ustinov, went on to become a much-beloved British actor, writer, and director. In his classic 1977 memoir, *Dear Me*, Peter wrote that Mr. von Ribbentrop arrived each morning "dressed like the rest of us but with the Nazi party youth badge—swastika, eagle all—prominently and incongruously displayed in his lapel."[76]

Joachim went on to play a key role in forging the short-lived pact with Joseph Stalin's Soviet Union, which led to the invasion and dissection of Poland.

Eager to support the Nazi cause, Rudolf joined an SS infantry regiment shortly after the war began in 1939 and went on to serve in military units in Czechoslovakia, France, and the Soviet Union. In December 1944, he was fighting in Normandy with the fanatic Twelfth SS Panzer Division Hitlerjugend (Hitler Youth), which he also served with during the Battle of the Bulge. He was wounded several times and was awarded the Iron Cross, Second Class, among other honors.

Thanks to the prominent position of his father, Rudolf had met many top Nazis and been in the company of Hitler himself on numerous occasions. He was very proud of his father. The von Ribbentrops were considered by many to be Nazi royalty. Shortly before the end of World War II in Europe, Rudolf even accompanied his father on a visit to see a paranoid and deluded Hitler in his bunker in Berlin.

It was February 3, 1945, while temporarily quartered with his regiment in Berlin that Rudolf met with his father. He asked if Rudolf would like to join him and Hitler in the bunke, beneath the Reich Chancellery building, which had already been hammered almost beyond recognition by Allied air raids. Rudolf initially refused, but while walking among the ruins of a nearby hotel, he accepted a sentry's invitation to enter the underground complex.

Only twenty-three at the time, Rudolf had known Hitler since his childhood and considered him a close family friend. He was shocked when he saw how far the Führer's health had deteriorated.

76   Peter Ustinov, *Dear Me* (Arrow, 2000).

Rudolf wrote, "His face was gray and puffy, his bearing bent in a way that looked as if he had a hump, holding one uncontrollably shaking with the other, his steps a shuffle."[77]

Rudolf recalled how he listened in silence as Hitler ranted about how the German army could fight the Allies to a standstill. Joachim von Ribbentrop then assured his son that a fresh regiment was being dispatched to the front every day. Rudolf was a soldier. He was extremely well educated and intelligent. He knew the reality of the situation full well and was somewhat taken aback when his father wholeheartedly agreed with Hitler's delusional procrastinations.

On April 30, 1945, Hitler and his wife of roughly thirty hours Eva Braun committed suicide in the bunker. At 3:15 p.m., they had closed the door and sat down together on a small sofa. He was fifty-six. She was thirty-three. They hadn't made plans for a honeymoon and didn't escape to South America as some deranged TV producers in Hollywood have falsely claimed. Germany surrendered unconditionally to the Allies in Reims, France on May 7, 1945, ending World War II and the Third Reich.

Rudolf was clever enough to hand himself over to American troops south of the Danube River and was sent to a succession of prisons and camps for three years before being released from a French military prison in 1948. His father, Joachim von Ribbentrop, was convicted at the Nuremberg trials on four counts, including deliberately planning a war of aggression and various other war crimes. Both father and son had anticipated the guilty verdict, so it came as no surprise when von Ribbentrop was hanged along with ten other significant Nazis on October 16, 1946.

Sir Hartley Shawcross, an English barrister and prominent politician who served as the lead British prosecutor at the Nuremberg War Crimes tribunal, summed up the prosecution case against Joachim von Ribbentrop by saying that "no one in history has so debauched diplomacy. No one has been guilty of meaner treachery."[78]

Many years after, Rudolph was still full of bitterness about the way in which his father had been treated at the trial. He wrote that

---

77   Rudolf von Ribbentrop, *Mein Vater Joachim Von Ribbentrop Erlebnisse Und Erinnerungen* (Graz: Ares-Verl, 2013).
78   Hartley Shawcross, *Life Sentence: The Memoirs of Lord Shawcross* (London, UK: Constable, 1995).

the court "had been so structured as to make unequivocally sure that the process taken was directed to capital punishment[79]," which although Rudolph felt was unfair, many were inclined to disagree.

After Rudolf's release from prison in 1948, he attempted to join the family liquor business, but some relatives felt, with some justification, that the name von Ribbentrop was a potential liability. His mother, who was no shrinking violet, threatened to sue them. One newspaper claimed that the company offered Rudolf's mother $100,000 to drop the suit. After a while, Rudolf got bored with the situation and decided to follow a career in banking, which he did until he retired. He died at the age of ninety-eight on May 20, 2019, in Ratingen, near Düsseldorf, Germany. His brother Adolf (wonder who inspired his name?) and sister Ursula Painvin survive him.

Gudrun Burwitz was the daughter of Reichsführer-SS, Heinrich Himmler, the infamous orchestrator of the "Endlösung der Judenfrage," the Final Solution to the Jewish question. She remained a dedicated Nazi until her death.

79   Mein Vater: Joachim von Ribbentrop: Erlebnisse und Erinnerungen: Ribbentrop, Rudolf von/ISBN 10: 3902732237 / ISBN 13: 9783902732231

When Gudrun Margarete Elfriede Emma Anna Burwitz died on May 24, 2018, aged eighty-eight, her funeral was well attended. Granted, a significant number of the hair-challenged attendees knew her maiden name and knew only too well that Gudrun was the daughter of *Reichsführer-SS*, Heinrich Himmler. Himmler was the infamous orchestrator of the *Endlösung der Judenfrage*, the Final Solution of the Jewish Question. He would have been mightily proud that his beloved daughter remained an unrepentant, vitriolic, Holocaust-denying Nazi until her last breath.

Gudrun maintained throughout her life that the Holocaust was little more than an Allied fabrication. She wasn't unique by any means. Insidious Holocaust deniers insist, among other things, that because there is not one signed document from Hitler ordering the Holocaust, the Holocaust itself is a huge hoax. Furthermore, some of these deniers insist that the Allies tortured perpetrators into testifying about their role in the killing process and that the survivors who testified about Nazi crimes against Jews were all lying merely out of self-interest. Their accusations and claims have about the same credibility as alien abductees.

Some Holocaust deniers even have the barefaced audacity to claim that those "few" Jews who perished died from natural causes or were legitimately executed by the Nazi state for committing criminal offenses. They further assert that the number of Jewish deaths during World War II has been grossly exaggerated.

Gudrun was Heinrich and Margarete's oldest and only legitimate child. She was born August 8, 1929, near Munich. She had a half-brother named Helge (born 1942) and a half-sister named Nanette Dorothea (born 1944). Both were a result of her father's illicit affair with his young secretary, Hedwig Potthast, that had started in 1939.

Himmler adored and doted on his daughter Gudrun. He even had her flown to his offices in Berlin on a fairly regular basis, and when she was at home with her mother, he would call her most days and made sure to write her a letter every week. He called her by her childhood nickname "Püppi" (doll) throughout his life. Gudrun even accompanied her father on a visit to the Dachau concentration camp, which she noted in her diary.

Himmler's extramarital affair was possibly incited by two of his SS subordinates, "golden boy" Reinhard Heydrich and Karl Wolff, who both had rather attractive wives. Previous to Himmler's affair, he had attended a Nazi banquet with his wife Margarete (or "Marga") who, according to Lina Heydrich (Reinhard's wife), wore "size fifty knickers, that's all there was to her."[80] Himmler was indeed embarrassed by her appearance and probably jealous of Heydrich and Wolff. According to Bella Fromm (a Jewish journalist living in exile in America who personally saw Margarete in July 1937), she was described as his dirty-blond, insipid, fat wife, adding that the pleasures of the table are apparently about the only pleasures she gets, since Himmler keeps her at home. It's good that Bella was writing from a safe distance when she published that.

On May 11, 1945, after the unconditional surrender, Himmler swapped his round-rimmed glasses for an eye patch, shaved his moustache, and went on the run disguised as Sergeant Heinrich Hitzinger. On May 21, 1945, Himmler was arrested by British soldiers at a checkpoint near Bremervörde, not far from Hamburg. Two days later while undergoing a medical examination by British army doctors, Himmler crunched a cyanide capsule in his mouth. Within minutes, he was as dead as a doornail.

Despite compelling evidence to the contrary, for the rest of her natural life, Gudrun continued to insist that the British had assassinated her beloved father. Holocaust deniers are not easily swayed by insignificancies such as proof and evidence. In April 1945, Gudrun and her mother were also apprehended and taken into custody. During a postwar interview in 1945, a British interrogation officer asked young Gudrun, "Do you know how many people your father cremated at Dachau? Or how many he gassed at Oranienburg? Of course you do. You're Herr Himmler's daughter, after all."

Gudrun later complained that she and her mother were held in various camps, and treated as though they had to atone for the alleged sins of her father. She continued to be loyal to her father,

---

80   James Wyllie, *Nazi Wives: The Women at the Top of Hitler's Germany* (St. Martin's Press, 2020).

even after he was captured and news of his war crimes was made public. They were both forced to testify at the Nuremberg trials and both were eventually released in November 1946.

Gudrun never renounced evil Nazi ideology and repeatedly sought to justify the actions of her father. Right up until her death, she helped run and was the figurehead of an organization known as *Die Stille Hilfe* (Silent Help). The sole initial purpose of this dark and secretive organization was to provide an assistance network for former SS personnel and SS camp guards. Among those Gudrun helped were Klaus Barbie (1913–1991), the "Butcher of Lyon"; Martin Sommer (1915–1988), the "Hangman of Buchenwald"; and Anton Malloth (1912–2002), convicted in 2001 of beating at least one hundred prisoners to death in Theresienstadt.

One of the original aspirations of the organization was to attempt to change public perception regarding Nazi war criminals. They arranged press campaigns, petitions, and wrote innumerable letters to try and convince the public these men had only been following orders, or *Befehl ist Befehl* ("an order is an order"). They further argued that the perpetrators of some of the most heinous acts in the history of the human race should be seen as innocent.

For obvious reasons *Die Stille Hilfe* became extremely popular with neo-Nazi groups around the world. Apparently the parameters for membership entail that the applicant should have at least two functioning brain cells. More would be superfluous.

It's remarkable that people living on a quiet, verdant side street in northern Virginia still have no idea that their innocuous-looking neighbor is the daughter of one of the most notorious murderers in human history. Brigitte Höss lived there under an assumed name, and her true identity had never been revealed. She was a former fashion model that lived and worked in the United States for over forty years. It's beyond ironic that the Jewish owner of the fashion store in Washington, DC, where Brigitte was gainfully employed, had fled Nazi Germany in 1938. She left just before Nazi authorities unleashed their seething hatred of the Jewish population in a series of carefully orchestrated acts of persecution. The most notorious became known as *Kristallnacht* (The Night of Broken Glass), due to all the shattered glass that littered the streets after the wanton vandalism and destruction of Jewish-owned businesses, synagogues, and homes. Back in the day, the shop in DC provided gowns and clothing for the wives of congressmen and senators.

According to the personnel records of the SS kept in the National Archives, Ingebrigitt Höss came into world on August 18, 1933, on a farm not far from the Baltic Sea. The farm run by her parents, Rudolf and Hedwig, was a magnet for errant German youths obsessed with ideas of racial purity. Brigitte was the third of five children (three girls and two boys). When her father, Rudolf Höss, joined the ranks of the SS in 1933, his career prospects improved dramatically, and he quickly rose to prominence. In 1934, he became part of the SS administration at the notorious labor camp Dachau. On August 1, 1938, Rudolf was appointed as adjutant of the Sachsenhausen concentration camp where he remained until early 1940, when he was appointed *Kommandant* of a newly built camp in the Polish town of Oswiecim, better known as Auschwitz.

In May 1941, SS commander Heinrich Himmler personally informed Rudolf that Hitler had authorized the Final Solution of the Jewish Question and that Auschwitz had been specifically chosen for this purpose. Rudolf dutifully converted Auschwitz into a mass extermination camp, eventually installing gas chambers and crematoria capable of killing and disposing of two thousand human beings an hour.

Brigitte had an extraordinary childhood, living an idyllic life in proximity to the mass extermination camp between the ages of seven and eleven. She was entirely ignorant that just a few yards from the garden where she played with her brothers and sisters people were living and dying in the most abhorrent conditions imaginable. Brigitte's mother described their villa beside Auschwitz as "paradise." They were provided with cooks, nannies, gardeners, chauffeurs, seamstresses, hairdressers, and cleaners, some of whom were actual prisoners, whose lives hung on a very fine thread indeed. They even ordered Jewish craftsmen to make toys for the children.

The palatial Höss residence was adorned with furniture and illicit artwork confiscated from mainly Jewish families. From an upstairs window, Brigitte and the rest of her family could even see the prisoner blocks and the crematorium that emitted a tower of pungent black smoke twenty-four-seven. She had long since buried these memories, preferring instead to recall visiting the horses and German shepherd dogs that were kept near the camp.

Brigitte was thirteen years old when British soldiers captured her father in March 1946 and handed him over to American forces. He was compelled to provide testimony at the Nuremburg trials and became the first senior person to admit the extent of the wholesale murder that had occurred under his direction at Auschwitz. After the trial had concluded, Rudolf Höss was given to the Polish who first prosecuted, then hanged him on makeshift gallows beside the only remaining gas chamber in Auschwitz. The rest had been destroyed shortly before the Soviet army liberated the camp on January 27, 1945.

Brigitte and the rest of the Höss family moved back to Germany after the end of the war and lived in abject poverty for many ensuing years. In the 1950s, Brigitte managed to get away from Germany and began to make a new life for herself. Her looks and figure came to the attention of the notable Balenciaga fashion house, and she was hired to work for them as a model for over three years. In 1961, she married an Irish American engineer who was working in Madrid for a Washington, DC-based communications company. They had a daughter and a son, and then in 1972, they all moved to America and bought a house in Georgetown. Brigitte had an agreement with her husband along the lines of, "Whatever you do, don't mention the war." When the couple divorced in 1983, her husband moved to Florida.

Brigitte's mother, Hedwig, visited her daughter in Washington, DC, every few years because there were no authorized travel restrictions imposed on the spouses of former Nazi war criminals. While in Washington, Hedwig spent her time babysitting her grandchildren while Brigitte worked at the clothes store. They never discussed the past. On September 15, 1989, Hedwig died in her sleep while visiting her daughter. It's a kind of poetic justice that her mortal remains were interned among the graves of Jews, Christians, and Muslims.

Brigitte, who was battling cancer when last heard from in 2012, made an annual flight to Florida to spend time with her sister Annegret, who flew in from Germany for the occasion and met her there. Their brother Klaus died in the 1980s somewhere in Australia. Her other brother, Hans Jürgen, and elder sister, Heidetraud, both still live in Germany. Whenever Brigitte was asked about her murderous father, she often said that "he was the nicest man in the world. He was very good to us."[81] This is probably why she was living covertly in northern Virginia.

She was a young child when her father commanded Auschwitz and cannot possibly be held accountable for his sins, but she never took the opportunity to condemn the man either! Some of the children of other high-ranking Nazi officials, such as Edda Göring, Wolf Rudiger Hess, and Gudrun Himmler, flatly refused to accept the fact that their fathers were guilty of indescribable war crimes and continually protested their innocence. But there were some who wanted to atone for their fathers, even though they were not personally responsible. Here's one in particular.

Anyone who saw *Schindler's List* knows the name of that murdering despot, Nazi camp commander Amon Leopold Göth. Ralph Fiennes accurately portrayed this bloodthirsty, swaggering Nazi in Steven Spielberg's epic movie about the Holocaust. Göth was little more than a vile Austrian sadomasochist who thoroughly enjoyed inflicting fear, pain, and death on his victims. As he arrogantly rode about the camp on his white horse, he literally had the power of life and death in his hands. He would kill prisoners, men, women, and children at random. So apart from Mozart, what good ever came out of Austria?

A survivor of Płaszów concentration camp who suffered daily abuse as one of the maids in Göth's villa later recalled, "When you saw Göth, you saw death." Helen Jonas-Rosenzweig, whose character was famously depicted in *Schindler's List*, also worked as one of Amon Goth's maids. She said, "As a survivor I can tell you that we are all traumatized people. It's inconceivable that any human being would be capable of such horror, of such atrocities. When we saw him from a distance, everybody was hiding, in latrines, wherever they could hide. I can't tell you how people feared him."[82]

81   Rudolf Höss, *Commandant of Auschwitz: The Autobiography of Rudolf Hoess* (Pan Books Ltd., 1974).
82   Brad Prager, *After the Fact: The Holocaust in Twenty-First Century Documentary Film* (New York, NY: Bloomsbury Academic, 2015).

Monika Göth, the illegitimate daughter of Amon Göth and his mistress Ruth Irene Kalder, was born in 1945. It was ten months before her father was sentenced to death on September 13, 1946, at the Montelupich prison in Kraków, not far from the site of the Płaszów camp where he worked. Her mother lived with Amon at the villa in Płaszów and did everything in her power to suppress information about her husband's infamous past. She often told Monika that he had been simply killed during the war and flatly refused to elaborate.

Amon Göth was a married to Anni, and they had two children who lived in Vienna. It was Oskar Schindler who introduced him to Ruth Kalder in 1942. She was a qualified beautician and aspiring actress originally from Gliwice near Kraków. At the time she met Amon, Ruth was working as a secretary at Schindler's famous factory.

The couple partied, played tennis, and rode horseback together. Ruth even witnessed him hunting humans. In a 1983 BBC interview, she vainly attempted to defend Amon Göth and claimed that she never personally visited the camp. During this interview, she was shown the transcripts of his war crimes trial, and a day later she took her own life.

When Monika was a mere eleven years old, she discovered that her father had been hanged for war crimes. When the movie *Schindler's List* was released, she went to see it and was apparently angry because her father had been depicted as a monster. Despite this, Monika participated in a documentary film in which she gave a full and frank account of what it was like living with the ghost of Amon Göth. She wrote to one of his former camp servants, Helen Jonas-Rosenzweig, and in 2004, they met for the first time at the memorial monument in Płaszów before visiting Amon's former villa. Helen was initially hesitant to agree to the meeting because her memories of the past were still simply too traumatic.

Now retired after working as a university administrator, Monika Hertwig (who, at the time of writing, is still alive), lives with her husband, Reinhart Hertwig, in Weissenburg, Germany, where she continues her efforts to educate young people about the real history of the Holocaust.

Club-footed nut job Joseph Goebbels, the Reich's minister of propaganda, was one of Hitler's closest confidants. He died with his dangerously deranged, fanatic wife Magda in the Berlin bunker. Their six children (Helga, twelve; Hildegard, eleven; Helmut, nine; Holdine, eight; Hedwig, six; and Heidrun, four, whose names all started with "H" in honor of Hitler) didn't survive the fall of the intended one-thousand-year Reich either. Magda could not bear the thought of her children having to live in a world without Hitler.

She even refused Albert Speer's offer to smuggle her kids out of Berlin and allegedly said to Hitler's secretary, Traudl Junge, "I would rather have my children die, than live in disgrace, jeered at. My children stand no chance in Germany after the war."[83]

Joseph Goebbels, the Reich's Minister of Propaganda and one of Hitler's closest confidants, died along with his dangerously deranged, fanatic wife Magda and their six children in the Berlin bunker.

Bearing this thought in mind, she approached Doctor Helmut Kunz, who on the evening of May 1, 1945, assisted Magda with the wicked infanticide of her own children. It was a macabre and horrific occasion when a very obviously deranged Magda Goebbels tenderly dressed the girls in long white nightgowns while gently combing and tying pretty ribbons in their hair. Then while the children were all together in one room, but not yet sleeping, the

83   Traudl Junge and Melissa Muller, *Until the Final Hour: Hitler's Last Secretary*, trans. Anthea Bell (New York, NY: Arcade Publishing, 2005).

doctor carried out his grim duty. "Have no fear," said Magda, "The doctor here is going to give you an injection of the sort that all children and soldiers get."[84] When she left the room, Kunz injected them all with morphine, beginning with the eldest daughter first, then the son, then the other daughters. It took around ten minutes for them all to die.

Another version of the story claims that Magda Goebbels wasn't able to kill her children alone, so Kunz called on Hitler's physician Ludwig Stumpfegger, who had provided the morphine. Stumpfegger entered the nursery with Magda and gave the kids something "sweetened" to drink. Later, Kunz claimed it was Magda herself who crushed the ampules of cyanide into the children's mouths.

Two hours later as they were leaving the room, Magda, her face pale and eyes reddened, said that it was all over. Then she went into the *Führerbunker* unattended. At about 9:00 p.m., Magda and Joseph Goebbels walked to the Reich Chancellery Garden and simultaneously swallowed cyanide capsules. Before they crunched the capsules, Joseph ordered an SS soldier to shoot him several times after they had ingested the poison to make sure that he was dead. Then the couple's bodies were doused with gasoline and incinerated.

Before she married wobbly Goebbels, she had another child by her first marriage, Harald Quandt, who survived the war. He became a successful industrialist in the postwar era and died in a private airplane crash in 1967. Other descendants of Nazis, such as Bettina Göring and her brother, have even gone as far as getting sterilized to avoid furthering their defiled blood lines.

It is morally and ethically wrong to inflict the sins of the father or mother on their innocent offspring, but it is equally immoral to venerate those who have inflicted untold misery and death on millions of innocents. Children of notorious or even lesser-known Nazis, who actively seek publicity for their associations, have a social obligation to condemn and prevent the dissemination of hatred.

Former German SS officer Oskar Gröning stood trial when he was ninety-four-years-old. Nicknamed the "Accountant of Auschwitz," he was charged by German prosecutors as an accessory

84   Roger Manvell and Heinrich Fraenkel, *Doctor Goebbels: His Life and Death* (New York, NY: Skyhorse Publishing, 2010).

to murder in 300,000 cases. He claimed in his defense that he didn't personally kill anyone in his role at the Auschwitz concentration camp. That's true. He didn't kill anyone, but he was an accessory to the fact, a cog in the evil machinery that murdered millions, and that alone made him culpable. He was found guilty but died while awaiting sentencing. Before he died, he expressed regret and spoke openly of his Auschwitz experiences on the premise that he wanted to counter Holocaust deniers, such as Gudrun Burwitz and her nefarious clique.

Thankfully Hitler did not have any children and neither did his sister, Paula (1896–1960). There are still five surviving descendants of Hitler's half-sister Angela (1883–1949) and half-brother Alois (1882–1956). They agreed among themselves not to have any children, assuring that the Hitler bloodline will definitively end with them.

I met a person by the name of Gudrun Burwitz at a secret location in Germany around fifteen years ago while researching and filming material for the TV series *Greatest Tank Battles* for the History Channel. What I didn't know was that Ms. Burwitz was the daughter of the man who orchestrated the murder of six million people the Nazis declared as undesirables or *Untermenschen*, which translates as "lesser humans." I wanted to know what legacy the children of top Nazis endured after the end of World War II. Did they carry a burden of guilt? Or did they venerate the actions of their fathers? This chapter explained who did and who didn't.

CHAPTER TWENTY:

LIKE IN THE MOVIES.

Over the years popular media has made much of sibling relations, toxic or otherwise. Stories of feuding families, solid sisters, and battling brothers usually have good ratings. One story that emerged shortly after the end of World War II touched millions of hearts and continues to do so even today.

Anne Frank's story based on her moving diary has been immortalized in books and various movies since her death in Bergen Belsen in 1945. Both sisters died of typhus.

A few hundred miles away in the Netherlands on July 6, 1942, a family went into hiding to escape the roundups of Jews that were occurring there on an almost daily basis. Anne Frank's story, based on her moving diary, has been immortalized in books and various movies since her death in the Bergen-Belsen concentration camp in 1945. After the family went into hiding, Anne, along with her older sister Margot and their parents, would spend the next two years concealed in a tiny attic apartment above their father Otto Frank's business at Prinsengracht 263 in Amsterdam.

On August 4, 1944, police in Nazi-occupied Amsterdam arrested eight Jews. Among those captured on that day were Anne, Margot, and their parents. They would have had little knowledge of the horrors they were going to witness, but the sisters would stay together.

Exactly one month later, the girls huddled together in a corner of a cattle wagon, which was part of the final transport of 2,087 Dutch Jews that left the Dutch internment camp at Westerbork. The destination? Auschwitz. They would spend tortuous days in a crammed cattle wagon with around forty other men, women, and children. The wagon was locked from the outside and everyone in that small space was breathing foul air, saturated with the nauseous stench of pungent human detritus, as they fought and jostled for space ravaged by hunger and thirst. The following day, September 5, became known as "Mad Tuesday" when in a fit of guilt and cowardice sixty-five thousand Dutch Nazi collaborators absconded and wormed their way to Germany.

On the Eastern Front, the Soviet army was making good progress. In late 1944, as they neared the locations of some of the concentration camps, thousands of prisoners from the east, many suffering from hypothermia and starvation due to forced marches, were sent to Bergen-Belsen concentration camp where conditions had deteriorated significantly during the past months. There were no sanitary facilities there at all, food was incredibly scarce, disease was rampant, and the water supply was grossly inadequate for the recent large influx of prisoners. According to official records, Anne and Margot Frank arrived in Bergen-Belsen from Auschwitz on October 30. By the time the harsh winter of 1944 set in, both sisters were suffering from typhus.

One prisoner, who was on one of the trains from Auschwitz to Bergen-Belsen, recalled the experience.

> *We were suffocating in a tiny space saturated filth, fumes, sweat…ravaged by thirst and lack of space….The Germans refused to open the train cars for even the most basic needs….At night, under a torrent of gunfire and machine-gun fire, the train crossed regions under attack by partisans or airplanes. There was one air raid siren after another. The Germans would get out of the train and take shelter wherever they could while we remained, piled up in the box cars, very visible on the tracks, panic-stricken.*
>
> *And when we finally arrived…not having the slightest idea where we were….Then the sad procession began: faded and yellow like the ground, starved, exhausted, pale…we dragged ourselves…along an endless road that led to the Bergen-Belsen camp.*
>
> *Many succumbed and fell exhausted by the wayside. The guards, not wanting to expend ammunition would simply cave in the brains of these unfortunates with the butts of their rifles. We resembled mute, deathly human shadows, moving along slowly toward a very uncertain future. I recall passing residents of local German villages dressed and well groomed in all their finery. They displayed only a passing interest in this ghastly parade. After the war many German civilians said that they had no idea, but they knew, they knew and they didn't care. I saw one young German boy draw his index finger across his throat indicating that we were going to die. Bergen-Belsen concentration camp was 5 long miles away from the train.*[85]

---

85   Hanna Lévy-Hass, *Diary of Bergen Belsen: The Story of How One Woman Survived the Holocaust* (Chicago, IL: Haymarket Books, 2009).

The rags Anne and Margot wore would have been soaked through as they struggled through the piercing wind and rain escorted by armed guards and vicious dogs. Inside the perimeter of Bergen-Belsen, fifteen large tents had been erected to accommodate the new arrivals. Anne and Margot were confined to the the tents for several weeks. There was no lighting in this section of the camp, and the water supply was primitive. A ditch served as a communal latrine. When it rained, the inhumanely-overcrowded tents leaked, the ditch flooded, and raw sewage flowed around the bare feet of the inmates. The wet straw that had been provided as bedding was teeming with lice.

Shortly after the sisters' arrival, a violent storm swept through Bergen-Belsen, causing widespread destruction especially in the tents. In the ensuing panic, many were killed and injured. Their screams were clearly heard in other parts of the camp where inmates had long since become impervious to death.

After the destruction of the tents, Anne and Margot, along with other inmates, were housed in camp barracks. Various infectious diseases, such as typhus and dysentery, were taking hold. As temperatures dropped and freezing cold set in, the inmates succumbed in the hundreds. The all-pervading stench of decaying corpses constantly permeated the air in the camp. In such deplorable conditions typhus spread like a forest fire. One doctor recalled, "Even the sick bay, was louse-infected from top to bottom, it was a breeding place for typhus and all our efforts to keep it in check were fruitless."[86]

Being a nurse in Bergen-Belsen was not an enviable task, but Dutch nurse Janny Brandes-Brilleslijper did her absolute best to provide clothing, medicine, and sustenance to fellow prisoners. Janny was one of the last people to see Anne Frank alive, two or three days before her death from typhus. She was little more than a skeleton. Her deathly pale emaciated body was shivering uncontrollably and loosely wrapped in a blanket because her own clothes were so infested with lice.

After the war, Janny met Anne and Margot's father Otto and delivered the tragic news that neither of his daughters had

---

86   Joanne Reilly, *Belsen: The Liberation of a Concentration Camp* (London, UK: Routledge, 1998).

survived Bergen-Belsen. On the basis of recent investigations, it is assumed that they died in February 1945, just a few weeks before the Allies liberated the camp in April 15, 1945. Anne was sixteen, and her big sister Margot was nineteen. Their mother, Edith Frank, died on January 6, 1945, three weeks before the liberation of Auschwitz-Birkenau.

Less than a month before Anne and her family were arrested by the Nazis, she wrote in her now famous diary: "It's difficult in times like these: ideals, dreams and cherished hopes rise within us, only to be crushed by grim reality. It's a wonder I haven't abandoned all my ideals; they seem so absurd and impractical. Yet I cling to them because I still believe, in spite of everything, that people are truly good at heart."

Not all Jews were prepared to die in mass executions or in Nazi extermination and labor camps. One of the better war movies to emerge from the last few decades concerned the true story of Tuvia, Asael, Zus, and Aron Bielski who were raised in Eastern Poland, which is now Western Belarus. The region had been annexed by the Soviet Union in 1939 in a pact that von Ribbentrop helped organize (known as the Molotov-Ribbentrop Pact).

These brothers lived in the village of Stankiewicze between the towns Lida and Nowogródek. It had been the home of the Bielski family for three generations. But this wasn't a Jewish community. They were the only Jewish family in a village where six other families resided. They enjoyed a relatively prosperous life farming the land and running the mill. Their parents, David and Beila, had twelve children: ten sons and two daughters. Tuvia, born 1906, was the second-oldest child. Despite the movie *Defiance* being a stylized version of their actual exploits, some of it was right on the nail.

Everything changed in Eastern Europe on June 22, 1941, with the launch of Operation Barbarossa, when Nazi Germany, along with its Axis allies, invaded the Soviet Union. Within two months they had occupied present-day Belarus. They razed over nine thousand Belarusian villages and deported around 380,000 people to work as slave labor. During the occupation, Nazi authorities imposed a savage racist regime that had mainly one purpose:

the systematic eradication of all Jews by some means or another. It is estimated that around 800,000 Jewish people died as a direct result of the Nazi authorities.

The people in the east were referred to as *Untermenschen* (lesser humans). This was the Nazi term for those regarded as hailing from inferior races. In the Nazi racial hierarchy, established in Hitler's *Mein Kampf* (my struggle), Jews were considered to be the lowest race, and they would be indiscriminately targeted and eventually exterminated. After the Jews, the Slavs were considered the next in line; it was the duty of the Germanic peoples to conquer land on which Slavs lived and incorporate it into the Reich. The Nazi policy of *Lebensraum* (room to live) implied that Slavs were to be kept alive so that they could provide manual labor in service to the German Reich. Nazi racial theory professed that the Slavic peoples were to be slowly worked to death. Other Nazis, such as Himmler and racial theorist Alfred Rosenberg, augmented Hitler's disturbed ideologies.

It is important to note that according to Nazi racial theory, the moral duty of the "superior" Aryan people was to conquer, subjugate, and destroy "inferior" races to ensure the continued development of the human species. It was an ersatz science derived from some rather questionable sources. The same applied to their concocted Aryan history. Nazi anti-Semitism wasn't an original concept either.

There had been a Jewish population in Belarus since the fourteenth century. During that time, the region was part of the Polish-Lithuanian union and, later, was incorporated into the Russian Empire. Right up until the first decades of the twentieth century, Jews in Belarus lived in small towns called *shtetls*, and most made a living in these self-contained communities as merchants and shopkeepers, artisans, craftsmen, and farmers. There was a lot of poverty, but the communities in the region developed an incredibly productive scholarship, literature, and cultural life, which became the center of the Jewish Hasidic movement.

An early instance of Jewish self-defense in the Russian Empire was organized during the 1903 pogrom in Gomel (or "Homel") during World War I when the western part of Belarus found itself in a combat zone. Russian military authorities expelled Jews from the area.

Shortly after the invasion, Jewish ghettos were established and paramilitary SS *Einsatzgruppen* (death squads) went about their heinous deeds. According to official data, Belarus suffered more than most other European countries in World War II; the human casualties amounted to more than 2.2 million people. The Bielski brothers decided rather early on that they had absolutely no desire to suffer the same fate. They fled to the nearby dense boreal forests of Zábiedovo and Perelaz in northwestern Belarus where they established the nucleus of a partisan group that initially consisted of about thirty family members and friends. If they were going to die anyway, they planned to die fighting.

One witness who joined the group had personally seen the slaughter of 5,500 people, who were herded to the outskirts of Lida and mercilessly shot point-blank as they stood helpless in preprepared mass graves. There were three trenches for children. Some members of the SS *Einsatzgruppen* were even seen actually shooting children with their lugers. Between July 1941 and the end of spring 1942, German authorities ordered the killing of tens of thousands of Jews in the Nowogródek (Novogrudok) District. In the first months of the occupation, Bielski family members managed to avoid the German onslaught, but by December 1941, the invaders had captured and killed the brothers' parents and two of their younger siblings. Tuvia could see only one alternative.

The primary rule for any army commander in the field is to know the terrain, so they hopefully used that knowledge to their advantage. The Bielski brothers had played in the dense, vertiginous forests of Zábiedovo and Perelaz all their lives and knew them intimately. It was going to be a good place to hide.

The main goal of Tuvia and the other leaders of the Jewish resistance was to attempt to protect all Jews regardless of the terrible consequences. Tuvia had served in the Polish army and had military training, but he soon discovered that most people from the towns did not have any knowledge of weapons or explosives and had to be taught from scratch.

As a rule, Tuvia preferred to avoid confrontations with the occupying forces. In his mind, saving Jewish lives superseded taking revenge against the Germans, and it was also a form of resistance (though some revenge would definitely occur). Women, children, and the elderly were accepted in the unit, including Jewish refugees who had fled other partisan units or escaped from one of the ghettos. Further south, Asael and Zus hid together and set about finding safe homes for a dozen or so of their surviving relatives, including their youngest brother, Aron.

The Bielskis did much more than provide a refuge and save lives. Every so often a group of them would emerge from the between trees on horseback, submachine guns strapped to their shoulders, ready to ambush the enemy. It is estimated that they killed more than three hundred enemy combatants. Bielski partisans were sent to the ghettos and hiding places of Jews in Nowogródek and Lida in an attempt to persuade people to escape from the ghettos and join the brothers in the forest.

It was by no means an easy task because many ghetto inhabitants feared the Germans even more than they feared living rough in the forests. They knew from experience that Nazi vengeance was callous, quick, and wholly disproportionate to whatever the misdemeanor was; moreover, they didn't believe that fighting the Germans would achieve anything except further punitive retribution.

Within time, the Bielskis' forest settlement became a fully-functioning micro society, reminiscent of a *shtetl*, complete with shoemakers, tailors, carpenters, and hat makers. There was a central square for social gatherings and a tannery that doubled as a synagogue. They even had a theater troupe. The Bielski brothers would collectively save the lives of 1,200 Jews. Asael was eventually conscripted into the Red Army and killed in action in February 1945. Tuvia, Zus, and Aron first immigrated to Israel, and both elder brothers later immigrated to the United States. Zus operated a trucking and taxi company and died in 1995. Tuvia drove a delivery truck and when he died in 1987, he was buried on Long Island. A year later, his mortal remains were exhumed and given a state funeral with military honors in Jerusalem. The Bielskis were heroes who lived in harmony with nature. Our next story began in harmony but sadly ended in acrimony.

The Andrews sisters, Patty, Maxene, and LaVerne, didn't fight in World War II, but that was the era when their fame peaked. They became great favorites of American troops overseas, performing regularly in United Service Organizations (USO) shows. They weren't afraid of performing in warzones either. They were nicknamed "America's Wartime Sweethearts" because that was when they rose to prominence. Their 1941 song "Boogie Woogie Bugle Boy," which tells the story of a musician who gets drafted into the US Army, became one of the Andrews Sisters' signature hits.

When the singing sisters appeared on the *Glenn Miller and his Orchestra* radio show in the early '40s, the audience response was so phenomenal that the broadcaster increased their appearances to three times a week. It was on Glenn Miller's show that the Andrews Sisters introduced their signature tune, a cover of Nora Bayes' "(I'll Be With You) In Apple Blossom Time." Apart from anything else, they were also one of the first groups to actually move on stage, and look like they were having fun. Previous performers had been, to put it mildly, a bit static.

When war was declared, the Andrews Sisters were quick to volunteer for the USO shows. The USO was the result of close collaboration between show business professionals and the military, with the goal of bringing morale-boosting entertainment to the troops. It definitely helped to do that in some of the direst of circumstances. The organization was initially funded entirely by public donation.

When they went overseas to warzones, the shows were mounted on the backs of flatbed trucks and driven from base to base. They featured some of the top talent of the day, artists such as Bob Hope, Bing Crosby, Ginger Rogers, Betty Grable, Abbott and Costello, Dorothy Lamour, and Clark Gable, along with the music of Tommy Dorsey, Glenn Miller, Benny Goodman and, of course, the amazing Andrews Sisters. They were all regulars.

During the ensuing four years overseas, they would be almost permanently on the road. For the armed forces' men and women, the Andrews Sisters represented home and family, the security and comforts of a youth they had so quickly lost. When they sang "(I'll Be With You) In Apple Blossom Time," the audience would listen in reverent silence until the last note. Then when they launched into "Boogie Woogie Bugle Boy," a veritable sea of olive drab would be on its feet clapping and dancing, ready to take on anything the enemy could throw at them. They were consummate crowd pleasers whose voices brought great comfort to countless young men and women serving their country. Making the right sound, in the right places, at the right time was the Andrews Sisters' legacy.

By the time World War II ended, the USO had staged 293,000 performances and entertained over sixteen million servicemen and women. It was the biggest production in show business history.

But the Andrews Sisters didn't confine their talents to the military. They also played to civilian audiences during the war. During a national tour in 1942, they set attendance records for their performances, and on Sunday nights they hosted their own half-hour, coast-to-coast radio show. Apart from that, the ladies appeared in more than a dozen films, and by 1944, they had sold over thirty million records for their record company Decca.

After the war, all three sisters and their parents permanently relocated to Los Angeles. Maxene had secretly married their manager, Lou Levy, in 1941, and LaVerne married a musician called Lou Rogers in 1948. After the hectic war years and multiple USO shows, their lives slowed down a little, but they were still playing to capacity crowds. Personality-wise, it would have been difficult to find more different siblings. Patty was an extrovert who loved attention and reveled in showing off. LaVerne was the antithesis, very quiet and unassuming. The real driver of the three was Maxene, who handled most of the trio's business dealings with their manager. According to Maxene, "Music is the one thing we had in common. We never agreed on hair styles or clothes, but we were always together on material and arrangements."[87]

Having such conflicting characters with such diametrically opposed opinions inevitably led to friction between the sisters. In 1953, the Andrews Sisters officially retired, and Patty signed with Capitol Records to follow a solo career in 1954. The sisterly relationships deteriorated even further when Patty sued her sisters, demanding a fairer share of their mother's estate. Then Maxene made the headlines on December 21, 1954, with a suspected suicide attempt, apparently incited by the domestic problems, but she always denied it.

After LaVerne died of cancer in 1967, Patty and Maxene rarely spoke to one another, but neither would ever divulge reasons behind their estrangement. In 1982, Maxene suffered a near-fatal myocardial infarction and had to have quadruple bypass surgery. In 1985, she recorded a solo album, and in 1989, she moved to Nevada. Her memoirs were published in 1991, a few years before she passed in October 1995.

Maxene never publicly admitted that she was gay; after all she had been married to music publisher Lou Levy for ten years until they divorced in 1951. She was with one female partner for thirteen

---

87   H. Arlo Nimmo, *The Andrews Sisters: A Biography and Career Record* (Jefferson, NC: McFarland, 2007).

years before she reconnected with her goddaughter Lynda Wells. She legally adopted Wells so they could be together because, according to Wells, a gay marriage was out of the question at that time. But surely adopting a goddaughter for a partner would raise other questions? Although Maxene didn't consider herself a lesbian, it was one of the areas of great contention between her and her sister Patty. Maxene said, "I tried to patch things up years ago, only to have Patty hang up on me…In fact, one time I called her and she told me that if I ever called again, she'd sue me! That's the last time I tried to fix things between us."

Maxene suffered another heart attack and died at Cape Cod Hospital on October 21, 1995. Patty did not attend her sister's memorial services in New York City, nor in California. Patty Andrews died of natural causes at her home in Los Angeles in 2013. She was ninety-four years old.

When we see the disclaimer "based on real events" on the big screen or the small screen, we immediately assume that everything we watch actually happened. I met many veterans whose stories referenced popular movies and TV series, such as *Band of Brothers*. The difficult aspect of this chapter was separating the public's assumptions from the reality of what really happened. On a few exceedingly rare occasions, Hollywood got it right, but every single story I looked at was embellished to some extent or another. Mark Twain said, "Never let the truth get in the way of a good story." Well, the purpose here isn't to dis Hollywood or its excellent productions. On the contrary, it's to provide the rest of the story about some of these real family members during times of conflict, so that the reader can draw their own opinions based on fact.

CHAPTER TWENTY-ONE:

WARS NEVER REALLY END.

No previous war had been so contentious, or raised more questions than answers, than the Vietnam War. It goes without saying that those who served in the Vietnam War ultimately deserve our respect and admiration for the amazing service they provided to a largely ungrateful nation. There were other wars before this one that affected more people, had a greater impact on the world, and entailed more devastation, but no previous war had the power to invoke images and sounds in people's minds like the Vietnam War. Popular media heavily influenced most opinions at the time and long thereafter. The mere mention of Vietnam conjures up images of Bell Huey helicopters flying to the musical accompaniment of Richard Wagner's "Ride of the Valkyries," "grunts" ascending steep mud-covered hills, jungles, napalm, and "humping the boonies."

It marred, and to some extent defined, a whole generation. Its theme tunes were the recognizable anthems such as Eric Burdon's rasping vocal hammering in "We Gotta Get Outta This Place" and Jefferson Airplane's "White Rabbit"; the Vietnam War had a million sounds and a million voices. The protagonists were mainly baby boomers raised on a tangible diet of fervent patriotism, anti-communism, Audie Murphy, John Wayne, and a veritable host of other indomitable heroes to emulate and admire. This was their war. The one they didn't want, but they would fight it anyway.[88]

During the Vietnam War, it was rare to see two members of the same immediate family serving in the same unit while "in country." The so-called Sullivan Rule from World War II prohibited two members of the same immediate family from serving together in a combat zone, but there were exceptions. In 1969, Ernie Gerhardt and his younger brother, Jim, served in the same National Guard unit at a "fire direction center" in southern Vietnam. Fiercely patriotic, they were both very proud to serve their country, and it was an added bonus to serve as part of the same unit.

Ernie joined the US Army in December of 1968 as a member of battery A, Third Battalion of the Twenty-Fifth Infantry Division's Thirteenth Field Artillery, and was shortly after sent to Vietnam. A few weeks later, Jim got his orders too. He wasn't married, and so he decided he would go. Those soldiers who had compatible Military Occupational Specialty Codes (MOS) could request to serve together. When Jim arrived in Vietnam in January of 1969, he discovered that Ernie was serving in Trung Lap, a suburb of Saigon (later Ho Chi Minh City) in southern Vietnam.

The brothers' job was to provided fire support for infantrymen. Ernie served as a gun chief, responsible for the firing of a 155mm Howitzer, while Jim compiled the firing coordinates for the men firing the six Howitzers in the unit. On one occasion, they were in the bunker while in radio contact with people out in the field who called in to request fire support. It was Jim's job to prepare the firing data, relay it to the guns, and get the rounds in the area as fast as was humanly possible.

Army engineers established a new firebase in the spring of 1969, and the brothers fired a lot of shells with those Howitzers but never came into close contact with enemy combatants. They didn't spend all their time in Vietnam together either. Sometimes they would go for weeks without seeing each other. But after eleven months, they made it back to "the world" and landed at home in northern Jackson County the day after Thanksgiving in 1969.

---

88   *To War with the 4th*: Martin King, David Hilborn, Jason Nulton. Casemate, 30 Nov 2016

Another Vietnam veteran who served with his brother "in country" was former Senator and Secretary of Defense during the Obama administration, Chuck Hagel. Being a noble veteran himself, he personally made it his goal to improve partnerships with the Department of Veterans Affairs, including health record interoperability, service treatment record transferability, and continuity of mental health services and support. His father, who had been a tail gunner on the World War II bombers that reduced Japanese cities to ashes, had trouble holding down a job. By the early 1960s, he was a chronic alcoholic, and on Christmas Eve of 1962 (after one of their frequent family debacles), he died in his sleep.

In 1967, Chuck landed at Tan Son Nhat Airport. He remembered that during the bus ride from Travis Air Force Base in California to board the plane, he noticed that the vehicle was full of innocent young army privates. They would have had no idea what was waiting for them in that faraway Southeast Asian land. At twenty-one, Chuck was one of the oldest on the bus of nineteen-year-olds. He recalled the large boombox radios that many of the troops carried with them. The songs that blared out from those music boxes during his tour included Otis Redding's "(Sittin' On) The Dock of the Bay" and Aretha Franklin's "Respect." Music was a defining aspect of most service personnels' Vietnam experience.

By 1967, soldiers were being sent to Vietnam as individuals to fill vacancies. Chuck's brother Tom had also volunteered for service in Vietnam, rather than accept orders for Germany. He joined Chuck's unit, company B, Second Battalion, Forty-Seventh Infantry, Ninth Infantry Division, soon after the start of the infamous Tet Offensive. Up until that juncture, Tom had been serving with the Third Squadron, Fifth Cavalry, attached to Colonel George S. Patton's Eleventh Armored Cavalry Regiment near the demilitarized zone. They both welcomed the opportunity to serve together because it was a rare situation indeed; however, because they both volunteered to join the army and volunteered go to Vietnam, the Sullivan Rule was ignored. They didn't just serve together in a full-strength division, they were in the same rifle platoon, which had between thirty and forty soldiers. So they really did serve side by side. It caused unlimited concern for their mother, who took some comfort knowing that her boys were together and that they would look out for one another.

Their new home for the ensuing ten months was along the brown water of the Mekong Delta, immediately to the west of Saigon (Ho Chi Minh City), where they both were wounded twice. Up until their deployment in Vietnam, their father and uncles who served in World War II provided the only knowledge they had about combat. But before long, they both saw the true horror of war first-hand, along with witnessing what Chuck considered to be the worst and best of human behavior.

The brothers' first experience of real combat occurred during the wee hours of January 30, 1968, at the start of the Tet Offensive, one of the largest military campaigns of the Vietnam War. Due to insufficient intelligence at the time, no one understood the strength of the enemy or their strategy. It was the most devastating coordinated attack by North Vietnamese and Viet Cong forces since the onset of the war. Even the headquarters of General William Westmoreland, commander of American forces in Vietnam, came under attack. Westmoreland's HQ was located at Long Binh, which was the site of the world's largest ammo dump (ammunition supply depot). The brothers' unit, a base installation known as Bearcat from the Ninth Infantry Division, received orders to engage the enemy at a place called Widows' Village, opposite the army's HQ. They all took a heavy battering that day, losing many of their officers and noncommissioned officers, who were either killed or wounded.

The whole experience had a deeply profound effect on Chuck and his brother. When Chuck got hit and was on his back, blood bubbling out of his chest with every breath, his nineteen-year-old brother, Tom, frantically crammed bandages into the holes to stem the bleeding, before noticing that his own arm had been reduced to a bloody pulp. Up until the attack, it was a day like any other in Vietnam.

They had always been two very opposing characters. Chuck had a reputation of shooting from the hip and telling it like it is. His brother Tom was the antithesis. He was known as a smart mouth, a wiseass who didn't exert himself, except when under duress, as they were when the Tet Offensive kicked off in Vietnam, and on many other occasions. Another marked difference was that Chuck supported the war, and Tom detested it. They were both affected by the growing up during anti-Vietnam War sentiment in the United States. The country was going through some radical changes at that time. When Dr. Martin Luther King, Jr. was assassinated, it affected relationships within the troops halfway around the world.

One day in July 1968, Tom saw a Viet Cong sniper fire several well-aimed rounds from his AK rifle into the belly of an American chopper, causing it to plummet to the swamp below. The crash killed Lieutenant Colonel Frederick Van Deusen, a high-ranking officer who also happened to be the brother-in-law of General William Westmoreland. Tom immediately crawled out toward where the shots came from and almost collided with the Viet Cong sniper but managed to fire a fatal bullet in the man's forehead and put him permanently out of action. It was the same day that Tom saw an American officer kill a young, pregnant Vietnamese woman he'd mistaken for Viet Cong. These terrifying images would be omnipresent in his mind until long after the war had ended.

During their year of service in Vietnam, they earned five Purple Hearts between them before they were both honorably discharged. Chuck got out first, followed several weeks later by Tom. Then they returned to Nebraska, but they had been to war. They had seen and experienced devastation, destruction, and death. Like many thousands of Vietnam veterans before them, the world felt different and would never be the same again. They lived together for the following two years and studied at the University of Nebraska on the GI Bill. They had survived Vietnam, but in some way or another it would always be there. Tom struggled with post-traumatic stress disorder, in an era whereupon the whole idea of PTSD was not widely appreciated. Former soldiers often struggled to suppress the internal demons and hide the mental scars as well as the physical ones. The Hagel brothers continued to harbor polarized views on the war, which often led to physical altercations between them. On one occasion neighbors became so alarmed at the sound of splintering furniture and breaking glass that they called the police. Thankfully tempers had calmed by the time they arrived, so no arrests were made.

Chuck and Tom's radically opposing views on the war finally found common ground when they were both invited by the Vietnamese government to visit their former battlegrounds.[89] It was a deeply emotional return that assuaged any remaining animosity they still felt for each other. More importantly, despite their political and moral differences, they realized that their fraternal bonds and the ties of shared experiences made petty squabbles pale into insignificance. They could be brothers again.

One of the many particularly disturbing legacies to emerge from the Vietnam War concerns the illegitimate children, better known as Amerasians. They grew up as the unwanted surplus product of a largely unpopular war, and most never knew their fathers. Their mothers abandoned many of these unfortunate children at the gates of orphanages. Some were even cast aside in garbage cans. At school, they were bullied and ostracized because of their round blue eyes and light skin, or dark skin and tight curly hair if their GI fathers were African Americans. Margaret Tran was one of these children. Her young birth mother, unable to live with the shame and social exclusion, gave Margaret away to a stranger in Saigon when she was just a few hours old. A few years later, Margaret and her adoptive mother started a new life in the United States. Margaret graduated from Garden Grove High School and later joined the Army Reserves. But despite her deep affection for her adoptive mother, she maintained an overwhelming desire to discover who her birth parents were. She wanted to know if she still had family out there somewhere.

Her natural father, Staff Sergeant Wayne Franklyn, served eight years in the United States Air Force during the Vietnam War, as part of the Forty-Sixth Communications Squadron. Wayne learned to speak Vietnamese. He met and fell in love with an orphaned Vietnamese woman named Mai, age eighteen. Wayne helped Mai to get

---

89   Nick Poppy, "How the Vietnam War Tore These Brothers Apart," *New York Post* (New York Post, November 11, 2017), https://nypost.com/2017/11/11/how-the-vietnam-war-tore-these-brothers-apart/.

her younger brothers out of an orphanage. They married in 1970 and had three daughters together.

Many years later after a DNA test, Margaret discovered that she had three half sisters. All four women have the same father, Wayne Franklyn, but different mothers. Thanks to Facebook, which can apparently be good for something apart from people displaying what they've eaten recently, the sisters connected and are now thankfully part of each other's lives.

Ann Marie Luc's case was similar to Margaret's. She was also a Vietnamese "war baby" who was just one year old when her mother gave her away in Vietnam. By the time she was seventeen years old, she had been passed around like an unwanted parcel between several families and had been known by four different names. Then she moved to the United States with a birth certificate that wasn't even hers. Several decades later, after getting married and having two children of her own, Ann discovered that she had a sister who was also born during the war.

Lisa Beresczky moved to America at the age of thirteen, also conceived during the conflict to a Vietnamese mother and an American soldier, but she knew neither of them. After years of struggling and living on welfare with her adoptive mom, Lisa finally settled in Arkansas, where she married. Throughout the following years, she struggled with an insuppressible feeling that there was something important missing in her life, but she couldn't pin it down. Using ancestry and DNA research, she discovered that the name of her Vietnamese birth mother was Tran thi Lan Huong. Then she hit a dead end.

Meanwhile Ann's friend, Jennifer, an amateur genealogist, spent months trawling DNA databases until she found Ann's father. Sadly, it was a decade too late. Ann's birth father had taken his own life. According to his sister, who didn't want to be named, he was never the same after he returned from the Vietnam War. His wasn't a unique case, in that respect at least. It is estimated that around fifty thousand Vietnam veterans had committed suicide before 1990. That's only eight thousand less than the number of fatalities that occurred during the actual war. The number of Vietnam veterans believed to have died as a direct result of being exposed to the chemical Agent Orange, is roughly three hundred thousand.

One day Jennifer contacted Lisa and asked if she was the daughter of Tran thi Lan Huong. Lisa replied that she was. Within days, Lisa booked a flight from Arkansas to South Carolina. There, she met Ann. They hugged and then played at the beach, more reminiscent of little girls, as they held hands and splashed in the ocean. The resemblance was very obvious, and although they didn't have a father anymore, their natural mother had died, and decades had passed since the end of the Vietnam War, they now at least had each other.

In 1987, Congress finally responded to the outcry over Vietnamese orphans with American faces, many abandoned in Vietnamese slums. On the strength of this, the Amerasian visa was created. It still isn't known precisely how many Amerasians were born in Vietnam, but so far the US has vetted and resettled nearly thirty thousand children of US troops and employees along with nearly eighty thousand Vietnamese relatives.

The United States federal government stated on October 2, 2012:

> *Individuals fathered by a U.S. citizen and born in Vietnam after January 1, 1962, and before January 1, 1976, are known as Amerasians and may be admitted to the U.S. as immigrants. Spouses, children, and parents or guardians may accompany the Amerasian.*

By the time the conflict came to a decisive end, the average age of male fatalities was 23.1 years. Despite the use of the draft, it's a little-known fact that two-thirds of the men who served in Vietnam were actually volunteers. These volunteers accounted for approximately 70 percent of those "killed in action," or KIA. In conclusion, the fall of Saigon occurred on April 30, 1975, two years after the American military had left Vietnam. The last American troops were recalled in their entirety on March 29, 1973. Just for the record, it's important to point out that it was the South Vietnamese who lost the war, not the Americans who fought it. It's also important to point out what should be self-evident by now, history really does repeat like a questionable burrito. Look at the fall of Kabul!

I have many friends who served in the Vietnam War, who still carry both internal and external scars from their combat experiences, which emphasizes the title of this chapter.

CHAPTER TWENTY-TWO:

THE CRIME FAMILIES.

In the past decades, movies and TV series about La Cosa Nostra (LCN) have enthralled audiences around the world, to the point of veneration. Therein lies the danger. These murdering mobsters shouldn't be venerated or romanticized at all. But such is the pervasive influence of the Mafia. One popular reader's website had an enquiry from a fourteen-year-old boy to the effect of, "How do I join the Mafia?" The young lad probably wanted to put a hit on his older sister or his parents, who in all likelihood have to prize him out of bed with a crowbar in the morning and stack his sheets against the wall. What the young lad should know is that anything conceived in crime will inevitably be consumed by crime, which is just another way of saying the proverb derived from the Gospel of Matthew: "Then said Jesus unto him, Put up again thy sword into his place: for all they that take the sword shall perish with the sword." Well it's true that many of the famous mobsters did, but some got away with it.

LCN and all affiliate organizations are, by their nature alone, inherently evil. So what does that have to do with families who go to war? Well, just about everything. It's often heard in the movies and TV series based around crime families, "We don't want to start a war with such and such a family, etc." Then they proceed to murder potential adversaries and family members alike. The murders are meticulously planned and executed by killers with antifreeze in their veins.

It isn't really worthy of veneration, but it doesn't prevent untold millions of viewers from reveling in the murderous antics of these sociopathic, homicidal maniacs—and maybe along the way unleashing their own inner Mafia aspirations on subjects such as "How to eliminate the mother-in-law?" or, "What's the going rate for hit men these days, and do they make a discount for bulk requests?" It's beyond ridiculous, but that's the all-pervasive power of both big and small screens.

Tony "fugghedaboutit" Soprano's serial philandering and tough-as-nails father approach can't detract from his rather unsociable inclinations, such as personally offing his own nephew Christopher, as well as about a half-dozen other members of his mob. Not particularly original. Michael Corleone had already trodden the path of fratricide in the 1974 epic *The Godfather: Part II* by putting a hit on his own brother Fredo; however, these characters couldn't hold a candle to the real LCN. These fictional crime families, such as those loveable Corleones or the Sopranos, continue to inspire and enthrall, but the basic truth is they're all remarkably unoriginal in their approach.

As this volume has already demonstrated, the machinations of murderous families are not an entirely new concept. Robert Graves's (previously mentioned) epic *I, Claudius* follows the history of the empirical Roman families, from Marcellus to the death of the eponymous Claudius in a gripping storyline. It basically reduces contemporary mob clans to the status of *Sesame Street* extras. Either way, just to be on the safe side, it's still a good idea to avoid accepting substantial cash donations from those with peculiar nicknames, although these days there are naturally multitudinous exceptions.

One family worth avoiding though is the Genovese crime family, which is still active in the deviant underworld of traditional organized crime. Having surpassed the once-dominant Gambino LCN group in both strength and numbers over the past decade, they are still considered the most formidable element in a perfidious league of ne'er-do-well contenders. The Genovese has far-reaching tentacles that stretch to incorporate a presence in portions of Connecticut, Massachusetts, Florida, California, and Nevada, but they're mainly active in the New York metropolitan region. Many decades ago, it was the first of the five New York-based families to expand its rackets to New Jersey (home of the Mafia soap *The Sopranos*).

Here comes the roll call. There are five infamous families that hail from New York. They are the Gambino, Genovese, Lucchese, Colombo, and Bonanno clans, which according to experts (who probably keep a low profile), still exist and still maneuver in the same tired realms of organized crime, extortion, loan-sharking, racketeering, gambling, prostitution, etc. Not forgetting the lucrative drug business of course, which despite insinuations to the contrary isn't entirely run by the Mexican cartels.

So the Genovese family is indubitably the largest of the aforementioned families. According to state and federal law enforcement authorities, it has a core membership of between 250 and 300, with well over 1,000 known criminal associates. The family has strong connections with other traditional and non-traditional organized crime groups throughout the United States. The Genovese group remains the most active, powerful, and resourceful LCN family in New Jersey, which has played a key role in its evolution and development. Historically, more high-ranking members of the Genovese family than any other LCN group have called New Jersey their home state.

This introduces the story of a notorious Genovese family don, who, to put it mildly, knew how to keep up appearances. He was once the most prominent defendant in a Housing Authority case, and was officially identified as the boss of the Genovese crime family. Vincent Gigante, (March 29, 1928–December 19, 2005) was known as "the Chin," an appellation that stemmed from his mother affectionately calling him "Chinzeeno," as a boy, which is a diminutive form of Vincenzo. Back in the day, Genovese members simply referred to him as "this guy" while simultaneously stroking their chins. To even mention his name on a telephone was a potential death sentence for the offender.

During the case, which directly implicated Gigante, a federal grand jury accused fifteen men of rigging bids for window contracts.

Some of the defendants were identified by colorful sobriquets such as Gaspipe, Baldy Dom, Benny Eggs, and Joe Cakes. This should have been a rather good indication that they were not dealing with the cast of *The Sound of Music*. Some nicknames were self-explanatory such as Peter (Fat Pete) Chiodo, who weighed in at around 350 pounds, and Dominick "Baldy Dom" Canterino who had a bad case of an expanding forehead and ingrown hair, but they didn't know the origin of the other colorful nicknames.

Vincent Gigante was a very strange and disturbed individual indeed. Born in New York City, he was one of five sons of Salvatore and Yolanda Gigante, both first-generation immigrants from the Italian city of Naples. His parents were decent, hardworking people. Salvatore was a watchmaker, and Yolanda was a seamstress. Vincent tried to learn various professions but failed miserably, because what he really enjoyed was intimidating and hitting people, and job opportunities in that department were limited. He began a career as a professional boxer, who, between 1944 and 1947, won twenty-one of his twenty-five bouts, which wouldn't have done his brain any favors. Then when his boxing took a dive, he took on a job as a Mafia enforcer for the Luciano crime family, predecessor of the Genovese family. While three of Vincent's brothers, Mario, Pasquale, and Ralph, followed in his criminal footsteps, brother Louis stayed out of organized crime and opted to become a priest. He would commit other crimes, but at least he could give his brothers absolution for their heinous deeds when he wasn't interfering with choir boys.

While Louis was getting up to no good in the confessional box, Vincent became known as the gunman who botched the murder of longtime Luciano boss Frank Costello in 1957. Vito Genovese made his move against Costello when he hired Vincent to do the hit. Well, things didn't go exactly according to plan. When Costello's cab pulled up to his apartment at 115 Central Park West, an ominous-looking black Cadillac pulled in behind it. Vincent jumped out of the car, followed Costello into the building's lobby, and fired a single shot at his head. When Costello collapsed into a leather couch, bleeding, Vincent raced back to his waiting car and vanished into the streets of Manhattan. He assumed that he'd done a good job, but this should have been a good indication that he didn't pay much attention to detail. This character deficit would improve with time.

In May 1958, Vincent went on trial for the attempted murder of Frank Costello. Vincent's criminal defense attorney, Maurice Edelbaum, exploited Costello's unwillingness to identify the shooter when he asked, "Do you know any reason why this man should seek your life?"

"None whatsoever," replied Costello.

Then Edelbaum demanded rather theatrically, "Who shot you?"

"I'll ask you who shot me," replied Costello with a wry smile. "I don't know. I saw no one at all."

With the victim respecting his sacred LCN omertà by refusing to identify the perpetrator, only one other potential eyewitness remained. Unfortunately, the apartment building doorman didn't have 20/20 vision. He was completely blind in one eye and visually impaired in the other—surprising that he got a job as a doorman in the first place, but there you go. Under fierce cross-examination, Edelbaum annihilated the sight-challenged doorman's testimony. Shortly before midnight, the jury returned a verdict of "not guilty." Loud applause erupted in the gallery as Vincent's wife Olympia and their four children burst into crestfallen tears, which raises other questions of course, such as, were they crying because he was aquitted? Anyway, when the applause had died down, Vincent walked over to Frank Costello, and said very simply, "Thanks, Frank," which was a little magnanimous, but not entirely out of character.

Vincent was home again, but not long enough to make a cup of coffee because that same year he was sentenced to seven years in prison for heroin trafficking. He was released on parole after five years. After sharing a prison cell with Costello's deadly rival, Vito Genovese, Vincent was given permission to run a caporegime with its own crew operating mainly out of Greenwich Village.

The American Mafia's hierarchy is intended to insulate the bosses from arrest and prosecution. They have a hierarchical chain of command reminiscent of a legitimate business corporation. Most Mafia families are headed by a boss, an underboss, and a consigliore (counselor). Associates (Giovone D'Honore) are not "made" members but rather made members direct their activities. Each coporesime oversees a "crew" of soldiers, who are made men (a fully-initiated member of the Mafia) and associates. The consigliere is an older member who has extensive expertise (and sometimes is an attorney). He advises the boss and also serves as a liaison between soldiers and administration. He may be a constable who serves as a financial advisor. A piciotto is usually a low-ranking soldier who serves as an enforcer (bit man).

In 1969, Vincent was charged again, this time in New Jersey, with conspiracy to bribe New Jersey police officers. He was prepared to pay a serious amount of money if they could possibly see their way to warning him of any intended surveillance operations by law enforcement agencies. On this occasion, at least, the cops didn't want to play ball; however, all charges were dropped after Vincent's legal team presented reports from psychiatrists claiming that he was mentally unfit to stand trial. Vincent's psychiatrist, Eugene D'Adamo, noted that since 1969, Vincent had been diagnosed as suffering from schizophrenia. He was also reported as being a paranoid type who had periods of acute exacerbations, sometimes resulting in hospitalization. His lawyers and relatives added fuel to his defense by saying that Vincent had been mentally retarded since the late 1960s and had a below-average IQ. Precisely what occurred in the 1960s to lower his IQ has never been revealed.

It's amazing that two legally court-appointed psychiatrists concurred with D'Adamo. The shrink angle was possibly the inspiration behind the main *Sopranos* character, Tony Soprano.

Sometime later, an old man was seen wandering around in his pajamas, a shabby bathrobe, and a dilapidated pair of house slippers muttering inanely to himself. He even stopped to have intense conversations with parking meters and fire hydrants, before urinating in the street. Surprisingly, these actions didn't impress fellow New Yorkers who considered such behavior a fairly typical sight in New York City, but Vincent was definitely not a typical person. To some he became known as the "Oddfather." While serving a twelve-year term for racketeering and conspiracy to murder, he was brought back to court on charges of obstruction of justice. This is when it all came out.

Vincent dropped his three-decades-long subterfuges and acknowledged that he had, in fact, conned doctors into believing he was mentally incompetent. Then he pleaded guilty as charged in US district court. He had even gone as far as checking himself into a suburban hospital for treatment on no less than twenty-two occasions, but now he knew that the game was up. Rumor was that he had made a deal with the federal authorities to prevent his sons and his *comare* (pronounced *goomah*, meaning Mafia man's mistress) from being charged with any misdemeanors. Incidentally, the name of his mistress was the same as his wife, Olympia. Smart move.

When Judge Leo Glasser read the charge he said, "You agree, that you knowingly, intentionally misled doctors who were evaluating your competency to stand trial?"

Vincent nodded wearily and answered in a low whisper, "Yes, your honor."[90]

His brother and most ardent defender, the Reverend Louis Gigante, was in court when Vincent finally admitted to faking his illness. But Louis must have known all along that it had all been a very cleverly orchestrated subterfuge. Despite this, the priest was prepared to swear on the Good Book and be diplomatic with the truth, under oath if it was necessary.

Under Vincent's leadership, the Genovese crime family became the largest and most powerful LCN organization in the United States. He skillfully expanded the operations of the family in all areas, from loan-sharking and bookmaking to extortion and bid rigging for New York City infrastructure contracts, one of which involved a former United States president. Under Vincent's watchful eye and at its height, the criminal enterprise earned around $100 million a year, making it the most lucrative Mafia enterprise in American history. According to *The Changing Face of Organized Crime in New Jersey: A Status Report* by the State of New Jersey Commission of Investigation published in 2004:

> *It [the Genovese family] runs the largest*
> *bookmaking and loan sharking rings in the New*
> *York/New Jersey metropolitan area. The family's*

---

90   John Pennisi, "Chin Flew over the Cuckoo's Nest," Sitdown News, December 4, 2020, https://sitdownnews.com/vincent-chin-gigante.

other major criminal enterprises include extortion and labor racketeering in the construction, demolition, asbestos removal, carting, recycling, trucking, and waterfront industries; theft and kickbacks from pension funds; insurance fraud; narcotics trafficking; infiltration of legitimate businesses; and public corruption. Its influence is particularly strong on the Port Newark/Elizabeth and Hudson County waterfronts. While the organization continues to commit traditional crimes such as murder, extortion, racketeering, loan sharking and illegal gambling, it has evolved into committing more sophisticated crimes, such as computer fraud, stock/securities fraud and health-care fraud.

Many of these crimes are committed with the assistance of non-traditional organized crime groups, such as those with Russian and Cuban members. Of all the traditional LCN families, the Genovese group has the most contact with non-traditional criminal organizations, and the money and power they command.[91]

It took the FBI many decades to nail their man, but nail him they did. After a more than fifty-year run as one of America's most notorious gangsters, Vincent "the Chin" Gigante died on December 19, 2005, at the Medical Center for Federal Prisoners in Springfield, Missouri. His funeral and burial were held four days later at St. Anthony of Padua Church in Greenwich Village.

In May 2021, a lawsuit was filed against Father Louis Gigante on the allegation that he molested a nine-year-old boy at St. Athanasius Church from 1976–1977. The retired priest reportedly subjected the unnamed victim to "endure prolific and profound abuse" during bible study sessions. Under normal circumstances, a priest would

91   "The Changing Face of Organized Crime in New Jersey: A Status Report," State of New Jersey (State of New Jersey Commission of Investigation, May 2004), https://www.nj.gov/sci/pdf/ocreport.pdf.

be suspended, pending investigations. But the Archdiocese of New York has repeatedly shown no commitment to previous pledges of zero tolerance of sexual abuse allegations, so it is possible that Louis will continue to minister as a priest in good standing indefinitely. He will, in all likelihood, get away with it. So even though Vincent feigned his mental illness, Louis is the one that definitely needs help, preferably from behind the bars of a secure facility. He has also proved that he is more than capable of telling fibs.

While Louis has been attracting unfavorable publicity around the Gigante name, he should also know that the mob doesn't appreciate unwelcome attention. Despite his clerical obligations, he cannot and should not reasonably be considered a man of God. But if he still believes, then he should be very worried because there's a wonderful reception waiting for him downstairs.

Hollywood knows full well that dysfunctional families are usually a great attraction. But some wise guys find out the hard way—that it's best to avoid too much attention. One famous movie depicted the frenetic life of Anthony "Tony the Ant" Spilotro and his brother Michael. According to the movie *Casino*, directed by the inimitable Martin Scorsese, Tony was a live wire who, with protection from the Chicago Mafia, had the run of Las Vegas. It was his playground to do whatever he so desired. That was the problem though. Tony had too many desires.

Monaco maybe the home of the rich and famous, but Las Vegas is the home of bachelorette parties, bachelor parties, excesses of the worst kind, along with polystyrene volcanoes, and good, old working-class greed. It's the place where former pop superstars go to sing and play their inevitable swan songs for a vaguely bemused audience. These days, it's a squeaky-clean operation, but that wasn't always the case. In the past, Las Vegas had been associated with some notorious mobsters such as Charles "Lucky" Luciano, Benjamin "Bugsy" Siegel, and Meyer Lansky. They were indeed a tough act to follow, but a few decades ago, everything was possible in Vegas.

By the mid-1980s, Mafia influence was on the wane. The Stardust became the last casino in Las Vegas to lose its license due to the uncovering of a major skimming operation. In 1983, a federal grand jury indicted fifteen people including Joey Aiuppa, head of the Chicago Outfit; Carl Civella, Mafia boss in Kansas City; and Milwaukee syndicate boss Frank Balistrieri. It was the Chicago Outfit, which had installed Frank "Lefty" Rosenthal, an infamous former Miami bookmaker, to run the Stardust and oversee a massive skimming operation. The problem was that Rosenthal had a bad reputation, and once his practices had been exposed, the Nevada gaming authorities placed Rosenthal in the "Black Book," banning him for life from Nevada casinos. The Chicago mob got around this minor setback by giving him less contentious positions such as entertainment director and food and beverage man. But by the end of 2006, the Stardust had closed its doors ad infinitum. It had been one of the Las Vegas Strip's most iconic casino resorts, renowned for its neon signage and topless *Lido* showgirls (and, of course, its nefarious underworld connections).

Tony Spilotro's involvement began in 1971 when Joey "Doves" Aiuppa, head of the Chicago mob, sent him out to Las Vegas to manage the loan-sharking business along with a few other lucrative street scams. More importantly, Tony was told in no uncertain terms to keep an eye on Rosenthal, who was in charge of the crime family's skimming operations at the Stardust and Fremont casinos. By December 1979, Tony had also been blacklisted by the Nevada Gaming Commission, preventing him from entering any casino. The crime syndicate also installed San Diego businessman Allen R. Glick at the helm of the Stardust and Fremont casinos as a licensed front man who surreptitiously answered to Rosenthal and Tony.

Tony had a bit too much fun for his own good. By all accounts, he was like a spoiled brat in a toyshop. His priority should have been to make money for the mob but some serious hedonistic tendencies got in the way of his objective. Nevertheless, there were some who genuinely admired and revered him. One particular eyewitness, who preferred to remain anonymous for obvious reasons and still lives in Vegas, said, "Fuck what everybody else says. Tony wasn't all bad. When I got sacked from my job running the tables at Caesars Palace, I told Tony. Within twenty-four hours I had my job back and a substantial raise. The boss didn't even dare to look at me after that. If Tony had your back you were as safe as Fort Knox, he saved my job and helped me feed my family. Nothing wrong with that, but there was a price. Because Tony was banned from entering the joint he asked me to be his eyes and ears there, and I was, for the duration. Made a shitload of cash thanks to him. Vegas was a better place back then, it was more exciting, more entertaining you know."[92]

Ah yes, the good old days. A smile, a song, and a bullet to the back of the head. The problem with Tony was that he had no brakes. He was full on twenty-four-seven, pedal to the metal, and he could do, more or less, whatever he wanted. He was a "made man," someone who had risen through the ranks of the Chicago LCN to achieve a kind of protected status within the organization. He had a fearsome reputation as a violent enforcer and hitman, hence his status made him practically invulnerable. He did as Joey Aiuppa asked and befriended Rosenthal. He also got very close to his wife, former showgirl Geri McGee. It was close enough to indulge a little horizontal jogging, which didn't particularly nurture his friendship with Rosenthal.

Before long, Tony's brothers Michael (a failed B movie actor) and John arrived on the scene. They helped run a front company called The Goldrush Ltd. Michael soon became embroiled in book-making, drug dealing, prostitution, robbery, extortion, and many other dubious activities, which were rife in Vegas at the time. The brothers took things a step further when they set up the Hole in the Wall Gang with a few other associates. It was a remarkably simple business model. They robbed and burglarized businesses in Vegas by drilling holes in their walls to gain access, and then plundering the place.

After a string of successful robberies, the gang eventually began to wind down their activities. Then, a carefully planned undercover sting at Bertha's Gifts and Home Furnishings (then on West Sahara Avenue) saw six members of the gang arrested and indicted for burglary, conspiracy to commit burglary, attempted grand larceny, and possession of burglary tools. A few months later, Frank Cullotta, a childhood Spilotro friend who was arrested with five others in the burglary, decided to rat out the rest of the gang and cooperate with Las Vegas police and FBI agents. Tony and his brothers were charged but later acquitted due to insufficient evidence and the fact that the

92   Author interview done in Las Vegas, 2020.

judge was in their payroll; however, Tony still faced three separate indictments, and was already on a downward spiral.

The top men in the Chicago mob were becoming increasingly uneasy at all the unwelcome attention the Spilotro brothers were attracting. Moreover, they hadn't sanctioned his little business venture. There are multiple theories about why Tony and his brother Michael were pursued by the Chicago mob. One claims that Tony was targeted because of his lurid affair with Rosenthal's wife.

Then there was the Rosenthal car bomb incident. It occurred on October 4, 1982, when Frank Rosenthal left Tony Roma's restaurant on East Sahara Avenue and got into his Cadillac, which then exploded into a ball of fire and flame. Amazingly, Frank survived with minor burns and small injuries. This was due to his robust 1981 car model, which had a steel-stabilizing plate beneath the driver's seat and had deflected the blast. It literally—quite literally—saved his ass. That same year, Rosenthal's by then ex-wife, Geri, was found dead in Los Angeles of an apparent drug overdose.

It has never been definitively ascertained who ordered the bomb hit, but most fingers pointed, albeit surreptitiously, at Tony Spilotro. In 1986, Chicago LCN boss Joey Aiuppa was charged and successfully convicted of skimming profits from Las Vegas casinos. For this, and other misdemeanors, he received a twenty-eight-year prison sentence. The word on the inside was that Tony had alban-pointed the federal authorities in the direction of Joey, but this, again, was pure speculation. Either way, when Joey overstepped the mark for the umpteenth time, the Chicago mob decided that there was only one option. Frank Cullotta said, "Tony's caused the Outfit a lot of problems, and he'd stopped generating money. Michael is cocky and has caused problems, too." After hearing of their disappearance, he said, "They aren't needed anymore. If you whack one, you gotta whack them both. I guarantee you they're both dead."[93]

Tony managed to incite the displeasure of his superiors when five of his subordinates decided to become government witnesses. Three of them personally testified against Joey, which went down like a digestive complaint in a diving suit and was largely the reason

93   Frank Cullotta and Dennis Griffin, *The Rise and Fall of a 'Casino' Mobster: The Tony Spilotro Story through a Hitman's Eyes* (Denver, CO: WildBlue Press, 2017).

Joey was sent to prison in the spring of 1986. He had heard enough. Joey reportedly ordered the hit when he said, "I don't care how you do it. Get him. I want him out."[94]

A hit team was assembled that included Nick Calabrese, who became a top government informant. A scheme was hatched to lure the brothers to a meeting in a Bensenville, Illinois, house with the promise of a mob promotion for Tony and Michael to become "made men." June 14, 1986, was the fateful date for the Spilotro brothers.

In 2007, during the government's Operation Family Secrets investigation aimed at clearing up unsolved gangland killings, several men confessed to the Spilotro murders. Calabrese testified that he—along with around ten other outfit killers, including James LaPietra, John Fecarotta, John DiFronzo, Sam Carlisi, Louie "The Mooch" Eboli, James Marcello, Louis Marino, Joseph Ferriola, and Ernest "Rocky" Infelice—was waiting in the basement as the two brothers entered. Tony suspected what was going down and asked his executioners if he could say a prayer. He didn't get a reply. Calabrese tackled him to the ground and held his legs while another mobster strangled Tony with a rope. Unlike the cornfield scene in *Casino*, no baseball bats were used, but both brothers were asphyxiated and savagely beaten to death by their captors. Then their battered, almost unrecognizable remains were buried in a cornfield in Enos, Indiana.

---

94   Ibid.

TO: DIRECTOR FBI

FROM: (ATTN SSA CHICAGO (281A-CG-88436)
SUBJECT: ANTHONY SPILOTRO
OC/DI – LCN – CHICAGO FAMILY

Reference Bureau airtel to Chicago, entitled Organized Crime/Drug Program (OC/DP) Matters, dated 5/19/93. For information of the Bureau, in June of 1986, ANTHONY SPILOTRO, a known Chicago LCN member and his brother, MICHAEL SPILOTRO, a known Chicago LCN associate and suspected LCN member, were murdered and buried in an Indiana cornfield located at the outskirts of Enos, Indiana. Autopsies conducted showed that both SPILOTROs were beaten. The cause of death was listed for each as asphyxia, due to blunt force trauma about the head, neck, and chest. The bodies of the SPILOTROs were positively identified through dental records supplied by PATRICK SPILOTRO, DDS, brother of the two deceased. As in most gangland slayings, cooperation with law enforcement officials by associates and members of the Chicago LCN is virtually non-existent. Several cooperating witnesses and sources were developed in this matter and have provided the following information concerning the time period just prior to the SPILOTROs disappearance and subsequent murders and events that followed the murders. [95]

---

95   Federal Bureau of Investigation, "Freedom of Information and Privacy Acts," 1980, https://vault.fbi.gov/Anthony%20Spilotro/Anthony%20Spilotro%20Part%2001%20of%2002

On June 23, 1986, the bodies of Tony and Michael were discovered by a farmer not far from a farm formerly owned by none other than Joey Aiuppa. Their faces had been battered beyond recognition. The person responsible for their burial, John Fecarotta, was killed in 1987 for bungling the burials of the brothers, which led to the bodies being discovered.

Forensic pathologist Dr. John Pless testified under oath that autopsies of the Spilotros determined that multiple blunt trauma injuries to the head, neck, and chest most likely were the result of punches and kicks (not bats), which caused the brothers' deaths. Pless added that the Spilotros died partly as a result of their lungs and airways being so full of blood, they couldn't breathe. The day after the bodies were discovered, the Archdiocese of Chicago ruled that the Spilotros could not be given a Catholic funeral because of their links to organized crime.

It's true that LCN takes dysfunctional families to another level, but there's nothing courageous or daring about beating somebody to a pulp when the odds are ten to two in the mob's favor. They still operate with an ersatz code of honor, which under scrutiny is anything but honorable; however, their antics still continue to enthrall audiences, which, although they may not deserve to be admired or hero-worshipped, it happens anyway. So what's the attraction? The attraction is simply this: they look great, they are feared and respected in the communities where they operate, they take care of their own in many different ways, and they talk tough. They live a life that many secretly dream of. That is what attracts all the admiration and veneration, and excites the imaginations of post-pubescent young men. But a word of advice: The authorities usually win in the end, and those who live by the sword....

There are still many who even claim that LCN was a philanthropic organization that protected its own, and there are plenty of instances where mob members have indeed stepped in to pay for medical interventions for people in their neighborhoods. But they were more likely to provide the actual reasons for those medical interventions. LCN further claim that "Family is everything," but domestic considerations don't just apply to them or their organization. In other parts of the world, there are families desperately struggling and suffering to maintain any semblance of cohesion.

In 2020, just before the big lockdown, I was touring around the United States promoting a book when I had the occasion to stay at the Hilton in Newark, New Jersey. I was actually a bit bored, drinking rather weak beer, and watching some college football in the bar when a guy sitting beside me mentioned that he didn't recognize my accent. After I explained, he introduced me to some of his friends, and a very friendly group they were indeed, with the addendum that they were all very well connected. I can't mention the person's name, for obvious reasons, but he claimed to be related to actor Joe Pesci.

I got a little overserved that night; they were such great company. They were telling stories about the Genovese crime family and other local notables. The previous day, I had been to see *Jersey Boys* on Broadway and knew the Pesci connection to the Four Seasons singing group. I mentioned that I was going to be in Vegas for a few days. The person told me to visit a certain restaurant where Pesci, Robert De Niro, and Martin Scorsese hung out while they were filming and/or researching *Casino*. My wife and I were there for five days, and we had a lot of time to kill. That's when I heard the story of Anthony and Michael Spilotro from a Las Vegas native, who praised them both to high heaven. I needed to know more. After I gave a lecture to a full house at the Four Seasons Hotel in Las Vegas, I visited the Mob Museum to get some background and then contacted a friend to get some documents on the brothers, which he dutifully provided.

Incidentally, when I left the extremely sociable Jersey boys at three in the morning, I was due to fly from Newark to Nashville one hour later. I got to the flight, but for some peculiar reason, I have absolutely no memory of it. I make no secret of my admiration and respect for the Italian and American mob, even if it based on a romantic ideal rather than actual reality. My first ever job when I was sixteen (while I was studying at college) was working for a Sicilian nightclub owner known as Gianni 'Big Eyes' Messina. He wasn't well liked by the rest of the staff, but I liked him. The club was a magnet for all the big stars of the day, and Gianni was always very decent to me, even when he discovered that I was running numbers in the car park. He just wanted a cut, which I duly gave him because those extra's helped me through college.

CHAPTER TWENTY-THREE:

THE TALIBAN CAN.

In a country where the average lifespan is forty-nine years old, it isn't surprising that more than half the population of Afghanistan is under twenty-five. The young get things done. Moreover, they have tasted freedom and democracy, and that experience will not lay dormant in their hearts and minds. But that was of little comfort when Kabul fell to the Taliban. Now, the population will witness a gradual eradication of their liberties and human rights. The future may look incredibly bleak, but when those seeds germinate, the Afghan people will rise and fight oppression. Until that time, and if one had any connection to British, NATO, or US forces or organizations, it was a sensible idea to get the hell out.

Marzia Sharifi was working as the director of a US Agency for International Development (USAID) project for women and young people in the western Afghan city of Herat. Her position rendered her and her family as targets of the "Shaving razor challenged hooligans," a.k.a. the Taliban. It's nothing short of tragic that for nearly two decades, USAID's Afghanistan mission was one of its largest in the world. In 2019, the organization invested almost $1 billion in the country, with much of its funding programs related to democratic governance, human rights, and economic development. Well, that's all gone with the wind now.

When Kabul fell and the Taliban seized power, Marzia was shuttling back and forth between California and Afghanistan. She was inadvertently caught on the wrong side of the world from her girls when it all went down, but like any mother who cares for her own, Marzia was determined to do everything she could to be reunited with her family. She watched the TV in horror as chaotic scenes unfolded at Kabul airport because she knew that members of her family were there.

It all began on August 12, 2021, when Marzia's hometown of Herat fell to the Taliban. Soon after, her daughter Maryam Mohammadi donned her school uniform and, accompanied by her grandmother Zahra Sharifi, set off for school. A few paces from her front door, a Taliban fighter stopped them on the street and immediately ordered them both to return home and remain there for the duration. They were told that they were to stay indoors unless they were accompanied by a male relative and wearing burqas. Then he told Maryam, "Next time I see you in this uniform, I will shoot you."

Must have taken an awful amount of courage to threaten a fourteen-year-old girl. Sometime later, a gang of Taliban officials appeared at the family home, looking for Marzia Sharifi. Her daughters Maryam, Mehrsa, and their grandmother had gone underground, spending days hiding in various dank basements as the Taliban menacingly stalked the desolate streets of Herat.

It's almost inconceivable that scenes such as these are occurring in these times. The family decided that the girls and their grandmother should attempt to reach Kabul, which is four hundred miles away from their home. It was going to be a long and perilous journey. On their first attempt to leave Herat, the Taliban halted the bus they were travelling on a few hours outside the town. Two disheveled-looking fighters boarded the vehicle and pointed their weapons at the passengers before ordering the driver to turn the bus around and return to Herat.

Determined to try again, the three wore veils and sat in silent terror as the bus drew to a shuddering halt at another Taliban checkpoint. Fighters boarded again, looked up and down the aisle at the mostly female passengers and then informed the driver that he could continue his journey. As the bus continued on its journey, an audible sigh of relief resonated through the vehicle. Kabul fell on August 15, 2021.

Despite these temporary setbacks, on August 17, 2021, Marzia's daughters and their grandmother finally made it to Kabul. Once there, they huddled together for safety while Taliban fighters armed with loaded AK-47s fired warning shots over the heads of a desperate, heaving, and jostling mass of humanity. Fourteen-year-old Maryam shuddered and drew her three-year-old sister, Mehrsa, closer in an effort to calm her down and dry her tears, which were coursing through the grime on her small, frightened face.

The blistering heat and pervasive stench must have been unbearable as people relieved themselves where they stood. They even occupied an open sewerage that ran beside the airport entrance. The incessant cries of children, augmented by yells of frustration and anger, fused into one long, earsplitting, continuous drone as steam rose from the assembled crowd as they pushed, shoved, and jostled to maintain their places in the ever-growing line.

It had taken many long, arduous days for the small group to reach the airfield (the hub of the US-led evacuation efforts). Now, as they waited, it looked like freedom was finally within their grasp, and they were going to get out of Afghanistan. They could see the US Marines waiting inside the airport gates to help them to safety. At that time, they were part of a larger group, which as far they understood, had been cleared to fly out of the Afghan capital, now firmly under the control of the Taliban. They made it completely obvious who was running the show as they lashed out indiscriminately at the waiting crowd with whips and rifle butts.

The scene was incredibly reminiscent of the ones the world witnessed during the fall of Saigon in 1975. Civilians fled a country that they knew would hold them accountable for whatever they deemed fit. The Taliban have every intention of implementing tough Sharia law, which would, by its nature alone, deny any freedoms or concessions for female members of the population. Sharia is Islam's legal system derived from the Quran (Koran). It literally means "the clear, well-trodden path to water," which was ironically

BLOOD IS THICKER THAN WAR

also in very short supply for those shuffling under the heat in the increasingly restless line outside Kabul airport.

Despite assurances from the Taliban, who have claimed that they've reformed their more extreme practices, their return to power will inevitably mean the return of their punitive approach by inflicting Sharia law on the whole population. The Taliban will use the rhetoric of Islam to try to convince their oppressed public that they are more legitimate than any secular invader or appointed authoritarian figure. But the truth of the matter is glaringly obvious: Whatever claims they make about being their version of extremist Islam, time will inevitably prove that they're just lying to their people. It isn't about religion; it's about power and control. At the end of the day, Sharia is a guide that decent, law-abiding Muslims use to live their lives by. It isn't a "law" in the western construal of the word.

There was little comfort to the sisters and their grandmother flinching as bullets flew over their heads. They saw planes taking off with frantic people attempting to cling on to the undercarriages and falling to their deaths on the runway. The day that they arrived at the airport, holding their precious travel documents, they waited patiently as American soldiers called out the names of travelers to allow these chosen ones inside. It's difficult to conceive the utter disappointment the two sisters and their grandmother must have felt when they discovered that their names were not on the list.

Meanwhile in the US, Marzia had engaged the assistance of a group of former American government officials to help obtain visas for her daughters. As the situation at Kabul airport deteriorated, Marzia went into overdrive in her frenetic attempt to get Maryam, Mehrsa, and their grandmother on the radar screens of US authorities in Washington and Kabul.

That was of little avail because while the wheels were slowly turning to have them all evacuated, there they stood exhausted, starving, and dehydrated. Suddenly and for no apparent reason as far as Maryam could see, the crowd surged forward crushing small children while trampling the elderly and infirm. Maryam looked down at Mehrsa who appeared to be sleeping but had in fact fainted due to the searing heat and lack of water. With the help of her grandmother, they managed to place Mehrsa's small body onto a cart and get her to a hospital, where the child received intravenous fluids and slowly revived. After that, they decided it was far too precarious for all of them to attempt to reach the gates again.

Just when Maryam thought that it was all over, she finally received some positive news from her mother. A few American volunteers, who were assisting the girls, had managed to establish contact with the Ukrainian government, which offered them seats on a plane designated to evacuate civic leaders. Ukraine dispatched a team of soldiers, along with numerous volunteers, to help escort the Afghans out of the country. One Ukrainian official and American volunteers helping the trio reported that they, along with around fifty others waiting in proximity to the airport, had been provided with orange balloons to distinguish them from the rest of the heaving mass. When it finally looked as if they were going to make it out, US Marines refused to open the gates again fearing that it would incite another disastrous stampede. Another day, another disappointment.

To Maryam it felt like time had run out, but she never lost hope and her faith was rewarded when, on August 26, with some assistance, they managed to board a Qatar Airways-sponsored minibus, which at the time offered the best option to reach the tarmac. Moments after they had seated themselves, a deafening explosion rattled the windows of the minibus and almost lifted it off its axles. A suicide bomb had been detonated right in the middle of the crowd outside the airport gates. The blast killed thirteen US soldiers and two hundred civilians. Panic and confusion ensued as all evacuation attempts were thrown into disarray. At that moment it appeared doubtful if the gates would ever be allowed to open again.

Maryam, Mehrsa, and their grandmother endured a long night on that minibus as it finally found a safe place to park. After twelve hours had elapsed, Maryam sent an impassioned plea to her mother with a voice mail saying that she was in pain and felt as if she was dying. Then on August 27, ten days since they had initially arrived at the airport, the minibus made a last-ditch attempt to reach the gates. Within no time, the Taliban had surrounded the vehicle with their loaded AK-47s and were banging on the windows with their fists and rifle butts, causing the bus to stop. At that very moment, a group of Ukrainian soldiers pushed their way through to the besieged vehicle and escorted it onto the runway. Their terrible ordeal was almost over, and a short while later they were all on a flight heading away from Afghanistan. They were out.

On August 30, 2021, Marzia arrived at the Kyiv Sikorsky Airport in Ukraine to meet her daughters and mother. It was a highly charged moment and tears flowed freely as the family was finally reunited.

At the time of writing, and since the mass evacuations began on August 14, approximately 116,700 people have been airlifted away from Afghanistan, including around 5,500 US citizens and their families. The war in Afghanistan may be over for now, but when thousands struggle to leave the country with such determination, it's possible that those left behind will eventually vent their anger and frustration against the regime inflicting hardship and terror on them. Only time will tell.

The twenty years of war has devastated some families and left an indelible mark on everyone who experienced it firsthand. Of the 3,502 coalition forces killed in the line of duty in Afghanistan, 2,312 were US military personnel and 457 were British. Two particular deaths attracted the attention of the US Department of Defense's "Sole Survivor" designation, which brought to light the experiences of three American brothers who all fought in the Afghan War.

In his memoir *Three Wise Men*, cowritten with author Tom Sileo, Beau Wise immortalizes his recollections of his two beloved brothers, Jeremy and Ben. Beau was the youngest with Jeremy being ten years his senior.

Ben, eager to serve, was the first to sign up, joining the army in 2000 at age twenty-three. He displayed exemplary commitment to his chosen métier and went on to become an elite Green Beret sniper. Jeremy enlisted shortly after the 9/11 attacks with the ardent ambition of becoming a Navy SEAL. He signed up at age twenty-seven, despite being enrolled in medical school at the time. He eventually realized his goal by working on clandestine CIA operations as a contractor. Beau had other military ambitions. He had been imbibed with stories of his Marine Corps relatives. One fought through the ferocious World War I Battle of Belleau Wood and another was a commando with the deadly Marine Raiders of World War II. At twenty-four, he joined the Corps' infantry as a machine gunner in 2008, a decision that initially devastated his parents.

When Beau was in Helmand Province, Afghanistan, he knew that his brother Jeremy was in the country, but had no idea that he was working for the CIA. Then one day when Beau was designated to go out on patrol, he was asked to visit the battalion chaplain, who delivered the tragic news that Jeremy had been killed. His death had been the result of a duplicitous al-Qaida agent, who had callously detonated a suicide vest at a Forward Operating Base (FOB), killing six other CIA operatives. This had been the CIA's highest death tally since the 1983 bombing in Beirut. In 2010, Jeremy was honored on the CIA's Memorial Wall at the agency's HQ in Langley, Virginia.

At Jeremy's funeral, Ben had remarked that he was the eldest brother now, but unfortunately that would be a temporary title. About two years later, on January 15, 2012, brother Ben was fighting for his life. While patrolling in Balkh Province, his body had sustained ten rounds from a concealed Taliban fighter, which resulted in both legs being amputated. Ben was airlifted to Germany where both Beau and Ben's wife Traci managed to see him before he eventually succumbed to his wounds. It was remarkable that he had hung on for a full six days, and it was meager compensation, but at least they had managed to bid a tearful goodbye before he died. Ben Wise was posthumously awarded the Silver Star, the United States military medal for valor.

Beau was now the sole surviving brother. Marine Commandant General James Amos informed him that in compliance with the Department of Defense's "Sole Survivor" designation, he would not be put in harm's way, a decision that Beau strongly resented at the time. He wanted to keep on fighting and honoring the warrior tradition of his departed brothers.

In 2016, much to the relief of his parents Mary and Jean Wise, Beau left active-duty service. Beau said that although the son and daughter he and his wife Amber adopted will never have the joy on knowing their heroic uncles, he will make it his solemn duty to remind them of the sacrifices they made. Memorial Day will have more significance for the family in the future, but for Beau, every day will be Memorial Day. More importantly, their story had been told before, in a different war and in a different scenario, but this only serves to reestablish the age-old premise about history repeating. As this volume has proven, young men and women, brothers and sisters have always stepped up to the plate, and in many cases, left their families bereft of their young lives. It has indeed happened before and doubtless it will happen again.

A joint deployment brings the spine-chilling possibility that siblings could be killed while on duty. While several sets of brothers, as well as a father and son, have served at the same time in Afghanistan, back in 2008, twenty-four-year-old twin sisters Calista and Cassandra Walker were assigned to different detachments of the 525th Battlefield Surveillance Brigade at Bagram Airfield in Afghanistan.

After completing high school and receiving college degrees in Criminal Justice, they enlisted in the US Army to attend basic and advanced individual training. They then embarked on their first duty assignment together, which included a three-month deployment to Iraq. The twins from Towanda, Pennsylvania, claimed to have done everything together, and continue to insist the importance of family in almost everything they do.

Despite being assigned to the same brigade, they supported the Combined Joint Special Operations Task Force from separate locations in Afghanistan. They were reunited briefly when Army Sergeant Calista flew to Kandahar, Afghanistan, to promote her sister, Army Specialist Cassandra, to sergeant. The ceremony was held at a firebase in Kandahar. Calista had been promoted a few days earlier but wished that they could have been promoted simultaneously.

Cassandra remarked that even though the sisters continually encouraged each other to achieve, they were also very competitive. While the friendly competition kept the sisters focused on improvement, it is also one aspect of their relationship that has kept them together for the past twenty-four years. Throughout their deployment, they managed to contact one another at least once a day by phone or by email. Either way, they kept permanent tabs on each other.

The final story in this chapter concerns the tumultuous lives of two accomplished journalists, Benesh and Esin (real names withheld),[96] who were devoted Afghan sisters that found themselves placed on the Taliban's list of undesirables, which is tantamount to a death sentence. They were tragically at opposite ends of the world when Kabul fell to the Taliban. Thanks to her connection with a British family, Benesh managed to secure a one-way ticket to the Netherlands, but the twenty-seven-year-old was compelled by force of circumstances to reluctantly leave her mother and her younger sister Esin behind in Kabul. At the time, Esin was currently residing at a military base until her final destination could be arranged.

It all began when Esin woke up in shock as she heard gunshots ringing out in the street. It was the Taliban celebrating the fall of Kabul. No one got any sleep during that night.

When the last US plane lifted off from Kabul, it left behind a country scarred and ravaged by terror, bloodshed, and heartache. Although the Taliban now had full control of Afghanistan, their archenemies ISIS were slowly beginning to emerge from the shadows. The two sisters never imagined a reality where they would be wrenched apart. While Benesh watched helplessly from a safe distance as the tragic sequence of events unfolded, her sister braced for what she felt in her heart would be very dark and sad days ahead. The last Benesh heard was that Taliban fighters had surrounded the perimeter of the building where Esin and the rest of her family were holding out. Regardless of all the adversity of their situation, the Afghan sisters cautiously grasped the faint hope of seeing each other again someday.

The airport was closed and that precious hope began to dissipate until Esin got a message from her older brother: he had managed to get out. He told her that many Afghans were escaping through the Pakistan border crossing, adding that she would have to move fast because there was a distinct possibility that the border was going to close indefinitely. Esin contacted Benesh to ask if she could get ahold of papers for the remaining members of her family, including her father Razziq, mother Mojdeh, and younger brother

---

96   Author interview done in 2021.

Malik. They would all travel as women except Razziq, who would be the obligatory male chaperone, so it was imperative that three of the documents were made using the women's names.

Sadly Benesh couldn't acquire the necessary documents, but she gave Esin the number of a contact in Kabul who was a forgery expert. He would provide four Pakistani passports, but it wouldn't be cheap. The price was $15,000, roughly $3,000 for each document. Time was not on their side, but Benesh sent the money and the forger promised to deliver in three days. Meanwhile, the Taliban were closing in, and the situation was becoming more precarious by the hour. Then as they waited to receive the passports, someone got word to Esin that the forger had been arrested and summarily executed. His lifeless body was hanging from a lamppost on the outskirts of Kabul. At that moment all hope faded.

As far as Esin was concerned, the game was up, and all they could do was wait for the Taliban to break into the compound and arrest them all. That night the whole family prepared themselves for the worst. At around midnight, there was a knock at the door. Fearful, nobody dared to open it. The knocking continued until Razziq decided to answer. He expected to see a gaggle of hairy mongrels holding AK-47s, but as he cautiously opened the door a few inches, he saw a young man standing there, holding what looked like a large leather purse. He handed it to Razziq and told him that he had been asked by his boss to deliver these to the family before he was arrested and hanged. Then the young man called out "inshallah" before he deftly disappeared down an alleyway and was never seen again. They didn't even know the name of this welcome messenger.

The passports looked genuine enough, but the photographs didn't correspond, so it was doubtful that they would be enough to convince Taliban control posts and Pakistani border guards. It was their only option. None of them got any sleep that night. At daybreak the following morning, as the sun cast its first hesitant shards of light across the rooftops of the parchment dry buildings in Kabul, the family loaded up their Hyundai minibus and headed out. They got lucky because the passports worked like a dream and completely confused the Taliban at every control post, which wasn't particularly difficult because most of the control post morons had the cerebral capacity of plankton. The Taliban had insisted that all women wear the full-length burqas, complete with eye mesh. Esin's family obediently complied. Power rarely exudes intelligence. Everything was going smoothly until they reached the Pakistan border crossing at Torkham, which was congested with desperate Afghans still attempting to escape overland. Razziq told his family to gather their belongings; he was going to abandon the vehicle.

Torkham is nestled into the mountainous valley of the famous Khyber Pass, previously used by traders and invaders from Alexander the Great to the British Empire. It was the route that the US-backed mujahideen took into Afghanistan in the 1980s and had been part of a region sandwiched between various empires for centuries. In recent years, Pakistan had tightened security considerably. In 2017, a 1,600-mile fence was erected by the Pakistani military. They also patrol the dry, craggy mountain slopes making nigh on impossible for Afghans to reach Pakistan without using the official crossing. At the time of writing, the Torkham border crossing is patrolled by heavily-armed Pakistani military and Taliban guards and is flanked by Taliban flags. Some Taliban guards wear green uniforms bearing the blue patch of the former Afghan National Police, the old US-backed force.

The family joined the massive queue to discover that some people there had been waiting for up to four days to get across, and now the rumor was that the border was going to close indefinitely, like the older brother had said. Pakistani border guards walked among the assembled crowd asking for documents. When they reached Esin's family, a guard belligerently held out his hand for their passports. Razziq confidently handed them over and waited. They all watched as the passports were passed from one guard to another for inspection. Then a Pakistani sergeant approached the family and addressed Razziq. He told him that there appeared to be a problem with the documents. Then the sergeant asked the whole family to follow him to a small office at the border crossing, where they were seated and asked to wait. After what felt like an age, Esin watched as each passport was stamped. The ruse had worked, and they were safe. Benesh immediately booked a flight to Islamabad, where they were eventually all reunited.

Their story isn't unique. War divides families, and has done so since the beginning of time. But history also teaches us that despots usually get theirs in the end; the problem is that the end can be a long time coming.

For countless centuries, the world has continued to turn throughout the heartache and desolate tears of those poor unfortunates caught in the middle of conflicts, and it's still going on today. So take a moment to look at a brother, sister, father, or mother. Tell them how much they are loved because while that isn't the only antidote available, it is a precious and vital one. Love doesn't assuage all the pain and suffering from the past, present, and future, but it helps, it really helps.

For many families, the most devastating event that occurred in 2021 was the fall of Kabul to the Taliban after twenty years of strife. My daughter, who's a nurse, had an Afghan friend who had a terribly sad story to impart. She wasn't unique. While the emphasis in most media was on the troops who made it out of there and the ones who had served with distinction in Afghanistan (and rightfully so), it isn't all about the soldiers. Families have been tearfully torn apart by this conflict and for many, the suffering is far from over. This chapter neither condones nor condemns the actual war, but it revealed some previously unknown stories of those who have been (and, in some cases, still are) directly affected by the events of 2021.

EPILOGUE

By Martin King

History has a tendency to venerate heroes, and in most cases rightfully so, but memory is subjective and highly selective. We forget the thousands of lives driven to dust by war and conflict until it directly concerns us. The world is so distracted and polarized by opinions on politics, climate change, and pandemics, it has caused people to become insular, to raise the drawbridge, and to look away or deflect the problem. The glorious information highway is gridlocked by those seeking immediate solutions to the puerile problems of the "look-at-me-society." We demand information, we want it yesterday, and the accuracy of that information maybe be negligible, but even that's considered a minor detail these days, which provides little comfort for refugees afflicted by war.

War underscores the plight of families, the nucleus of everything, and nothing transcends or is more precious than that. Self-preservation and self-interest have exceeded the needs of those we see almost daily on the net and on the news, but the war in Ukraine has reminded us that geography is no guarantee of security. They struggle to escape to a fresh horizon, and they struggle to maintain some meager semblance of cohesion—even when everything they possess has gone, including their home. That doesn't stop us from incongruously demanding the new iPhone or buying a new Mac computer. We have become impervious to suffering, and we have a disturbing tendency to only make exceptions when it directly concerns our possessions or our overfull stomachs. All these bountiful years have rendered western society complacent and indolent. Therein lies the danger.

That's the way it is, but someday we will all have to take stock and hopefully realize that concern for the future of our species must entail respecting the past, having consideration for others, and not turning a blind eye in the hope that the situation will resolve itself. It won't. But we can change the status quo, and that is the vital lesson we need to learn from history, because we haven't learned much so far. We still pander to the whims of self-aggrandizing politicians who rarely have any other consideration that exceeds matters of self-interest.

As I write the Ukraine government, which was so integral to helping Afghan refugees is now dealing with it's own refugee crisis. It's all so terribly heartbreaking and so implacably inevitable, because it could have all been avoided.

So in conclusion, while you're looking after yourself, no matter how inept or maladjusted your family is, there are considerably worse cases in this volume. Now take a moment to care for each other, and you will be glad you did because the glaringly obvious truth of the matter is this. We are *all* members of one big dysfunctional family living in the same house. Love, light, and peace.

BIBLIOGRAPHY AND REFERENCES

"Anniversary of the Battle of Messines: 7 - 14 June 2017." Visit Flanders. Flanders State of the Art. https://www.visitflanders.com/en/binaries/BattleofMessines_tcm13-87760.pdf.

"The Beechey Boys." The Royal Anglian & Royal Lincolnshire Regimental Association. The Lincoln Branch of The Royal Lincolnshire and Royal Anglian Regimental Association. http://www.thelincolnshireregiment.org/beechey.shtml.

Bihet, Molly. *A Time for Memories*. Molly Bihet, 2005.

Bolger, Daniel P. *Our Year of War: Two Brothers, Vietnam, and a Nation Divided*. Da Capo Press, 2017.

Booth, John. *The Battle of Waterloo: Containing the Accounts Published by Authority*. London, UK: R. R. Howldt, 1815.

Borneman, Walter R. *The French and Indian War: Deciding the Fate of North America*. New York, NY: Harper Perennial, 2007.

Bradbury, Jim. *Philip Augustus: King of France 1180-1223*. Routledge, 2015.

Burns, Eric. *The Golden Lad: The Haunting Story of Quentin and Theodore Roosevelt*. New York, NY: Pegasus Books, 2016.

Cappart, Marie. "La Famille Fabry: Trois Frères à La Guerre." RTBF. https://www.rtbf.be/14-18/thematiques/detail_la-famille-fabry-trois-freres-a-la-guerre?id=8303083.

Carter, Miranda. *George, Nicholas and Wilhelm: Three Royal Cousins and the Road to World War I*. New York, NY: Vintage Books, 2011.

Collings, Michael R. *Milton's Century: A Timeline of the Literary, Political, Religious, and Social Context of John Milton's Life.* San Bernardino, CA: Borgo Press, 2013.

Collins, Max Allan. *Saving Private Ryan.* Signet Books, 1998.

Collins, Michael, and Martin King. *Voices of the Bulge: Untold Stories from Veterans of the Battle of the Bulge.* Minneapolis, MN: Zenith Press, 2011.

Commonwealth War Graves. Commonwealth War Graves Commission. https://www.cwgc.org/.

"Comprehensive List of Investigations." New Jersey State Commission of Investigation. https://www.state.nj.us/sci/reportsall.shtm.

Conner, Thomas H., and James Scott Wheeler. *War and Remembrance: The Story of the American Battle Monuments Commission.* Lexington, KY: University Press of Kentucky, 2018.

Crasnianski, Tania, and Molly Grogan. *Children of Nazis: The Sons and Daughters of Himmler, Göring, Höss, Mengele and Others—Living with a Father's Monstrous Legacy.* New York, NY: Arcade Publishing, 2019.

Cromwell, Glayds. *Poems.* Macmillan Company, 1919.

Crowe, David. *Oskar Schindler: The Untold Account of His Life, Wartime Activities and the True Story behind the List.* Cambridge, MA: Westview Press, 2004.

Cullotta, Frank, and Dennis Griffin. *The Rise and Fall of a 'Casino' Mobster: The Tony Spilotro Story through a Hitman's Eyes.* Denver, CO: WildBlue Press, 2017.

D'Ewes, Simonds. *The Autobiography and Correspondence of Sir Simonds D'Ewes, Bart: During the Reigns of James I. and Charles I.* Edited by James Orchard Halliwell. Wentworth Press, 2016.

Danziger, Danny, and John Gillingham. *1215: The Year of Magna Carta.* Hodder & Stoughton, 2003.

DeStefano, Anthony M. *Deadly Don: Vito Genovese, Mafia Boss.* Citadel Press, 2021.

Doopsgezinden Tijdens De Tweede Wereldoorlog. Amsterdam: Doopsgezinde Historische Kring, 2015.

Duffy, Peter. *The Bielski Brothers the True Story of Three Men Who*

Defied the Nazis, Built a Village in the Forest, and Saved 1,200 Jews. New York, NY: HarperCollins, 2004.

Durso, Pamela R. *The Power of Woman: The Life and Writings of Sarah Moore Grimké*. Mercer University Press, 2004.

Dwyer, Bill. "Details of Spilotro Murders Revealed in Mob Trial." Wednesday Journal of Oak Park and River Forest, August 14, 2007. https://www.oakpark.com/2007/08/14/details-of-spilotro-murders-revealed-in-mob-trial/.

Eddé, Anne-Marie. *Saladin*. Cambridge, MA: Belknap Harvard, 2014.

Elms, Matthew. *When the Akimotos Went to War: An Untold Story of Family, Patriotism, and Sacrifice during World War II*. Arlington, VA: American Battle Monuments Commission, 2015.

Falkner, James. *Great and Glorious Days: Marlborough's Battles 1704–09*. Spellmount, 2007.

Falkner, James. *The War of the Spanish Succession, 1701–1714*. Pen & Sword Military, 2015.

Fenelon, Holly S. *That Knock at the Door: The History of Gold Star Mothers in America*. Bloomington: iUniverse, Inc, 2012.

Fuchs, Lawrence H. *The American Kaleidoscope Race, Ethnicity, and the Civic Culture*. Hanover, NH: Wesleyan University Press, 1990.

"Get a Copy of Military Service Records." GOV.UK, September 24, 2015. https://www.gov.uk/get-copy-military-service-records.

Ghauri, Iftikhar Ahmad. *War of Succession between the Sons of Shah Jahan, 1657-1658*. Lahore, Pakistan: Publishers United, 1964.

Graves, Robert. *I, Claudius*. Camberwell, Vic: Penguin Books, 2011.

Greeson, Janet, and Patricia Rose Mulvihill. *An American Army of Two*. Minneapolis, MN: Carolrhoda Books, 1992.

Griffin, John. *The Diary of Anne Frank: Longman Literature Guidelines*. Pearson School, 1989.

Grimké, Angelina Emily. *Appeal to the Christian Women of the South*. American Anti-Slavery Society, 1836.

Hansen, Waldemar. *The Peacock Throne: The Drama of Mogul India*. Delhi, India: Motilal Banarsidass, 1986.

Hart, B. H. Liddell. *A History of the First World War*. London: Pan Macmillan, 1972.

Helm, Toby. "Five Sons Killed. Then a Town's Pleas to Save the Last Were Heard." The Guardian. Guardian News and Media, November 4, 2018. https://www.theguardian.com/world/2018/nov/04/barnard-castle-pauses-remember-five-sons-who-never-came-home-first-world-war-rememberance-day.

Hill, Christopher. *The World Turned Upside Down: Radical Ideas during the English Revolution*. Penguin Books, 2021.

Hinze, Maxi. *The Third Crusade and Its Impact on England*. GRIN Publishing, 2007.

Holmes, Richard. *Marlborough: Britain's Greatest General*. London, UK: Harper Perennial, 2009.

Holt, Tonie, and Valmai Holt. *My Boy Jack: The Search for Kipling's Only Son*. Pen & Sword Military, 2008.

Hughes, John McKendrick. *The Unwanted: Great War Letters from the Field*. Edmonton, Alta.: The University of Alberta Press, 2005.

IrishCentral Staff. "An Untold Story of Six Irish-American Brothers Who Fought in WWII." IrishCentral, January 6, 2017. https://www.irishcentral.com/roots/an-untold-story-of-six-irish-american-brothers-who-fought-in-wwii-97261184-237701951.

Jackson County, Ohio Genealogical Society. *Jackson County, Ohio: History and Families*. Paducah, KY: Turner Pub. Co., 1991.

Jacob, Happymon. *The Rise, Fall, and the Resurgence of the Taliban*. New Delhi, India: Samāskrāit, in association with Observer Research Foundation, 2006.

Jacobs, James B, Christopher Panarella, and Jay Worthington. *Busting the Mob: The United States V. Cosa Nostra*. New York University Press, 1996.

Johnston, Terry A, ed. *Him on the One Side and Me on the Other: the Civil War Letters of Alexander Campbell, 79th New York Infantry Regiment and James Campbell, 1st South Carolina Battalion*. Columbia, SC: University of South Carolina Press, 1999.

Johnstone, Hilda. *Oliver Cromwell and His Times*. Batsford Books, 1962.

Jones, Dan. *The Plantagenets: The Warrior Kings and Queens Who Made England*. New York, NY: Penguin Books, 2014.

Jones, Dan. *The Wars of the Roses: The Fall of the Plantagenets and the Rise of the Tudors*. New York, NY: Penguin Books, 2015.

Jones, Terry L. *Historical Dictionary of the Civil War*, vol. 1. Lanham, MD: Scarecrow Press, 2011.

Kendall, Paul Murray. *Warwick the Kingmaker*. London, UK: Phoenix, 1957.

King, Martin. *Lost Voices: The Untold Stories of America's World War I Veterans and Their Families*. Lyons Press, 2018.

Kinra, Rajeev. *King of Delhi, King of the World: Chandar Bhan's Perspective on Shah Jahan, the Mughal Court, and the Realm*. Berkeley, CA: University of California Press, 2015.

Koop, Volker. *The Commandant of Auschwitz: Rudolf Höss*. Frontline Books, 2021.

Laplander, Robert. *Finding the Lost Battalion: Beyond the Rumors, Myths and Legends of America's Famous WW1 Epic*. Waterford, WI: Lulu Press, 2017.

Lee, Carol Ann, and Marja de Bruijn. *Anne Frank: 1929-1945: Het Leven Van Een Jong Meisje: De Definitieve Biografie*. Amsterdam: Balans, 2012.

Lindwer, Willy. *The Last Seven Months of Anne Frank*. Knopf Doubleday Publishing, 2011.

The London Gazette, October 12, 1816.

"The Lost Battalion," After Action Report, 77th Infantry Division, National Archives, Maryland.

MacDowall, Simon. *Malplaquet 1709: Marlborough's Bloodiest Battle*. Illustrated by Graham Turner. Oxford: Osprey Publishing, 2020.

Malsin, Jared, and Dion Nissenbaum. "Two Young Afghan Sisters' Journey across Afghanistan to Escape the Taliban." The Wall Street Journal. Dow Jones & Company, September 6, 2021. https://www.wsj.com/articles/two-young-afghan-sisters-journey-across-afghanistan-to-escape-the-taliban-11630964304.

"Margaret and Kate Carruthers, MM, Territorial Forces Nursing Service." Scotland's War. http://www.scotlandswar.co.uk/pdf_Margaret_and_Kate_Carruthers.pdf.

Massie, Robert K. *Romanovs: The Final Chapter*. Random House, 2012.

McPherson, James M. *This Mighty Scourge: Perspectives on the Civil War*. Oxford University Press, 2007.

McShane, Larry. *Chin: The Life and Crimes of Mafia Boss Vincent Gigante*. Citadel Press, 2018.

Messenger, Charles. *Call to Arms: The British Army 1914-18*. London, UK: Hachette, 2015.

Milton, John. *The Doctrine & Discipline of Divorce Restor'd to the Good of Both Sexes from the Bondage of Canon Law and Other Mistakes to the True Meaning of Scripture in the Law and Gospel Compar'd 1645*. Facsimile Publisher, 2013.

The Newsroom. "Astonishing Story of Ten Yorkshire Brothers Who Went to Fight in First World War and Nine Survived." Yorkshire Evening Post. Yorkshire Evening Post, November 8, 2018. https://www.yorkshireeveningpost.co.uk/news/astonishing-story-ten-yorkshire-brothers-who-went-fight-first-world-war-and-nine-survived-223043.

Niemi, Robert. *History in the Media: Film and Television*. Santa Barbara, CA: ABC-CLIO, 2006.

Nimmo, H. Arlo. *The Andrews Sisters: A Biography and Career Record*. Jefferson, NC: McFarland, 2007.

O'Brien, Toby. "Hitler Has Only Got One Ball." Antiwar Songs (AWS). https://www.antiwarsongs.org/canzone.php?id=60260&lang=en.

"Orders, Decorations, Medals and Militaria (17 September 2020)." Dix Noonan Webb: London Specialist Auctioneers. DNW, September 17, 2020. https://www.dnw.co.uk/auction-archive/past-catalogues/lot.php?auction_id=533&lot_uid=377030.

Orr, Timothy. "'Each Died For His Cause': Marylanders in the Army of the Potomac, Part 7." Tales from the Army of the Potomac, May 1, 2020. http://talesfromaop.blogspot.com/2020/05/each-died-for-his-cause-marylanders-in.html.

Ottaway, Susan. *Sisters, Secrets and Sacrifice: A True Story*. London, UK: Harper Element, 2013.

Owtram, Jean, and Patricia Owtram. *Codebreaking Sisters: Our Secret War*. United Kingdom Baker & Taylor, 2020.

Pershing, John J. *General Pershing's Official Story of the American Expeditionary Forces in France*. New York, NY: Sun Sales Corp., 1919.

Phillips, Douglas W. *Letters and Lessons of Teddy Roosevelt for His Sons*. San Antonio, TX: Vision Forum, 2001.

Pietras, David J. *A Look inside the Five Mafia Families of New York City*. David Pietras, 2013.

Prysor, Glyn. *CWGC Battlefield Companion Somme 1916*. Bloomsbury Publishing, 2016.

Puzo, Mario. *The Godfather*. Berkley, 1983.

Rash, Felicity, and Christophe Declercq. *Great War in Belgium and the Netherlands: Beyond Flanders Fields*. Palgrave Macmillan, 2018.

Regan, Geoffrey. *Lionhearts: Saladin and Richard* I. London, UK: Constable, 1998.

Reuth, Ralf Georg. *Goebbels Eine Biographie*. München: Piper, 2013.

Ribbentrop, Rudolf von. *Mein Vater Joachim Von Ribbentrop Erlebnisse Und Erinnerungen*. Graz: Ares-Verl, 2013.

Richman, Jeff. "Brothers Divided by the Civil War." Green-Wood. The Green-Wood Historic Fund, November 26, 2018. https://www.green-wood.com/2018/brothers-divided-by-the-civil-war/.

Rimmer, Monica. "The Eight Brothers Who Fought in World War One." BBC News. BBC, November 11, 2018. https://www.bbc.com/news/uk-england-birmingham-46044001.

Ritchie, John. *Lachlan Macquarie: A Biography*. Carlton, Vic.: Melbourne University Press, 1986.

Roland, Paul. *Nazi Women: The Attraction of Evil*. London, UK: Arcturus Publishing, Ltd, 2014.

Roosevelt, Kermit. *The Long Trail 1921*. Facsimile Publisher, 2013.

Roosevelt, Kermit. *War in the Garden of Eden*. C. Scribner's Sons, 1919.

Russell, Thomas H. *The World's Greatest War and Triumph of America's Army and Navy*. New York: L. H. Walter, 1919.

Sanders, Brian. "Brothers Served in Same Military Unit during Vietnam War." The Holton Recorder, November 9, 2015.

https://www.holtonrecorder.net/news/brothers-served-same-military-unit-during-vietnam-war.

Satterfield, John R. *We Band of Brothers: The Sullivans and World War II*. Parkersburg, IA: Mid-Prairie Books, 2000.

Schneid, Frederick C. *Napoleon's Conquest of Europe: The War of the Third Coalition*. Westport, CT: Praeger, 2005.

Schröm, Oliver, and Andrea Röpke. Stille Hilfe Für Braune Kameraden Das Geheime Netzwerk Der Alt- Und Neonazis. Berlin: Aufbau-Taschenbuch-Verl, 2006.

Seitz, Matt Zoller, and Alan Sepinwall. *The Sopranos Sessions*. Harry N. Abrams, 2019.

Shiffrin, Gale Hamilton. *Echoes from Women of the Alamo*. San Antonio, TX: Clarke, 1999.

Snow, Peter. *To War with Wellington: From the Peninsula to Waterloo*. London, UK: John Murray Publishers, 2011.

Standke, Corinna. "Sharia - The Islamic Law," GRIN Verlag, 2008. https://www.grin.com/document/113665

Swift, Johnathan. *The Conduct of the Allies, and of the Late Ministry, in Beginning and Carrying on the Present War*. Delhi, India: True World Books, 2018.

Tang, Albert. *Road to Freedom: A Young Refugee's Journeys*. iUniverse, Inc, 2021.

Taylor, Amy Murrell. *The Divided Family in Civil War America*. University of North Carolina Press, 2009.

Thomas, David, and John A. Chesworth. *Christian-Muslim Relations. A Bibliographical History. Volume 12: Asia, Africa and the Americas (1700-1800)*. Leiden: Koninklijke Brill NV, 2018.

Tyerman, Christopher. *God's War: A New History of the Crusades*. London, UK: Penguin, 2007.

"U.S. Army Twin Sisters Reunite for Promotion in Afghanistan." Defense Visual Information Distribution Service, February 10, 2008. https://www.dvidshub.net/news/16206/us-army-twin-sisters-reunite-promotion-afghanistan.

The United States Army and World War II: The Collected Works. Washington, DC: U.S. Army Center of Military History, 2011.

Van Walleghem, Achiel. "Oorlogsdagboeken 1914-1918." Translated by Willy Spillebeen. Uitgeverij Lannoo.

Voltaire. *The Age of Louis XIV*. Translated by William F. Fleming. e-artnow, 2016.

Von Muenchhausen, Friedrich Ernst. *At General Howes Side 1776 1778: The Diary of General William Howes Aide De Camp, Captain Friedrich Von Muenchhausen*. Phillip Freneau Press, 1974.

Von Peters, Dr. William. *Comparative Gospels - King James/ Rheims 1582*. Lulu.com, 2018.

Vries, Susanna De. *Australian Heroines of World War One: Gallipoli, Lemnos and the Western Front*. Chapel Hill, Qld.: Pirgos Press, 2013.

Walsh, Michael. *Brothers in War*. Ebury Press, 2007.

White Francis and co. *Nottinghamshire. History, Directory and Gazetteer of the County, and of the Town and County of the Town of Nottingham. To Which Is Added, the History and Directory of the Port of Gainsborough*. Delhi, India: True World of Books, 2021.

Whitehead, Dennis. *Shell Shock: Twin Sisters Born Into New York's Gilded Age Struck Down by the Horrors of War*. Kindle Direct Publishing, 2018.

"Who We Serve - Amerasians." Office of Refugee Resettlement. The Administration for Children and Families, October 2, 2012. https://www.acf.hhs.gov/orr/policy-guidance/who-we-serve-amerasians.

Wise, Beau, and Tom Sileo. *Three Wise Men: A Navy SEAL, a Green Beret, and How Their Marine Brother Became a War's Sole Survivor*. St. Martin's Griffin, 2021.

Yarborough, Trin. *Surviving Twice Amerasian Children of the Vietnam War*. Herndon: Potomac Books, 2014.

CreateSpace Independent Publishing Platform, 18 Dec 2014 - 30 pages

ACKNOWLEDGMENTS

Warm thanks to my wife Freya and to my son and daughter, Ashley Rae and Allycia, not forgetting my publisher Roger S. Williams, Aleigha Kely and Kiera Baron. My family in the UK, Sandra, Mick, Rachel, Graham and Anne, Debbie and Marc, Ben, Becky and Pipa, Jake and Rachel. Also my excellent New Zealand family, Parei, Cliff, Jodi, Julian Jolene, Wendy and Joef Dusevich Barnard, not forgetting top mates Andy Kirton, George Lee and Wayne Kidd. Profound thanks also to my fellow author Mike Collins and to John and Joanne Collins, my Irish/American family. This volume wouldn't have been possible without the wonderful support and encouragement of Jeff Barta (Ret. Commander US Navy), Brigadier General Rob Novotny USAF (Ret.), Colonel Rob Campbell 101st Airborne (Ret.), and Madonna Roberts ROTC Ansbach. Thank you also to Randy and Staci Garcia, my Vegas connection, Ms. Helen Patton, Hans Van Kessel at the 101st Airborne Museum in Bastogne, and the excellent team at the Bastogne War Heritage Institute Bastogne. Vietnam Veteran and dear friend Mr. Bob Babcock of Deeds Publishing USA. Profound thanks to Prof. Carlton Joyce, Brian Dick, Bob Allen, Doug and Diane Haven, John Taylor and Martina Steffens Taylor not forgetting the Shape Middle School kids. Mike, Tiffany and Clan Edwards, Lisa Hockley and Rick Beyer (Ghost Army). These notables deserve a mention too, Phyllis Pennings, Cindy

Livingstone, Andrew Wakeford and Christa, Ray Wheatley and Vicki, Steve Highlander and Geneva,Guy and Hilde, Frank E Jackson Jr. Linda Washington, Wanda Stump, Mark Chernek USMC, Ellen Bailey, my nieces Jill and Erin, and last but not least Nico the top man. You are all wonderful.